Digital Public Relations and Marketing Communication Trends in Africa

The uptake of digital media platforms necessitates the need to understand how digital cultures of consumers and brands are unfolding. Despite the increase in usage and adoption of the internet in Africa, there is limited information about digital marketing trends on the continent. This book is among the first to present an edited collection of chapters on digital and influencer marketing authored by many who are either from or have close ties to Africa.

This book showcases digital marketing trends in Africa that are burgeoning at the same speed as the uptake of technology in the continent. With this in mind, the contributors seek to interrogate digital marketing trends in two stages: the status of digital marketing on the African continent, including cases from Nigeria, Egypt, Uganda and Kenya, and an analysis of the rise of influencer marketing, including cases from Nigeria and Uganda. This book will explore factors driving the increase in digital media platforms in Africa as well as an analysis of the implications of the growth in digital marketing, using various theoretical and methodological underpinnings to probe trends.

Digital Public Relations and Marketing Communication Trends in Africa provides significant implications for marketing scholars and researchers and will be relevant to those looking to understand the opportunities and challenges ahead.

Anne W. Njathi (Ph.D. North Carolina State University) is a data-driven digital marketer and chartered marketer (ACIM) with over 10 years of industry experience in building sustainable brands in Africa. As an assistant professor at Pepperdine University, her research focuses on digital technologies, the creator economy, internet governance and FinTech, from an emerging market perspective.

Brandi Watkins (Ph.D., APR, The University of Alabama) is an associate professor in the School of Communication at Virginia Tech. Her research examines the role of digital and social media in facilitating organization-public relationships, brand communication and social change.

Routledge New Directions in PR & Communication Research
Edited by Kevin Moloney

Current academic thinking about public relations (PR) and related communication is a lively, expanding marketplace of ideas and many scholars believe that it's time for its radical approach to be deepened. Routledge New Directions in PR & Communication Research is the forum of choice for this new thinking. Its key strength is its remit, publishing critical and challenging responses to continuities and fractures in contemporary PR thinking and practice, tracking its spread into new geographies and political economies. It questions its contested role in market-orientated, capitalist, liberal democracies around the world, and examines its invasion of all media spaces, old, new, and as yet unenvisaged.

The New Directions series has already published and commissioned diverse original work on topics such as:

- PR's influence on Israeli and Palestinian nation-building
- PR's origins in the history of ideas
- a Jungian approach to PR ethics and professionalism
- global perspectives on PR professional practice
- PR as an everyday language for everyone
- PR as emotional labor
- PR as communication in conflicted societies, and
- PR's relationships to cooperation, justice, and paradox.

We actively invite new contributions and offer academics a welcoming place for the publication of their analyses of a universal, persuasive mindset that lives comfortably in old and new media around the world.

Workplace Culture in Mass Communication Industries
Martina Topić

Digital Public Relations and Marketing Communication Trends in Africa
Edited by Anne W. Njathi and Brandi Watkins

For more information about this series, please visit: www.routledge.com/Routledge-New-Directions-in-PR--Communication-Research/book-series/RNDPRCR

Digital Public Relations and Marketing Communication Trends in Africa

Edited by
Anne W. Njathi and Brandi Watkins

Routledge
Taylor & Francis Group
LONDON AND NEW YORK

First published 2024
by Routledge
4 Park Square, Milton Park, Abingdon, Oxon OX14 4RN

and by Routledge
605 Third Avenue, New York, NY 10158

Routledge is an imprint of the Taylor & Francis Group, an informa business

British Library Cataloguing-in-Publication Data
A catalogue record for this book is available from the British Library

ISBN: 978-1-032-68961-6 (hbk)
ISBN: 978-1-032-68963-0 (pbk)
ISBN: 978-1-032-68965-4 (ebk)

DOI: 10.4324/9781032689654

Typeset in Times New Roman
by codeMantra

Contents

Contributors

Yinka Ajibola is a Ph.D. student at the University of Wisconsin-Madison (iSchool). He holds a double master's degree in information communications sciences and political science from Ball State University. His research areas include information communications technologies (ICTs), development, artificial intelligence for development.

Christiana Alex-Ojei (Ph.D.) lectures at the Department of Demography and Social Statistics, Federal University Oye-Ekiti, Nigeria. She specialises in quantitative, qualitative and mixed-method research approaches. Her research examines the nexus between social issues, dynamics and population health access and outcomes.

Amany Bassyouny (Ph.D., Ain Shams University) is an associate professor in the Faculty of Communication and Mass Media at the British University in Egypt where she teaches public relations and crisis communication courses. Her research scans digital marketing trends and the opportunities and challenges of the use of social media in public relations in Egypt from the perspective of professional experts.

Akwasi Bosompem Boateng, Ph.D., is a lecturer in the School of Communication and Media Studies, University of Education, Winneba, Ghana. Akwasi received his Ph.D. in Cultural and Media Studies from the University of KwaZulu-Natal, South Africa. Akwasi is Member of several academic and professional bodies.

Luke Capizzo (Ph.D., APR) is an assistant professor of strategic communication at the University of Missouri, USA. A PR researcher, educator and practitioner, his scholarly interests include social issues management, corporate social advocacy, dialogue and organizational listening.

Tendai Chari is an associate professor of Media Studies and a National Research Foundation (NRF) C3 rated researcher at the University of Venda, South Africa. He holds a Ph.D. in Media Studies from the University of Witwatersrand, South Africa.

Adeola Kayode works at the intersection of strategy, marketing and technology. He has an MBA (Unilag) and a Diploma in Marketing (CIM, UK). He works as Head of Brands in Nigeria and wrote *Digital Epidemic* – a book on Marketing in Africa.

Tabani Moyo (Ph.D.) combines academia and practice in leadership. He is an adjunct faculty member at ESAMI, Arusha, Tanzania and a researcher at the Graduate School of Business and Leadership, University of KwaZulu-Natal (UKZN). He is the regional director at MISA.

Emmanuel Mutambara (Ph.D.) is with the School of Management and Governance. He holds a Ph.D. in Business Administration from North-West University, South Africa. Professor Mutambara has published more than 100 academic peer-reviewed papers in local and international journals.

Grace Mutung'u is a technology policy researcher based in Kenya. Her interests include information controls and civic space, digital rights and public digital projects. She is currently a Ph.D. student at the University of Nairobi, researching on digital identities and social justice.

Teresia Nzau is a Ph.D. student of strategic communication at the University of Missouri, USA. Broadly, her research examines risk and crisis management from a global perspective. Teresia is a member of the Public Relations Society of Kenya (PRSK).

Cecile Gerwel Proches (Ph.D.) is an academic in the Graduate School of Business and Leadership at the University of KwaZulu-Natal (UKZN), South Africa. Her teaching, research, supervisory and consulting interests include leadership, change management, organizational behaviour, leading in complex and disruptive times, and complexity theory.

Upasana Singh (Ph.D.) is the academic leader and a senior lecturer in the Discipline of Information Systems and Technology at the University of KwaZulu Natal (UKZN), Durban, South Africa. She holds a Ph.D. in Information Systems from the University of South Africa.

Eric Wamanji is a public relations practitioner based in Nairobi, Kenya. He is interested in researching political communication in the age of social media and how brands are using social media in crisis management and brand building.

1 Africa

An Introduction to a Growing Digital Market

Anne W. Njathi and Brandi Watkins

Introduction

Due to the increasing digital connectivity, Africans are leveraging the internet for socializing, communicating, entertainment, information-seeking, digital entrepreneurship, and as a thriving digital marketplace. Africa has the fastest growth rates in internet penetration, increasing from 2.1% in 2005 to 24.4% in 2018 (Internet Society, 2022; ITU, n.d.). Just like other parts of the world, Africans are consuming and enjoying digital products and services, plugging the African continent into the global digital economy. As such, Africa represents a "potentially vast, and untapped market, the world's next great consumer market" (Mersham et al., 2011, p. 195). Beyond market potential, Africa has a large youth concentration who embrace modernity and actively engage in online activities, including a growing creator economy. Taken together, this points to an inflection point in terms of the need for effective communication management in an African-specific context. Effective communication management and continued professionalization of the industry are supported by a rich body of academic research, something scholars have been calling for since the early 2000s. For example, in making a case for the development of African-centric communication management theories, Ronél Rensburg (2007) wrote:

> Scholars and practitioners should scrutinize the state of theory, research, and practice of communication management in Africa with Afro-optimism. They must determine not only how the field can make a contribution to development and empowerment in Africa, but also how Africa can contribute to the field and body of knowledge of communication management on the global stage. The African continent is a greenfield for research, and scholars have finally realized that some, but not all, aspects of Anglo-European-American concept and practice of communication management can be transplanted onto the field in Africa. The composition of the social fabric and the value system of Africa is still far too different from that of the developed world.
>
> (p. 38)

DOI: 10.4324/9781032689654-1

This book is an answer to this call for research within the digital marketing, public relations, and communication disciplines that focus on the complexity that is the African continent. Examples discussed in this chapter, and throughout this book, contribute to larger dynamics of the unfolding of the African digital economy. Simultaneously, it highlights a couple of critical insights, including the fast-evolving African digital landscape, and how African consumers are responding to the transition by embracing digital technology. In addition, these examples underscore a drastic shift in the minds of African consumers, reflecting changes in their needs and behaviors. Before engaging in discussions of research, it is prudent to highlight some of the unique characteristics of the African continent and foreground the events that led to the growth of digital life in Africa including the rapid growth of internet use among Africans, the emerging digital economies, and interest from multinational corporations.

About the African Continent

The African continent is home to 54 countries, each at its own stage of economic development and with different political, cultural, and socioeconomic dynamics. Africa is divided into two regions—Northern Africa, which includes the countries of Algeria, Libya, Egypt, and Sudan, among others, and is often grouped with the Arab nations of the Middle East. Sub-Saharan Africa is the second region, which consists of countries located geographically below the Sahara Desert. Africa is the second most populous continent in the world and accounts for about 18% of the world's population (World Population Review, 2023). In fact, the combined populations of Europe and North America (1.3 billion) are just shy of the African population. Moreover, Africa is the only continent where the population is on the rise, and projections suggest it will have the largest population of people below the age of 25 by 2030 (Bordia Das & Espinoza, 2020; UN, 2017) at 60% of its population (El Habti, 2023). Rapid population growth translates to a larger and younger workforce than in India and China (Jackson, 2020; Tanzi & Lu, 2019). Due to this unprecedented growth, African cities will join globally ranked megalopolis status between 2021 and 2100, as predicted by recent studies compiled by the *Washington Post* (Bearak, Moriarity, & Ledur, 2021). By the year 2100, one in every three people on earth will be Africans and almost half of the young people in the world will be African (Sierra, 2020).

The nations that make up the African continent are as diverse as the people that inhabit it. African countries range from impoverished to wealthy and rural to urban. Many developing countries are still trying to overcome a past ravaged by colonialism and occupation (Ngondo & Klyueva, 2023). On the other hand, some countries, particularly KINGS countries (Kenya, Ivory Coast, Nigeria, Ghana, South Africa; Osiakwan, 2017), have been propelled to massive technological advancement; the reality, as this book shows, is much more complex. These countries have captured the attention of large global corporations and technology companies seeking to take advantage of a youthful population and growing economic status.

Africa Online

The growing importance of the African continent for global technology and multinational companies results from the exponential penetration of the internet. Individuals value convenience and rely on technology for this provision. Digital technology is becoming an integral part of daily life for millions of Africans. A continent with an estimated population of 1.35 billion people, 43% of its population, 601,940,748 according to Internet World Stats (2023), has access to the internet. The exponential uptake of the smartphones (DataReportal, 2023; GSMA, 2023) has permitted a plethora of digital possibilities in the everyday lived digital experiences of millions of Africans. The smartphone, having become less expensive over the years, is the main force behind the expansion of social media advertising. As access to the internet has increased, so has social media use among Africans. Africa's social media users have continuously been on an upward move, with the most recent data indicating over 384 million users on leading platforms (Galal, 2023). Facebook maintains its position as the largest market share among social media platforms in Africa. The platform has 170 million users with traffic generated on the platform sitting at 79.4% while dominating traffic referrals to other websites on the African continent over the observed period. YouTube is the closest, with a share of 6.6% (Statista, 2023).

WhatsApp is a particularly important social media platform for Africans. For instance, on a typical day, 200 million Africans exchange messages via WhatsApp, making it the most popular instant messaging platform (Badenhorst, 2023). Because of the platform's functionality, which includes content sharing, messaging, and payment all coming together, WhatsApp has become a critical tool for many Kenyan small and medium enterprises in running their day-to-day business (Mureithi, 2021), a concept known as social commerce platform for small businesses. In emerging markets, Small- and Medium-Sized Enterprises (SMEs) use WhatsApp to reach, sell, and engage their customers (Caribou Data, 2020). In Nigeria, for example, retailers are using WhatsApp to reach more buyers and navigate the skyrocketing inflation rates. Emeka, a local computer seller, has been using WhatsApp for the past six years selling goods worth millions in the local currency, Naira (Paul, 2023).

Digital Economies

The drastic shift in internet access is transforming the way people shop, communicate, learn, socialize, and work in the continent—an opportunity for most businesses to meet the needs of their consumers at their convenience. The fast-growing African digital market, with enormous potential, is emerging as a vibrant digital e-commerce, advertising space, and creator economy.

Troves of Africans order products online through thriving e-commerce platforms such as Jumuia, Takealot, Konga, and Kilimall, among others (Webretailer, 2023). Online retail revenue in Africa is estimated at around $20 billion annually. At the same time, Sub-Saharan Africa's subscription video-on-demand (SVOD) market is on the rise. There are over 2.6 million Netflix subscribers and estimated to rise to 5.8 million by 2026 (Digital TV Research, 2021). These numbers are outside of other thriving local streaming platforms such as Multichoice, IROKOTV, and iBAKATV (Wang, 2023), an indication of untapped growth for the subscriber base in Africa (Lodderhose, 2023).For example, the usage of ride-hailing apps from big players like Uber and Bolt to local ride-sharing players such as Little Cab in Kenya and Africa Ride in South Africa (Sagaci Research, 2023) showcases the total addressable market potential the African continent holds. Drivers on Uber only have completed over one billion trips in Africa (Kene-Okafor, 2022). Since 2013, Uber, and Uber Eats, cumulatively reached more than 30-million riders and eaters in Sub-Saharan Africa (Khaole, 2022; Venter, 2022).

A study on the Social Media Usage Trends in Africa by *GeoPoll* showed that 80% of the respondents had purchased a product or service advertised on social media (Adika, 2023). Given the existing popularity, penetration, and functionality of Facebook, WhatsApp, Instagram, and YouTube, 92% of SMEs in Kenya use these social commerce platforms to carry out their businesses (Caribou Data, 2020). Since the COVID-19 pandemic, social media usage has increased, especially for video content, which has caused exponential growth in social media advertising. Ad spending in the African social media advertising market is projected to reach US $1.08 billion in 2023 (Statista, 2023). A majority of Africans are increasingly spending more time on social media, prompted by the TikTok's boom during the pandemic and the significant increase in Instagram's video content. Because of increased content consumption, social media advertising has grown significantly (Statista, 2023).

Africa's social media boom has led to the rise of the creator economy (Adeleke, 2021). The creator economy includes influencer marketing, fueled by local content creators, and is transforming the advertising landscape, as suggested by country-specific empirical studies (Eltringham, 2018; Iqani, 2019; Kleintjes, 2017; Njathi, 2023; Njathi & Lee, 2021; Otiende, 2018; Wilson, 2019) that showcase in-depth accounts of influencers' visibility in Sub-Saharan Africa. Altogether, these studies discuss partnerships between brands and influencers to reach consumers, leading to an increase in popularity in Africa. The integration of e-commerce capabilities on social networking sites like Facebook and Instagram is enabling brands to reach customers directly by streamlining the process of selling goods and services online. In addition, the new and innovative payment technologies, and infrastructures such as mobile payments, for example, Mpesa are enabling faster and easier consumer and retailer transactions, while offering new business models (Mckinsey & Company, 2022).

Global Corporate Interest in Africa

As more Africans take advantage of the digital marketplace, global companies are deeply entrenching themselves into the African ecosystem, scouting for their next market. As part of this effort, brands are investing in internet infrastructure on the continent to leverage the vast, budding, youthful population; growing economies; and high internet access and adoption rates. Therefore, it should come as no surprise to see global players who are already well established in Western and European countries such as Google, Amazon, Facebook, Apple, and Microsoft (a.k.a. the GAFAM companies), Netflix, Uber, TikTok, Airbnb entering Africa with multiple technology projects, such as investing in internet infrastructure. For instance, Facebook and Google have been building an undersea cable to allow people to have high-speed internet access (Business Insider SA, 2019; FitzGerald, 2019; Kazeem, 2019; Shapshak, 2019a). Facebook's Free Basics access program has been offered across 20 countries in Africa (Couldry & Mejias, 2019). Microsoft Corporation has invested $100 million in African technology development centers in Kenya and Nigeria (Microsoft, 2019; Miriri, 2019)—proposed hubs for engineers working on artificial intelligence (AI), machine learning, and mixed reality (Morgan, 2019). Google has funded the AI Lab in Ghana (Adeoye, 2019; Morgan, 2019; Shapshak, 2019b), and it launched the Project Link Fiber in Ghana for internet access on a wholesale basis (Osiakwan, 2017).

Africa has also caught the attention of China with Mersham et al. (2011) noting that "China is poised to have more impact on Africa over the next 20 years than any other country" (p. 205). The "Forum on China-Africa Cooperation" in 2000 signaled China's interest in developing a strategic partnership with African countries, and as a result, the Chinese government has encouraged many Chinese companies to establish factories in African countries (Mersham et al., 2011). Chinese companies are also investing in the digital infrastructure in Africa. For example, Alibaba, a Chinese e-commerce company, developed an "inclusive development strategy" for local SMEs in 14 African countries, aiming to open them up for a more inclusive globalized trading network (Caslin, 2019; CNBC, 2019).

The technology sector is not the only sector to find a promising new market of savvy consumers in Africa. Luxury brands like Porsche, Tom Ford, Gucci, and LVH, among others, are scaling up their presence on the continent to meet the demands of the emerging African digital consumer. A report by KPMG (n.d.) on the luxury goods sector in Africa indicates that the continent holds significant potential for the luxury goods segment on the back of a high demographic dividend and rising per capita GDP levels (KPMG, n.d). Africa has a young population, fast-growing cities, and rapidly increasing disposable income.

Implications

Modernization in many African countries coupled with improved internet access, a growing online economy, and interest from global corporations (and countries) has far-reaching implications for the continent. Arora (2019) noted that as people in developing countries are becoming consumers of new media technologies as global, multinational corporations are targeting them as an opportunity for future market growth. Global companies are seducing young people by advertising North American and European brands to African users. Although some view tech companies like Facebook as an equalizer between the rich and the poor in online corporate marketing (Arora, 2019), some brands do not discriminate algorithmically and attempt to lure the poor with choices beyond their means, contributing to the already existing aspirational economy fed by conventional mass media. But what worsens the situation for the Global South, in Arora's (2019) argument, is that they live in areas with weak institutions, few privacy and data protection laws, and vast semiliterate populations. Moreover, there are few checks and balances in these conglomerates. This position places Africa as part of the Global South at odds regarding understanding the uptake of digital media products and services. These peculiarities provide a precursor to exploring how Africa's digital consumption is distinct from other markets.

Another emerging implication of digital growth in Africa concerns data. The panoply of data available on the continent makes Africa irresistible to Digital International Companies (DICs), which view Africa as a suitable uncharted market for testing out new technical products and expanding their market shares (Njathi, 2023). And, if people produce data, Africa has over 70% of its population under 25 (Hinshaw, 2015). As a result, much of the data from Africa will come from a younger population, turning the continent into a rich resource. First, Africa's web traffic (internet clicks and views) comes from the youth population, producing more data than older generations (Silver & Johnson, 2018; Wangari, 2017). If people produce data, then much of the data coming from Africa will come from a younger population. Data is the new form of capitalist accumulation used as a business model by tech giants to maximize profits (Couldry & Mejias, 2019; Kwet, 2019; Srnicek, 2018; Zuboff, 2019). No technology company can ignore the growing market and data opportunities that Africa represents (Ehimuan, 2021).

A third implication for the expansion of digital technology in Africa is a growing digital divide within the continent itself. Although digital connectivity rapidly evolving in Africa varies by country, several African markets have emerged as hotbeds for opportunities discussed above. Despite lagging digital infrastructure, a significant percentage of the African population is out of range for digital connectivity (Bukht & Heeks, 2017; Graham et al., 2017), including inadequate electricity supply and erratic internet connectivity. In addition, as the next billion users in developing countries are becoming consumers of new media technologies as tech giants target them online (Arora, 2019), there are few or nonexistent tech and digital policies such as privacy and data protection laws, making them susceptible to foreign powers. This position places Africa as part of the Global South at odds regarding understanding the uptake of digital media products and services. These peculiarities provide a precursor to exploring how Africa's digital consumption is distinct from other markets, as digital consumers navigate these challenges within the digital landscape.

Book Overview

Businesses leverage digital online platforms, like social media and mobile apps, for public relations and marketing communications. And, as explored in this book, are leveraging communication management techniques to tap into the massive African user base for brand exposure, sales, and customer engagement. The uptake of digital media platforms necessitates the need to understand how digital cultures of consumers and brands are unfolding on a continent once regarded as the "Dark Continent." Despite the increase in usage and adoption of the internet, there is limited information about digital marketing trends in Africa. The research presented in this book is a step in advancing research on public relations and marketing communications from an African-specific context.

As evidenced in the chapters presented herein, the African continent is a rich tapestry of countries, with cosmopolitan countries that have embraced globalization and modernity and countries that are still quite rural and remote. Moreover, there are some parts of the continent still reeling from the effects of colonialism. The diversity of the countries that make up the continent reflects its people. Communication professionals working in African countries must balance the needs of diverse publics with varying communication expectations and preferences. For example, there are parts of the continent that prefer indigenous methods of oral communication whereas the citizens of the more populous, industrialized countries have preferences reflecting those of their Western counterparts (Holtzhausen et al., 2003). The political, economic, and sociocultural complexities of countries in Africa, therefore, necessitate the development of theory, research, and practice that reflects the continent, which as Rensburg (2007) noted can also make significant contributions to our global understanding of communication management.

At the time of publication, there is limited published research on the development of the digital marketing and public relations industries situated in the African context. Moreover, there is a noted lacuna of research on the usage and influence of digital and social media, this despite the marked increase in internet and social media in Africa, particularly among young people, due to the rise in mobile phone penetration in countries across the continent. The chapters in this book represent a step in addressing this gap in the body of knowledge.

The chapters are organized into two discipline-specific categories—studies focusing on public relations (Chapters 2–6) and studies focusing on marketing (Chapters 7–9). Chapter 2 sets the stage with an overview of the existing academic research on African public relations and provides insights into the factors that make practicing public relations in Africa different from elsewhere in the world. With Zimbabwe as a backdrop, Chapters 3 and 4 look at the use of social media as a tool for brand and reputation management. Chapter 3 applied relationship management and agenda-setting theories to qualitatively examine the opportunities and challenges of social media in corporate reputation management. Likewise, Chapter 4 presents a theory-based model to demonstrate the effectiveness of Twitter as a tool for managing corporate reputation management. Chapters 5 and 6 take on social media and crisis communication in Kenya, both examining aspects of the Kenyans on Twitter (KOT) phenomenon. Chapter 5 features a content analysis of KFC's Twitter response to a recent scandal while Chapter 6 examines the role of humorous tweets in addressing political conflict between Uganda and Kenya. Transitioning to more marketing-oriented research, Chapters 7, 8, and 9 look at various applications, opportunities, and challenges of digital marketing. Chapter 7 represents a Northern African perspective and investigates the opportunities and challenges of using social media in digital marketing and public relations in Egypt.

Chapter 8 includes a qualitative assessment of how the University of Cape Coast in Ghana uses social media as a marketing tool, which provides a unique view of the African higher education market. Chapter 9 looks at the growing influencer and creator economy in Nigeria with a quantitative study on the impact of online influencers on consumer purchase intentions. Chapter 10 features a trend analysis of regulatory policies in Kenya and Nigeria. The book concludes with the editors' reflections on the research and suggestions for continued research (Chapter 11).

Bibliography

Adeleke, D. I. (2021, October 5). *Communiqué 16: How to think about Africa's creator economy*. Communiqué. https://cmqmedia.substack.com/p/africa-creator-economy

Adeoye, A. (2019, April 16). Google has opened its first Africa artificial intelligence lab in Ghana. *CNN.* https://www.cnn.com/2019/04/14/africa/google-ai-center-accra- intl/index.html

Adika, N. (2023, September 6). *Social media usage trends in Africa: GeoPoll report*. GeoPoll. https://www.geopoll.com/blog/social-media-usage-trends-in-africa-geopoll-report/#:~:text=Download%20Infographic-,Internet%20Penetration%20and%20Social%20Media%20User%20Base,Africa%20than%20in%20other%20regions

Arora, P. (2019). *The next billion users: Digital life beyond the West*. Harvard University Press.

Badenhorst, H. (2023, March 2). *Africa's WhatsApp economy is on the rise*. IT-Online. https://it-online.co.za/2023/03/02/africas-whatsapp-economy-is-on-the-rise/

Bearak, M., Moriarty, D., & Ledur, J. (2021, November 19). *AFRICA'S RISING CITIES how Africa will become the center of the world's urban future*. Washington Post. https://www.washingtonpost.com/world/interactive/2021/africa-cities/

Bordia Das, M., & Espinoza, S. A. (2020, December 11). *Inclusion matters in A*frica. World Bank. https://documents1.worldbank.org/curated/en/245561571158107064/pdf/Main-Report.pdf

Bukht, R., & Heeks, R. (2017). *Defining, conceptualizing and measuring the digital economy* (Development Informatics Working Paper No. 68). SSRN. https://doi.org/10.2139/ssrn.3431732

Business Insider SA. (2019, May 29). Google to build a powerful new internet cable from Europe to South Africa. *Business Insider*. https://www.businessinsider.co.za/google-is- building-a-powerful-new-internet-cable-from-europe-to-south-africa-2019-6

Caribou Data. (2020, June 1). *Digital behaviors of Kenyan micro-entrepreneurs; Doing business in the age of social commerce*. Finance Digital Africa. https://www.financedigitalafrica.org/wp-content/uploads/2020/06/Caribou-Data-Digital-behaviors-of-Kenyan-micro-entrepreneurs.pdf

Caslin, O. (2019, September 9). *China e-giant Alibaba searching for African gems*. https://www.theafricareport.com/17036/china-e-giant-alibaba-searching-for-african-gems/

Couldry, N., & Mejias, U. A. (2019). *The costs of connection: How data is colonizing human life and appropriating it for capitalism*. Stanford University Press.

CNBC. (2019, June 9). Chinese internet giant Alibaba shares its plans for Africa. *CNBC*. https://www.cnbcafrica.com/news/technology/2018/07/09/chinese-internet-giant-alibaba-shares-its-plans-for-africa/

DataReportal. (2023). *Africa — Reports — DataReportal – Global digital insights*. Data Reportal. https://datareportal.com/reports/tag/Africa

Digital TV Research. (2021, January 1). *African OTT to generate $1.7 billion*. Digital TV Research. https://digitaltvresearch.com/wp-content/uploads/2021/01/Africa-OTT-TV-and-Video-Forecasts-2021-TOC_toc_306.pdf

Ehimuan, J. (2021, May 24). *What my decade at Google taught me about Africa's tech future*. Africa Report. https://www.theafricareport.com/90339/what-my-decade-at-google-taught-me-about-africas-tech-future/

El Habti, H. (2023, September 19). *Why Africa's youth hold the key to its development potential*. World Economic Forum. https://www.weforum.org/agenda/2022/09/why-africa-youth-key-development-potential/

Eltringham, P. (2018, December 1). *Taking play seriously: Exploring the work of Instagram influencers in South Africa* [Honors research report]. Academia.edu. https://www.academia.edu/44658658/Taking_Play_Seriously_Exploring_the_Work_of_Instagram_Influencers_in_South_Africa

FitzGerald, D. (2019, April 7). Facebook looks to build underwater ring around Africa. *Wall Street Journal*. https://www.wsj.com/articles/facebook-looks-to-build-underwater-ring- around-africa-11554649200

Galal, S. (2023, August 31). *Social media in Africa - statistics & facts*. Statista. https://www.statista.com/topics/9922/social-media-in-africa/

Graham, M., Ojanperä, S., Anwar, M. A., & Friederici, N. (2017). Digital connectivity and African knowledge economies. *Questions de Communication*, *32*, 345–360. https://doi.org/10.4000/questiondecommunication.11579

GSMA. (2023). *2023 The mobile economy Sub-Saharan Africa*. GSMA. https://www.gsma.com/mobileeconomy/sub-saharan-africa/

Hinshaw, D. (2015). For a growing Africa hope mingles with a fear of the future. *Wall Street Journal*. http://www.wsj.com/articles/for-a-growing- africa-hope-mingles-with-fear-of-the-future-1448632865

Holtzhausen, D. R., Petersen, B. K., & Tindall, N. T. J. (2003). Exploding the myth of the symmetrical/asymmetrical dichotomy: Public relations models in the new South Africa. *Journal of Public Relations Research, 15*(4), 305–341. https://doi.org/10.1207/S153275XJPRR1504_02

Internet Society. (2022, June 9). *The internet society pledges to expand internet access in Africa*. Internet Society. https://www.internetsociety.org/news/press-releases/2022/the-internet-society-pledges-to-expand-internet-access-in-africa/

Internet World Stats. (2023). *INTERNET USAGE STATISTICS the internet big picture world internet users and 2023 population stats*. Internet World Stats. https://www.internetworldstats.com/stats.htm

Iqani, M. (2019). Picturing luxury, producing value: The cultural labor of social media brand influencers in South Africa. *International Journal of Cultural Studies*, *22*(2), 229–247. https://doi.org/10.1177/1367877918821237

ITU. (n.d.). *Internet statistics*. https://www.itu.int/en/ITU- D/Statistics/Pages/default.aspx

Jackson, P. (2020, January 30). This will be Africa's century. *Financial Times*. https://www.ft.com/content/65e74935-3217-4528-9eab-0c0c4ed170f3

Kazeem, Y. (2019, May 1). Google and Facebook are circling Africa with huge undersea cables to get millions online. *Quartz*. https://qz.com/africa/1656262/google- facebook-building-undersea-internet-cable-for-africa/

Kene-Okafor, T. (2022, May 24). *Uber hits 1 billion rides in Africa*. TechCrunch. https://techcrunch.com/2022/05/24/uber-hits1-billion-rides-in-africa/?guccounter=1&guce_referrer=aHR0cHM6Ly93d3cuZ29vZ2xlLmNvbS8&guce_referrer_sig=AQAAAN3_IEuNYTKXFec9gBiM2lFA5aU0hB-N9CCFH_-EmjqyIKvhFvqtl9

TEYt2Osf_qgOpXAK0Wj9MOepBF-Q3TFNmmXPtvEw2W3bcLxngPvWnkWgy4cDld2rnB1CR_ld8FBSc7McMxCqXIPL8C2aFD2yN3Ewy2Fhq7_cTXlYMm4NfZ#:~:text=Uber%20today%20announced%20a%20significant,covered%2C%20according%20to%20the%20company

Khaole, K. (2022, October 24). *Uber expands African offering; Uber Eats sees healthy growth in SA*. Creamer Media Engineering News. https://www.engineeringnews.co.za/article/uber-expands-african-offering-uber-eats-sees-healthy-growth-in-sa-2022-10-24

Kleintjes, A. (2017). The rise of the 'Instagram economy 'phenomenon in a South African context: An exploration of how conspicuous consumption on Instagram contributes to brand value creation [Master's thesis, University of Cape Town]. OpenUCT. http://hdl.handle.net/11427/27242

KMPG Africa. (n.d). *Luxury goods in Africa*. KMPG. https://assets.kpmg.com/content/dam/kpmg/za/pdf/Luxury-Goods-in-Africa.pdf

Kwet, M. (2019). Digital colonialism: U.S. empire and the new imperialism in the Global South. *Race & Class*, *60*(4), 3–26. https://doi.org/10.1177/0306396818823172

Lodderhose, D. (2023, October 17). *All eyes on Africa: Global streamers & local players are toughing it out in the next frontier of growth — Mipcom Cannes Special*. Deadline. https://deadline.com/2023/10/mipcom-cannes-africa-streaming-1235568865/

Mckinsey & Company. (2022, September 7). *The future of payments in Africa*. Mckinsey & Company. https://www.mckinsey.com/industries/financial-services/our-insights/the-future-of-payments-in-africa

Mersham, G., Skinner, C., & Rensburg, R. (2011). Approaches to African communication management and public relations: A case for theory-building on the continent. *Journal of Public Affairs, 11*(4), 195–207. https://doi.org/10.1001/pa.413

Microsoft. (2019, May 13). *Furthering our investment in Africa: Microsoft opens first Africa Development Centre in Kenya and Nigeria*. https://news.microsoft.com/en-xm/features/furthering-our-investment-in-africa- microsoft-opens-first-africa-development-centre-in-kenya-and-nigeria/

Miriri, D. (2019, May 14). Microsoft to spend $100 million on Kenya, Nigeria tech development hub. *Reuters*. https://www.reuters.com/article/us-africa-microsoft/microsoft-to-spend-100-million-on-kenya-nigeria-tech-development-hub-idUSKCN1SK1BT

Morgan, R. (2019, December 30). Rwanda is bringing tech buzz to Africa. *Fortune*. https://fortune.com/2019/12/30/rwanda-kigali-tech-africa/

Mureithi, C. (2021, October 7). *Social commerce is becoming an important business model in Africa*. Quartz. https://qz.com/africa/2069970/importance-of-whatsapp-facebook-instagram-for-african-businesses

Ngondo, P. S., & Klyueva, A. (2023). Inviting an *Ubuntu*-based approach to public relations theory building in Sub-Saharan Africa. In C. H. Botan & E. J. Sommerfeldt (Eds.) *Public relations theory III: In the age of publics* (pp. 374–392). Routledge.

Njathi, A. W. (2023). The glitz and glamour platform economy: Issues for Instagram monetization for influencers in Nairobi, Kenya [Doctoral dissertation, North Carolina State University]. NC State University Libraries. https://repository.lib.ncsu.edu/handle/1840.20/40891

Njathi, A. W., & Lee, N. (2021). Social media influencers in Africa: An analysis of Instagram content and brand endorsements. In B. Watkins (Ed.) *Research perspectives on social media influencers and their followers* (pp. 91–109). Lexington Books.

Osiakwan, E. M. (2017). The KINGS of Africa's digital economy. In B. Ndemo & T. Weiss (Eds.) *Digital Kenya* (pp. 55–92). Palgrave Macmillan.

Otiende, L. N. (2018). Impact of social media influencers on social brand communication for Kenyan tech brands on Instagram [Doctoral dissertation, United States International University-Africa]. USIU Digital Repository. http://erepo.usiu.ac.ke/11732/4177

Paul, D. S. (2023, April 20). *Nigeria's retailers are using whatsapp to reach more buyers and navigate inflation.* Emerging Markets Today. https://emergingmarkets.today/nigerias-retailers-are-using-whatsapp-to-reach-more-buyers-and-navigate-inflation

Rensburg, R. (2007). Communications management in the Africa context: Implications for theory, research, and practice. *International Journal of Strategic Communication, 1*(1), 37–51. https://doi.org/10.1080/15531180701285269

Sagaci Research. (2023, May 12). *Revolutionising transportation: Analysis of the market of Ride-Hailing Apps in Africa.* Sagaci Research. https://sagaciresearch.com/revolutionising-transportation-analysis-of-the-market-of-ride-hailing-apps-in-africa/

Shapshak, T. (2019a, June 3). Google and Facebook to build own undersea cables around africa. *Forbes.* https://www.forbes.com/sites/tobyshapshak/2019/07/03/google-and-facebook-to-build-own-undersea-cables-around-africa/#306d64cbde16

Shapshak, T. (2019b, December 6). Tech CEOs visit Africa as "source of innovation and talent." *Forbes.* https://www.forbes.com/sites/tobyshapshak/2019/12/06/tech- ceos-visit-africa-as-source-of-innovation-and-talent/#77b4b1ada04e

Sierra, G. (2020, December 11). *The future is African.* Council on Foreign Relations. https://www.cfr.org/podcasts/future-african

Silver, L., & Johnson, C. (2018, October 9). *Internet connectivity seen as having positive impact on life in sub-Saharan Africa.* Laura Silver, Courtney Johnson. https://apo.org.au/node/197261.

Srnicek, N. (2018). *Platform capitalism.* Polity.

Statista. (2023, August 1). *Social media advertising - Africa.* Statista. https://www.statista.com/outlook/dmo/digital-advertising/social-media-advertising/afric

Tanzi, A., & Lu, W. (2019, June 20). Africa's working-age population to top Asia's by 2100. *Bloomberg.* https://www.bloomberg.com/news/articles/2019-07-20/africa-s-working-age-population-to-surpass-china-s-by-2100

United Nations. (2017). *World population.* United Nations. https://population.un.org/wpp/publications/files/wpp2017_keyfindings.pdf

Venter, Irma. (2022, October 24). *Uber expands African offering; Uber Eats sees healthy growth in SA.* Engineering News. https://www.engineeringnews.co.za/article/uber-expands-african-offering-uber-eats-sees-healthy-growth-in-sa-2022-10-24

Wang, Z. (2023, June 26). *Global streaming giants are looking to sub-Saharan Africa as the next engine of subscriber growth.* The Current. https://www.thecurrent.com/global-streaming-sub-saharan-africa-subscriber-growth-amazon-netflix

Wangari, N. (2017, February 27). African millennials; mobile usage and media consumption. *Geopoll.* https://www.geopoll.com/blog/african-millennials-mobile-usage-and-media-consumption

Webretailer. (2023, June 26). *Online marketplaces in Africa: Fast growth, enormous potential.* Webretailer. https://www.webretailer.com/marketplaces-worldwide/online-marketplaces-africa/

Wilson, B. (2019). Review of the book digital influence: Unleash the power of influencer marketing to accelerate your global business, by Joel Backaler. *Information, Communication & Society, 22*(10), 1528–1530. https://doi.org/10.1080/1369118X.2019.1578398

World Population Review. (2023). *Population by Continent.* World Population Review. https://worldpopulationreview.com/continents

Zuboff, S. (2019). *The age of surveillance capitalism: The fight for a human future at the new frontier of power.* Public Affairs.

2 The State of Public Relations Research in Africa

Brandi Watkins

Introduction

In a seminal paper proposing African-centric scholarship on communication management, Mersham, Skinner, and Rensburg (2011) wrote, "Africa can provide a unique contribution to the global practice of public relations" (p. 197), and they assert that Africa represents a "potentially vast and untapped market, the world's next great consumer market" (Mersham et al., 2011, p. 195). Africa also has a high concentration of youth across the continent who have been exposed to a global worldview (Rensburg, 2007), thus increasing the need for the development of modern public relations practices in countries throughout the continent. As such, there is considerable interest in improving the public relations and communication practices across countries on the continent.

Public relations, as a profession, has been practiced for over 50 years in Africa (Nutsugah & Anani-Bossman, 2023); and in many ways is still evolving (Sule & Ridwanullah, 2023). However, scholarly inquiry into the practice on the continent has been sparse (Rensburg, 2007). Research on public relations is an integral part of the professionalization and legitimization of the profession and advances the profession by highlighting the business value of communication and documenting the ever-evolving roles and practices of professional public relations practitioners (Ngondo, 2019). Africa remains "the most underrepresented continent regarding public relations scholarship" and the "lack of visibility of public relations practice and scholarship makes Africa's contributions to the discipline mostly unrecognized" (Nutsugah & Anani-Bossman, 2023, p. 1). Journals such as *The Journal of African Media Studies* and *The African Journal of Information and Communication* are based in Africa and publish public relations research, but in order to determine where African public relations fits into the global perspective of research, it is necessary to assess the contribution of African-based public relations research in Western research journals. To that end, the purpose of this chapter is to investigate the ways in which African public relations has been studied in Western contexts, as defined by publication in journals published predominantly in the United States and Europe. Doing so will provide scholars with an overview of the contexts, methods, and theories in the discipline and point to directions for future research needed to give Africa a more prominent position in discussions of global public relations.

DOI: 10.4324/9781032689654-2

As such, this chapter functions as a snapshot of the current state of public relations research in Africa through a literature review of Western-based academic journals on public relations. The literature review presented in this chapter provides an in-depth analysis of the current state of research on public relations practice on the African continent. Leading U.S. and European-based peer-reviewed academic journals in public relations were analyzed to determine (1) the extent of published public relations research centering on Africa, (2) public relations topics and countries represented in the research articles, (3) theory and methods used in the research, and (4) an analysis of the research findings.

The National Communication Association (n.d.) lists seven journals for the public relations discipline: *Case Studies in Strategic Communication,*[1] *International Journal of Strategic Communication, Journal of Communication Management, Journal of Public Relations Research, Public Relations Inquiry, Public Relations Journal,* and *Public Relations Review,* and were used as source material to identify relevant research articles. To identify eligible articles for the study, a keyword search was conducted using the search function on each journal's website. The keyword "Africa" was searched, and results were reviewed for relevance to the study. Articles had to meet two criteria to be included in this literature review. First, the article had to be a published research paper (full-length articles and research-in-brief were included). Book reviews, commentary, conceptual papers, editorials, and essays were excluded from this analysis. Second, the article had to have an Africa-specific focus as indicated in the article's title, abstract, research context, and data collection/sample information. Articles failing to meet either criterion were excluded from the analysis. Data collection yielded 40 articles available for analysis.

An additional source, the chapter "Inviting an *Ubuntu*-Based Approach to Public Relations Theory Building in Sub-Saharan Africa" by Prisca S. Ngondo and Anna Klyueva (see Ngondo & Klyueva, 2023) in the book *Public Relations Theory III* provided a rich background on the practice of public relations in the African context and, therefore, was used throughout the analysis to provide additional background information. *Public Relations III* is a continuation of previous volumes seeking to advance theory building in public relations and is an important reference for public relations researchers.

The chapter is organized into three sections. First, pertinent background information on public relations on the African continent is provided to identify characteristics of the continent that makes public relations practice different than other global regions. Second, statistical results and synthesis of articles from the literature review are provided. Finally, the chapter concludes with a section on Africa-centric trends that points to directions for future research.

Background on African Public Relations

Much of the criticism of international public relations scholarship centers on the application of Western and Euro-centric models of public relations (Krishna et al., 2020) without regard for the cultures of individual countries. Ngondo and

Klyueva (2023) explained, "applying Western theoretical thought without regard for particularities of local contexts and cultures overlooks the need for public relations theories to be applied differently due to the difference in societal systems and philosophical backgrounds" (p. 387). Moreover, successful public relations practice is largely influenced by the political and cultural environment of a country (Holtzhausen et al., 2003). As such, Krishna et al. (2020) reiterated the call for continued research on models of public relations practice that are "informed by the cultures and societies in which they are set rather than applications of models from the West" (p. 1).

Scholars have argued that approaches to public relations practice and theory building in Africa should center on the distinct characteristics of the continent (Holtzhausen et al., 2003; Mersham et al., 2011; Ngondo & Klyueva, 2023). As Ngondo and Klyueva (2023) argued "country is unique, as not all African countries have the same ecological, political, media, economic, or cultural structures" (p. 378). For example, a defining feature of public relations practice in Africa is balancing indigenous African communication practices (Holtzhausen et al., 2003) with the needs of modern, multinational corporations (Kiambi & Nadler, 2012). Rural populations in Africa preferred indigenous African forms of communication "oral communication through drama, storytelling, proverbs, and poetry" the urban, industrialized populations preferred communication through technological means (Holtzhausen et al., 2003, p. 317). Thus, inter-African and inter-cultural communications are essential to successful public relations in Africa (Mersham et al., 2011).

Culture is an essential component of public relations practice because communication is a byproduct of culture (Ngondo & Klyueva, 2023). Holtzhausen et al. (2003) summarize key differences in Western and African approaches to cultural heritage and knowledge

> Whereas the Western cultural heritage was literature, art, technology, religion and documentation, African cultural artifacts were rituals, symbols, oral story telling (sic), oral literature, music, dance, and spirits. The Western intellectual base was analytical, methodology driven, individualistic, and based on documentation. In contrast, the African intellectual base was rituals, symbols, intuition, community, group, and Ubuntu.
>
> (p. 317)

Many African nations embody a collectivist culture in contrast to the more individualistic cultures of the United States and European countries. The collective culture permeates through the public relations practice in these countries. For example, in Ghana, public relations practitioners work to help clients better understand the public's attitudes and behaviors in an effort to build organization-public relations through two-way communication (Wu & Baah-Boakye, 2009). Ghanaian public relations professionals also help international clients with potential cultural barriers that will allow them to better make local connections. Further, the collectivist culture aligns with the implementation of the cultural interpreter and personal influence models of public relations (Wu & Baah-Boakye, 2009) commonly practiced throughout Africa.

Ubuntu in Public Relations

One way that collective culture manifests in African culture, and by extension public relations practice, is through the philosophy of Ubuntu. Scholars have noted that for African countries, Ubuntu has potential far-reaching implications for public relations practice in a collectivist culture (Mersham et al., 2011; Ngondo & Klyueva, 2023). As Mersham et al. (2011) suggest

> Any normative theory or framework must take into account indigenous and global influences. In such a post-colonial and postmodern perspective for public relations in Africa, a case can be made for the central position of indigenous frameworks based on indigenous epistemologies, namely the African moral philosophy of Ubuntu.
>
> (p. 205)

Ubuntu is value-based, African humanist philosophy popularized by Archbishop Desmond Tutu and Nelson Mandela (Ngondo & Klyueva, 2023), and as Mersham et al. (2011) note, "it runs deeply throughout African thought and action" (p. 196). Ubuntu can be translated as "a person is a person through other people" or more commonly as "I am because we are" (Ngondo & Klyueva, 2023, p. 378). Ubuntu, as a philosophy reflecting a collective culture, presents an interesting juxtaposition to the more Western, individualistic notions of culture (Ngondo & Klyueva, 2023). According to Mersham et al. (2011), Western cultures emphasize isolation and "its penchant for automation often appears designed to reduce face-to-face interaction with others to an absolute minimum" (p. 197), whereas socialization and interaction are defining features of everyday life in Africa.

For public relations, the goals of Ubuntu include creating and maintaining "harmony and reconciliation in society between organizations and their publics" (Ngondo & Klyueva, 2023, p. 382) and working toward "equality, emancipation, and social change, in general" (Holtzhausen et al., 2003, p. 337). Mersham et al. (2011), who proposed Ubuntu public relations, add that Ubuntu "places a high premium on negotiation, inclusiveness, transparency, and tolerance" (p. 196). Ubuntu in public relations is achieved by "incorporating Ubuntu values such as inclusivity, tolerance, transparency, and consensus-building into the organization's relationship-building and communication practices" (p. 382). Further, Holtzhausen et al. (2003) note that Ubuntu-based public relations would "bring joy and harmony to the workplace because at is base were powerful African communication principles of collective work and hospitality, and continuous consultation, and consensus" (p. 317). Ubuntu's emphasis on relationships aligns with some Western notions of public relations as a strategic management function whose end goal is to build mutually beneficial relationships between organizations and publics. Ubuntu differs from Western tradition in that it "emphasizes individual rights and power in the communication process" (Ngondo & Klyueva, 2023, p. 382).

Despite not catching the wider attention of public relations scholarship (Ngondo & Klyueva, 2023), Ubuntu has influenced African public relations practices. Ubuntu public relations was applied during the Covid-19 pandemic with messaging centered around bringing people together for a common purpose, which in that case was to protect each other from the Covid-19 virus (Ngondo & Klyueva, 2023). In a study of South African public relations practitioners, Holtzhausen et al. (2003) found that the Ubuntu model of public relations was practiced and provided evidence for the adoption of culturally specific public relations practices.

The State of African Public Relations Research

A total of 40 articles spanning six public relations journals were used in this analysis. *Public Relations Review* had the most articles on African public relations research (n = 24, 60%), followed by *Journal of Communication Management* (n = 7, 17.5%), *International Journal of Strategic Communication* (n = 5, 12.5%), and *Public Relations Inquiry* (n = 2, 5%). *Public Relations Journal* and *Journal of Public Relations Research* each had one article (n = 1, 2.5%). The timeframe for published articles ranged from 1986 to 2023. The year 2014 saw the most published articles at eight, followed by 2011, 2012, 2020, and 2023 with three articles each year. 2009, 2019, and 2022 were the only other years with multiple articles (n = 2).

A total of nine, all Sub-Saharan countries, were represented in the research. South Africa (n = 19) was the most represented making up 47.5% of the sample followed by Ghana and Nigeria with six articles each (15%). There were two published studies on Zimbabwe and Kenya (5%). The remaining countries had one published study each (n = 1, 2.5%): Botswana, Gabon, Sudan, and Uganda. One study examined several Sub-Saharan countries at once.

Inductive coding revealed 15 public relations topics covered across the research articles. The majority of studies examine public relations practice in the respective country (n = 12, 28.6%). Studies of public relations campaigns was the next most researched topic (n = 5, 11.9%) followed by crisis communication (n = 4, 9.5%). Nonprofit communication and technology/social media each had three articles (7.1%). The following categories had two published articles (n = 2, 4.8%): activism, corporate social responsibility (CSR), internal communication, public relations education, public relations roles, public relations theory and model development. Finally, there was one published article on the following topics (n = 1, 2, 7%): leadership communication, nation-building, and public affairs.

For methodology, the studies were marginally more qualitative (n = 21, 53.8%) than quantitative (n = 15, 38.5%). Three studies utilized mixed methods (7.7%). Survey was the most popular methodology used in 36.4% of the studies (n = 16) and was used to collect both quantitative and qualitative data. The interview methodology was a close second, with 13 studies using either an in-depth interview method or semi-structured interview method (29.5%). Case studies accounted for 11.4% of the methods (n = 5) and content analysis (n = 3, 6.8%). Critical discourse analysis and focus groups appeared in two studies (4.5%) and archival data analysis and textual analysis each appeared in one study (2.3%).

The studies were mostly atheoretical, with only 10 of 40 studies explicitly stating a theoretical framework to guide the work (25%). Among the theories used were relationship management theory, organization-public relationships theory, situation crisis communication theory, stakeholder theory, social representation theory, dialogic principles, two-way symmetrical model of public relations, systems theory, circuit of culture, and Nieman Strategic Integrated Communication model.

Extant research on public relations practice on the African continent can be divided into three broad categories: (1) professionalization of the practice, (2) how Africa fits into the global public relations landscape, and (3) country-specific research. The following sections will explicate these categories.

Professionalization of Practice

Rensburg (2007) argued for the importance and urgency of establishing a professionalized communication management (public relations) industry in Africa. Particularly as research has found that despite finding public relations messaging to be credible, most of the public (of Nigeria) were less trustful of public relations because of the view that they are more beholden to their employers or clients than the public (Olatunji, 2014). Likewise, when surveyed, South African public relations practitioners view the continued professionalization of the industry as important (Niemann-Struweg & Meintjes, 2008). Scholars have put considerable effort into studies describing the professionalization of public relations practice across African countries. The professionalization of practice category includes studies related to the history of professional development, state of public relations education, and research into public relations roles.

History of Professional Development

The professionalization of public relations practice in Africa dates back at least 50 years (Nutsugah & Anani-Bossman, 2023), and some individual countries have professional public relations organizations that predate that. For example, public relations practice was formalized in South Africa in 1957 with the establishment of the Public Relations Institute of South Africa (PRISA; Holtzhausen et al., 2003). Another example is Zimbabwe, which has an active chapter of the International Public Relations Association and its own Institute for Public Relations dating back to 1966 (Ngondo & Klyueva, 2020). Similarly, in Ghana, public relations has existed as far back as the British colonialism era, but Thompson (2018) dates modern public relations practice in the country to the development of The Public Relations Department (now Information Services Department) in 1957. The arrival of multinational companies in the 1960s first introduced public relations practice to Gabon (Oksiutycz & Enombo, 2011). In an attempt to advance the profession of public relations, Nigeria enacted a law that required all public relations practitioners to register as such, which public relations professionals in Nigeria support because they think that "licensing enhances not only the legitimacy of their profession but also think it benefits their clients and organizations" (Molleda & Alhassan, 2006, p. 67). The African Public Relations Association (APRA) serves as an "umbrella body for all national public relations associations in African and consultant to African governments and to the African Union" (Mersham et al., 2011, p. 196).

State of Public Relations Education

An important component of institutionalizing public relations practice is how professionals working in the field are educated and trained. Local universities with robust research programs provide public relations practitioners with a better understanding of the best practices for public relations (Ngondo, 2019). Public relations education and training varies across the countries in Sub-Saharan Africa with some countries providing access to undergraduate and graduate degrees and other countries relying more on on-the-job training and workshops to train prospective practitioners (Ngondo & Klyueva, 2023). For example, strategic communication education in Nigeria is growing with several universities offering undergraduate and master's degrees in the field (Sule & Ridwanullah, 2023). Additionally, the universities that offer degrees in public relations generally have an applied or work experience requirement (Benecke & Verwey, 2020).

Research on public relations education in Ghana and Zimbabwe demonstrates the varying levels of public relations education development. Public relations education in Ghana dates to the 1960s (Thompson, 2018). The University of Ghana was the first, and for a while only, university to offer a master's course in public relations. However, as Nutsugah and Anani-Bossman (2023) note, public relations education in Ghana has seen a tremendous amount of growth in the offerings of diplomas at the undergraduate and postgraduate levels. Thompson (2018) examined the status of public relations education in Ghana by interviewing public relations lecturers and found that PR education in Ghana is highly influenced by Western and U.S.-based approaches, particularly the use of Grunigian theories and systems theory. Moreover, Thompson (2018) suggested that the Ghanaian education system is more akin to the Canadian system with a distinct difference between training future professionals at the technical level (through diploma-level education) and management (at the bachelor's-awarding education level). Anani-Bossman (2021) noted that despite not being fully immersed in organizational strategic management, the practice of public relations in Ghana is becoming more professionalized through advancement in public relations education in the country. While the progress in formalized public relations education is inspiring, it's not the case in all African countries. For example, formal public relations education in Zimbabwe is still developing. Ngondo and Klyueva (2020) note that no Zimbabwean university offers a degree in public relations and most practitioners get on-the-job training or postgraduate diplomas offered by professional organizations or some South African companies. Moreover, most public relations professionals come from other fields like journalism and media studies with various professional and educational backgrounds (Ngondo & Klyueva, 2020).

Of the countries that do offer a specialized degree in public relations, the approaches to practice are heavily influenced by Western, specifically European approaches to the discipline (Ngondo & Klyueva, 2023). However, most of the resources available to would-be public relations practitioners in African countries are U.S.-based (Ngondo & Klyueva, 2023), which by default means it does not account for the philosophies and characteristics that make countries on the African continent unique. Continued scholarly research on public relations practice in Africa would allow for the development of an African-specific public relations curriculum that takes into account the different socioeconomic and cultural situations that will prepare aspiring practitioners for work in African countries (Thompson, 2018). As Venter's (2010) study of South African public relations practitioners revealed, there is room for improvement and growth in African public relations education, specifically citing the need for more business-oriented courses.

Research into Public Relations Roles

A third stream of research into the professionalization of public relations practice in Africa is examination of the various roles that public relations practitioners take on. Benecke and Verwey (2020) noted a shift in public relations research from a near-exclusive focus on organizations to interrogations of the practitioners of public relations. However, as Anani-Bossman (2022) counters, there is no codified typology of public relations roles specific to the African context as most of the existing research applies the normative roles of public relations practitioners in the United States. There is some existing scholarship making inroads to developing such a typology. For example, Ngondo and Klyueva (2020) surveyed public relations practitioners in Zimbabwe to better understand their role. They found that while Zimbabwean public relations professionals adhere to the three traditional roles – technician, manager, and strategist – they also differ from practitioners in neighboring countries. Tindall and Holtzhausen (2011) identified strategists, media specialists, communication liaisons, cultural interpreters, and personal influencers as the roles of strategic communication practitioners in South Africa. In their study of early-mid-career public relations professionals in South Africa, they found that PR practitioners take on an activist role to promote the interest of marginalized populations and also the legitimacy of their own role as activists (Benecke & Verwey, 2020). According to Mersham et al. (2011), cultural intermediary within the larger economy is a common role among African public relations practitioners.

Africa & Global Public Relations Practice

Western and Euro-centric public relations research has shifted away from conceptualizing the discipline and describing roles to research focused on theory development and the use of digital technology (Sule & Ridwanullah, 2023). Extant research on public relations in Africa focuses more on the profession and roles within the profession, models of practice, and strategic communication campaigns

(Ngondo & Klyueva, 2020). Ngondo and Klyueva (2020) go on to note that much of the findings of this research yielded mixed results with "roles blurred and merged" (p. 8). Researchers on public relations in Africa have sought to apply the four historical models of public relations (public information, press agentry, two-way asymmetrical, and two-way symmetrical) to public relations. However, in international settings, the use of the models of public relations is not part of normative public relations practice and should be avoided (Anani-Bossman, 2021; Holthauzen et al., 2003). As Holtzhausen et al. (2003) argue:

> The basis of symmetry as a normative approach to international public relations is a dangerous one. The question might well be asked how a social norm applied and formulated in one country can be applied to a country with a very different social, cultural, and economic climate.
>
> (p. 332)

Instead, researchers should seek to better understand how local public relations professionals engage in the practice (Anani-Bossman, 2021). For example, in the case of South Africa, practitioners developed their own approach to practicing public relations based on the economic, social, and political context of their own country rather than relying solely on Western and Euro-centric public relations models (Holtzhausen et al., 2003).

Still, some research has looked beyond the typical Western approach to public relations to better understand the practice of public relations across African countries. Extant research has found that international models of public relations, cultural interpreter and personal influence, are practiced in Ghana, South Africa and Kenya (Kiambi & Nadler, 2012; Wu & Baah-Boakye, 2009), which indicates an increased emphasis on networking and relationship building in public relations practice (Kiambi & Nadler, 2012). The personal influence model emphasizes the development of relationships with external stakeholders (Anani-Bossman, 2021). Specific to Ghana, Wu and Baah-Boakye (2009) suggest that the interpreter model reflects the importance of international trade and multicultural characteristics of the country while the personal influence model emphasizes the networking capabilities of Ghanaian public relations professionals who "help their organizations and clients socialize and communicate with key publics in order to build good relationships with them" (p. 84). On the other hand, the cultural interpreter model puts more emphasis on helping multinational corporations and clients better understand the local language, culture, customs, and political systems of the host country (Anani-Bossman, 2021). Taken together, these two models of public relations practice reflect the collectivist, interpersonally oriented structure of many African countries (Anani-Bossman, 2021; Wu & Baah-Boakye, 2009). In a nod to the ever-evolving public relations profession in Africa, Tindall and Holtzhausen (2012) introduced a new model of public relations in South Africa – the integrated marketing communication model. These results support Anani-Bossman's (2021) assertion that "the need for African PR scholars and practitioners to critically examine the current trends in PR and communication management and develop a model that reflects the African situation" (p. 91) and goes on to suggest scholars consider the African principle of Ubuntu as a key factor in developing an African model of public relations.

Beyond research on models of public relations practice, some published research investigates other public relations functions like crisis communication and dialogic communication. For example, Adamu and Mohamad (2019) looked at internal crisis communication within the Nigerian Electricity Distribution Industry. Kiambi (2012) analyzed political apologia among Kenyan politicians as contributions to crisis communication research in Africa, while Simon et al. (2023) examined the use of Facebook for crisis management. Madichi and Hinson (2014) applied the dialogic principles to content analyze the websites of the Sub-Saharan Police Service. CSR in Africa has also received attention from scholars with studies looking at the CSR practices in the retail sector (du Plessis & Grobler, 2014) and the insurance industry (Appiah et al., 2016). Pratt and Omenugha (2014) applied relationship management theory to better understand how counties can use strategic communication practices and public relations principles to communicate in a manner that is mutually respectful for Sub-Saharan African countries facing ethnopolitical and ethnoreligious conflicts. Similarly, Kiambi et al. (2023) used the organization-government relationship framework to study the development of public affairs in Kenya. Using focus groups and interviews with communication officers from four South African-based child welfare organizations, Degenaar et al. (2022) extended Niemann's Model of Strategic Integrated Communication, a model specific to public relations practice in South Africa.

Country-Specific Research

Scholars have taken to task researching and discussing public relations in Africa over the last ten years, but still the depth of research and emphasis on sociocultural contexts is lacking (Ngondo & Klyueva, 2020, 2023). For example, Ngondo and Klyueva (2023) note that of the 46 countries that make up Sub-Saharan Africa, only eight have been the subject of academic scholarship. Kiambi and Nadler (2012) remark that most public relations studies center on South Africa, Nigeria, and Ghana. The findings of this analysis support this in that South Africa, Ghana, and Nigeria account for 77.5% of the studies in this sample.

South Africa

South Africa is one of the most researched countries within public relations scholarship. Researchers have noted that South Africa provides a rich tapestry for studying public relations. Benecke and Oksiutycz (2015) explained "South Africa is a truly multicultural society, with many languages, tribes, and ethnicities living together" (p. 4). Holtzhausen (2005) emphasized the opportunities available to study the impact of political change, "While the country has undergone one of the most drastic political changes of the late 20th century, it also has a 45-year tradition of public relations practice and education" (Holtzhausen, 2005, p. 408). In 2003, Holtzhausen et al. wrote that despite being the leading economic power in Sub-Saharan South Africa, there is limited extant research on the country. Twenty years later, Ngondo and Klyueva (2023) remarked that "South Africa is the most researched African nation" (p. 378).

Extant research on public relations in South Africa has covered important issues like nation-building through presidential speeches (Chaka, 2014) and public relations activism in South Africa (Benecke & Oksiutyca, 2015). Other studies have examined public relations practice in South Africa. In a study of South African public relations practitioners, Holtzhausen et al. (2003) found that the Ubuntu model of public relations was practiced and provided evidence for the adoption of culturally specific public relations practices. Research situated in South Africa has contributed to the discussion of global public relations more so than other countries on the continent (Anani-Bossman, 2021) while also emphasizing the need for African-specific public relations practice. For example, South African public relations practitioners noted the importance of social value of the practice over the contribution to the client's bottom line (Holtzhausen et al., 2005), thus emphasizing the need to take into account the impact of cultural differences in public relations practice in Africa.

Ghana

Ghana is another African country that has been the focus of scholarly inquiry within the public relations discipline. Nutsugah and Anani-Bossman (2023) conducted a systematic review of ten years of public relations in Ghana. The analysis included 26 articles from peer-reviewed academic journals and found that most of the research conducted focused on CSR and CSR communication, public relations in higher education, and dialogic principles. Their findings indicate that despite recent progress in studying public relations in Ghana, more work is still needed as the "current status of public relations scholarship is very limited and narrowly focused" (p. 8). They call on Ghanaian public relations scholars to step up and contribute to the body of knowledge through theory development from a Ghanaian public relations perspective. Krishna et al. (2020) contributed to the growing body of literature on West Africa by conducting a case study of how Ghanaian citizens implemented a football (soccer) tournament strategy to improve community relations. This research moves beyond studies of public relations practitioners and situates everyday citizens as purveyors of public relations. Anani-Bossman (2022) found that in Ghana, public relations practitioners took on a combination technician/manager role simultaneously, which implies a lack of difference between the practitioner as technician and practitioner as manager. This is consistent with findings of similar studies of the roles of public relations practitioners across Africa (Anani-Bossman, 2022). In general, Ghanaian public relations has its own characteristics centered on "strong interpersonal relationships, informal relations, and the cultural environment of the country" (Anani-Bossman, 2021, p. 92).

Nigeria

Recent research has addressed public relations practice in Nigeria as well. Sule and Ridwanullah (2023) traced the origins of strategic communication from Nigeria's precolonial era to the present. Adegbola and Okunloye (2022) investigated the Nigerian government's response to actions from terrorist group Boko Haram representing an application of crisis communication to two African-specific events (i.e., 2014 Boko Haram kidnapping of 276 schoolgirls from Chibok and a 2018 Boko Haram kidnapping of 100 schoolgirls from Dapchi). Their study applied situational crisis communication theory to the government's response to these two events. Findings revealed that the government had a delayed response to the initial Chibok incident and attempted to distance itself from the event, but in 2018 the government response was timelier and more demonstrated an acceptance of responsibility.

Zimbabwe and Kenya

Despite not receiving as much attention as South Africa, Ghana, or Nigeria, Zimbabwe and Kenya are starting to capture the attention of public relations scholars. Of interest to note, Ngondo and Klyueva (2020) found that Zimbabwean public relations practice is different from that of its neighbor, South Africa, particularly in the ways that Zimbabwean practitioners execute the roles of technician, manager, and strategist. In regard to social media in Zimbabwe, Ngondo (2019) found that social media has changed the way Zimbabwean public relations professionals manage both internal and external communication. This is the first study on social media use among public relations practitioners in Africa. Findings indicate that they are aligned with other studies on social media and public relations.

Kenya is becoming a central location for multinational corporations seeking to invest in the African market due to its status as a "relatively politically stable country in a region rocked by intermittent political and economic turmoil" (Kiambi & Nadler, 2012, p. 505). In their study on Kenyan public relations professionals, they found that rather than employ Western models of public relations, practitioners tended to favor the personal influence and cultural interpretation models, two important international models of public relations. The use of international models of public relations is consistent with findings in other countries like South Africa and Ghana (Kiambi & Nadler, 2012; Wu & Baah-Boakye, 2009).

Africa-Centric Trends

This chapter provided an extensive overview of the current state of public relations in Africa. Research on public relations practice in Africa is still in its early days. Results of this analysis revealed that most of the published research has made its way into disciplinary conversation in the mid-2010s; despite the practice of public relations in Africa dating back at least 50 years. The findings of this analysis point to three key Africa-centric trends that can inform future scholarship into public relations as practiced in countries on the African continent. First, future scholarship must acknowledge and incorporate the cultural, political, and economic complexities of business in African countries. Second, much of the current research is still sorting and categorizing the nature of public relations practice in Africa, but this is happening concurrently with great technological advances worldwide (e.g., artificial intelligence, data mining, and augmented/virtual reality). Finally, the studies discussed in this literature review are largely from either an organizational or practitioner point of view. There is a dearth of research on publics and stakeholders who are an important consideration in the practice of effective public relations. The following sections will explicate these trends and point to directions for future research.

Complexity of Public Relations in Africa

Despite the great advancements in the public relations profession in Africa, scholarly research focusing on the unique attributes of the countries that make up Africa and their approach to public relations practices is limited. Scholarly inquiry into the public relations practices in a more collectivistic culture will not only benefit public relations development in Africa but can also inform and improve practices in Western countries. As such, scholars should note the ways in which countries in Africa are distinct from one another and from Western and Euro-centric countries. For example, the African population is among the most diverse and complex regions in the entire world (Mersham et al., 2011). The continent is made up of 54 countries and is divided into two regions – North Africa and Sub-Saharan Africa. Countries in Africa range from "large and prosperous and cosmopolitan to impoverished and troubled" (Mersham et al., 2011, p. 195). Sub-Saharan Africa, the geographic region of 46 countries geographically located fully or partially south of the Sahara Desert, is one of the most impoverished areas in the world due to the "legacies of colonial conquest and occupation, neo-colonialism, inter-ethnic conflict, and political strife" (Ngondo & Klyueva, 2023, p. 376) but has recently experienced an economic boon due to its "plentiful mineral and energy resources….prompting rapid development of the communication industry in SSA [Sub-Saharan Africa] nations, including public relations" (Ngondo & Klyueva, 2023, p. 376). Thus, necessitating the need for advanced research on public relations practices in the African context. However, it is important to note that African countries are not a monolith and require individual study to account for ecological, political, economic, and cultural differences (Ngondo, 2019). In a study on public affairs in Kenya, Kimabi et al. (2023) cautioned that findings of a single study, such as theirs, should not be interpreted as capturing the entirety of the continent but rather as a single snapshot of a specific country. They go on to recommend that scholars study public relations practice in other Sub-Saharan and Northern African countries.

Lack of Research on Digital and Technological Advances

This literature review indicated a lack of focus on digital and technological advances with public relations research in Africa. In fact, studies on technology and social media accounted for less than 10% of the sample (n = 3). The practice of effective public relations is dependent on local media infrastructures (Mersham et al., 2011), which varies greatly from country to country with combinations of state-owned and operated media structures and privately owned media organizations (Ngondo & Klyueva, 2023). Notably, access to communication and media development has hindered progress in some African countries (Mersham et al., 2011), but new developments such as mobile phone and broadband internet access have prompted growth in public relations practices (Mersham et al., 2011; Ngondo & Klyueva, 2023). In particular, the high usage rate of mobile phones has greatly impacted the African information ecosystem with most Africans turning to social media as their main source of content and information (Ngondo & Klyueva, 2023). Increased mobile phone usage has important implications for the practice of public relations as it is the primary means for accessing the internet for many Africans (Ngondo & Klyueva, 2023). As such, scholars should prioritize digital technology, particularly mobile, as it is an important information source for many Africans.

A considerable amount of Western public relations research has looked at the impact of new technology on the practice (Sule & Ridwanullah, 2023); however, studies on the use of technology in African public relations, specifically, have not kept pace. Among the studies in the sample of articles, one study looked at how Zimbabwean public relations practitioners used digital and social media (Ngondo, 2019). Findings of this study revealed that digital and social media is an important component of public relations practice with respondents indicating they spend a little more than half of their time on digital media. Other studies in the sample looked at the organizational use of the internet (Madichi & Hinson, 2014; Naudè et al., 2004). More studies of this ilk are necessary to get a more comprehensive look at the impact of digital technology not only on the practice of public relations but also on how it has changed the day-to-day activities of African citizens.

Lack of Research on Publics and Stakeholders

While not explicitly coded for in the study, the review of literature demonstrates that much of the published public relations research in Africa is void of the perspective of publics and stakeholders, opting instead to capture the perspectives of the organization or practitioner. One study in this sample, Olatunji (2014) examines the general public of Nigerians' perceptions of public relations practice in contrast to that of public relations practitioners. The omission of the publics and stakeholders that organizations and practitioners serve fails to capture the full picture of public relations practice. Mersham et al. (2011) noted that public relations in Africa have "yet to realize its full responsibility to the urban and rural classes in Africa" and to meet the "needs and aspirations, a new approach to public relations practice needs to be devised through communication and collaboration with the African social and political order" (p. 205).

The absence of audience-centered research is particularly notable given the emphasis on the collective and inherently social nature of African life. As Ngondo and Klyueva (2023) suggest, "culture plays a crucial role in public relations because public relations is a communication function, while communication itself is a cultural phenomenon" (p. 387). By extension, the people of a culture are an important component of the equation. One area of potential for public relations scholarship is the inclusion of the Ubuntu philosophy. Ubuntu recognizes the interdependence of members of the community along with organizations and emphasizes nurturing relationships differs from Western approaches to public relations that has a tendency to prioritize the organization and power in communication (Ngondo & Klyueva, 2023). Ubuntu provides public relations researchers with a research context that is uniquely African to continue developing the field of public relations research.

Conclusion

Inroads are being made to improve the visibility of African public relations research globally. As evidenced by the data presented in this study, there has been a slight uptick in the publication of African-based public relations research in Western journals starting in the 2010s. Additionally, at the time of publication, scholars are working to establish a presence for African-based research within U.S.-based academic communication associations. But, as this literature review reveals, more work is needed to advance African public relations research. Specifically, research that integrates African-specific philosophies and culture into the practice of public relations is necessary. Rather than relying on application of the often-ill-fitting Western theories and models of public relations, scholars should embrace the diversity of the African continent to develop an understanding of public relations practice that is distinct to Africa. In doing so, the contributions of African public relations can be more readily realized on a global stage.

Note

1 At the time of publication, *Case Studies in Strategic Communication* is on hiatus and was not included in this literature review.

Bibliography

Adamu, A. A., & Mohamad, B. (2019). Developing a strategic model of internal crisis communication: Empirical evidence from Nigeria. *International Journal of Strategic Communication, 13*(3), 233–254. https://doi.org/10.1080/1553118X.2019.1629935

Adegbola, O., & Okunloye, O. (2022). A tale of two kidnappings: Government response to Chibok & Dapchi attacks in Nigeria. *Public Relations Review, 48*, 1–8. https://doi.org/10.1016/j.pubrev.2022.102248

Anani-Bossman, A. A. (2021). An exploration of strategic public relations management in Ghana. *Public Relations Inquiry, 10*(1), 73–96. https://doi.org/10.1177/2046147X20979292

Anani-Bossman, A. A. (2022). An empirical investigation of public relations roles: A case study of the financial service sector of Ghana. *Corporate Reputation Review, 25*, 94–105. https://doi.org/10.1057/s41299-021-00114-8

Appiah, K. O., Amankwah, M. A., & Asamoah, L. A. (2016). Online corporate social responsibility communication: An emerging country's perspective. *Journal of Communication Management, 20*(4), 396–411. https://doi.org/10.1108/JCOM-06-2015-0048

Benecke, D. R., & Oksiutycz, A. (2015). Changing conversation and dialogue through LeadSA: An example of public relations activism in South Africa. *Public Relations Review, 41*, 816–824. http://dx.doi.org/10.1016/j.pubrev.2015.06.003

Benecke, D. R., & Verwey, S. (2020). Social representation of PR activism: Perceptions of early career public relations professionals in South Africa. *Public Relations Review, 46,* 1–9. https://doi.org/10.1016/j.pubrev.2020.101978

Chaka, M. (2014). Public relations (PR) in nation-building: An exploration of the South African presidential discourse. *Public Relations Review, 40*, 351–362. https://dx.doi.org/10.1016/j.pubrev.2013.11.013

Degenaar, A., Fourie, L. M., & Holtzhausen, L. (2022). A strategic integrated communication framework for child protection organizations in South Africa, *16*(5), 700–721. https://doi.org/10.1080/1553118X.2022.2093204

du Plessis, N., & Grobler, A. F. (2014). Achieving sustainability through strategically driven CSR in the South African retail sector. *Public Relations Review, 40*, 267–277. http://dxdoi.org/10.1106/j.pubrev.2013.11.009

Holtzhausen, D. R. (2005). Public relations practice and political change in South Africa. *Public Relations Review, 31*, 407–416. https://doi.org/10.1016/j.pubrev/2005.05.011

Holtzhausen, D. R., Petersen, B. K., & Tindall, N. T. J. (2003). Exploding the myth of the symmetrical/asymmetrical dichotomy: Public relations models in the new South Africa. *Journal of Public Relations Research, 15*(4), 305–341. https://doi.org/10.1207/S153275XJPRR1504_02

Kiambi, D. (2012). Ethnic appeal: A self-defense tool for Kenyan politicians. *Public Relations Review, 38*, 144–146. https://doi.org/10.11016/j.pubrev.2011.08.019

Kiambi, D., Arceneaux, P., & Golan, G. (2023). Organization-government relationships in sub-Saharan Africa: The emerging public affairs industry in Kenya. *Journal of Communication Management, 27*(4), 433–450. https://doi.org/10.1108/JCOM-07-2022-0093

Kiambi, D., & Nadler, M. K. (2012). Public relations in Kenya: An exploration of models and cultural influences. *Public Relations Review, 38*, 505–507. https://doi.org/10.1016/j.pubrev/2012.01.007

Krishna, A., Connaughton, S. L., & Linabary, J. R. (2020). Citizens' political public relations: Unpacking choices, and emergent and deliberate strategies in building trust and relations among groups in conflict. *Public Relations Review, 46*, 1–10. https://doi.org/10.1016/j.pubrev/2023.101853

Madichi, N. O., & Hinson, R. (2014). A critical analysis of the "dialogic communications" potential of sub-Saharan African Police Service websites. *Public Relations Review, 40*, 338–350. https://doi.org/10.1016/j.pubrev.2013.10.009

Mersham, G., Skinner, C., & Rensburg, R. (2011). Approaches to African communication management and public relations: A case for theory-building on the continent. *Journal of Public Affairs, 11*(4), 195–207. https://doi.org/10.1001/pa.413

Molleda, J.-C., & Alhassan, A. D. (2006). Professional views on the Nigeria Institute of Public Relations' law and enforcement. *Public Relations Review, 32*, 66–68. https://doi.org/10.1016/j/pubrev.2005.10.008

National Communication Association. (n.d.). *Journals publishing communication research.* https://www.natcom.org/academic-professional-resources/research-and-publishing-resource-center/journals-publishing

Naudѐ, A. M. E., Froneman, J. D., & Atwood, R. A. (2004). The use of the internet by ten South African non-governmental organization – a public relations perspective. *Public Relations Review, 30*, 87–94. https://doi.org/10.1016/j.pubrev/2003.11.008

Ngondo, P. S. (2019). An exploratory study: Digital and social media use by Zimbabwean public relations practitioners. *Public Relations Journal, 12*(3), 1–26.

Ngondo, P. S., & Klyueva, A. (2020). Exploratory study of public relations roles in Zimbabwe. *Public Relations Review, 46*, 1–10. https://doi.org/10.1016/j.pubrev.2020.101961

Ngondo, P. S., & Klyueva, A. (2023). Inviting an *Ubuntu*-based approach to Public relations theory building in Sub-Saharan Africa. In C. H. Botan & E. J. Sommerfeldt (eds.) *Public relations Theory III: In the age of publics* (pp. 374–392). Routledge.

Niemann-Struweg, I., & Meintjes, C. (2008). The professionalism debate in South African public relations. *Public Relations Review, 34*, 224–229. https://doi.org/10.1016/j.pubrev.2008.03.029

Nutsugah, N., & Anani-Bossman, A. (2023). Development of public relations research in Ghana: A systematic review. *Public Relations Review, 49*, 1–10. https://doi.org/10.1016/j.pubrev.2023.102348

Oksiutycz, A., & Enombo, M. P. (2011). Public relations in private sector companies in Gabon. *Public Relations Review, 37*, 274–280. https://doi.org/10.1016/j.pubrev.2011.03.011

Olatunji, R. W. (2014). As others see us: Differing perceptions of public relations in Nigeria among practitioners and the general public. *Public Relations Review, 40*, 466–472. http://dx.doi.org/10.1016/j.pubrev.2014.02.007

Pratt, C. B., & Omenugha, K. A. (2014). "My God is Not Your God": Applying relationship management theory to managing ethnoreligious crises in Sub-Saharan Africa. *International Journal of Strategic Communication, 8*, 100–125. https://doi.org/10.1080.1553118X.2014.882338

Rensburg, R. (2007). Communications management in the Africa context: Implications for theory, research, and practice. *International Journal of Strategic Communication, 1*(1), 37–51. https://doi.org/10.1080/15531180701285269

Simon, C., Rees, S., & Thomas, R. (2023). Behind the scenes: A critical discourse analysis of Botswana government power plays on Facebook during two post-millennial state-owned organizational crises. *Public Relations Inquiry, 12*(3), 321–341. https://doi.org/10.1177/2046147X231200891

Sule, S. Y. U., & Ridwanullah, A. O. (2023). The evolution of strategic communication practices and reflections in Nigeria. *Public Relations Review, 49*, 1–11. https://doi.org/10.1016/j.pubrev.2023.102323

Thompson, E. E. (2018). Public relations education in an emerging democracy: The case of Ghana. *Journal of Communication Management, 22*(4), 476–489. https://doi.org/10.1108/JCOM-04-2018-0038

Tindall, N. T. J., & Holtzhausen, D. R. (2011). Towards a roles theory for strategic communication: The case of South Africa. *International Journal of Strategic Communication, 5*, 74–94. https://doi.org/10.1080/1553118X.2011.561075

Tindall, N. T. J., & Holtzhausen, D. R. (2012). Toward an integrated model of communication: The case of South Africa. *Journal of Communication Management, 16*(4), 371–387. https://doi.org/10.1108/13632541211279003

Venter, B.-P. (2010). Views of PRISA-members on South African public relations: An exploration. *Public Relations Review, 36*, 281–284. https://doi.org/10.1016/j.pubrev.2010.04.007

Wu, M-Y., & Baah-Boakye, K. (2009). Public relations in Ghana: Work-related cultural values and public relations models. *Public Relations Review, 35*, 83–85. https://doi.org/10.1016/j.pubrev.2008.09.015

3 Corporate Reputation Management Opportunities and Challenges in the Social Media Age

Experiences of Public Relations Practitioners in Zimbabwe

Tendai Chari

Introduction

Social media networks have fundamentally transformed public relations, albeit in a contradictory way. On the one hand, public relations practitioners have at their disposal a global communication vehicle that reaches millions of people instantly at very little or no cost. The viral nature of social media means that public relations practitioners have been gifted with a medium that can propel an organization's brand to "instant fame and fortune" (Scott, 2008, p. 8). In addition, social media enables public relations practitioners to bypass mainstream media gatekeepers, making it possible for organizations to publish creative digital content and provide or receive real-time feedback through discussions, commentaries, evaluations, and corrections to the original content (Wright & Hinson, 2008, 2009). On the other hand, social media has made corporate reputation "more fragile and more open to attack" than before (Stern, 2015, p. vii) as everybody becomes a producer of content. Thus, the power of public relations practitioners in shaping corporate agendas is being whittled down, particularly as publics can write and whatever they want however they want about the quality of an organization's goods and services. A key assumption made in this chapter is that corporate reputation is the most intangible asset of any organization (Bechan, 2008; Lee, 2022; Mikola, 2016; Pires & Trez, 2018; Pollak & Markovic, 2022; Sirzad, 2022). Consequently, building, protecting, and sustaining corporate reputation is crucial for organizations to be successful in the long run. In the era of social media networks, whereby news and information travel very fast and reach many people, corporate reputation has become more vulnerable than ever before.

Existing studies mainly focus on how organizations in industrialized countries of the West leverage on digital media communication technologies to manage their corporate reputation (McCorkindale & Distaso, 2013). This literature has neglected the impact of social media on corporate reputation management in the global South, particularly in Africa. Consequently, there is a knowledge lacuna with regard to how public relations practitioners in Africa perceive the impact of social media on corporate reputation. Combining insights from the relationship management theory and agenda-setting theory, this chapter is a qualitative exploration of opportunities

DOI: 10.4324/9781032689654-3

created for and challenges presented to corporate reputation management by social media in Zimbabwe. How public relations practitioners perceive, opportunities created, and challenges posed by social media on corporate reputation are questions at the core of this paper. The ultimate objective of the chapter is to present an African, particularly Zimbabwean, perspective of the impact of digital communication technologies on public relations.

Zimbabwe is suited for this nature because it is the only African country that has experienced protracted economic volatility spawned by stagflation during an onslaught from global and local online media since the early 2000. The hyperinflationary environment has portended different types of business malpractices as organizations try to remain afloat in the turbulent economic environment which fosters immense customer dissatisfaction and often finds an outlet through the various social media networks. A case in point is the 2020 viral video of an angry customer who alleged that he had been poisoned by milk produced by a leading milk processing company in Zimbabwe. In the videos, the customer was seen uttering damaging words and using the milk to wash his toilet and bicycle, claiming that the milk was not fit for "human or dog consumption". Earlier, he had approached the company demanding $500,000 (USD) as compensation for the sickness he allegedly suffered because of the bad milk, but the company refused to do so (Netsianda, 2020). The company went to court to force the customer to take down the videos and interdict him from "recording videos, audios, or publishing anything which damaged the company's reputation" (Netsianda, 2020, para 11). This highlights the emerging conundrums that corporate reputation managers must contend with in the social media era.

The rest of this chapter unfolds as follows: After this introduction, which is the first section, section two surveys literature related to the study and discusses the theories underpinning the study, namely the corporate reputation management theory and the agenda-setting theory. After that, section three discusses the methodology employed in the study. Section four presents study findings based on themes gleaned from the electronic questionnaire administered to 15 purposively sampled public relations practitioners who are the target of this study. Finally, section five provides concluding remarks and critically reflects on the unique trends in relation to the social media-corporate reputation nexus in the African, particularly the Zimbabwean, context.

Corporate Reputation Management

Corporate reputation has become one of the most valuable intangible assets in an organization and needs to be managed proactively, particularly in view of emerging threats entering the business environment (Bechan, 2008, p. 1). Lee (2022) argues that corporate reputation needs to be protected proactively because it takes many years to build, yet it can be destroyed in a few minutes; particularly, in the era of new technologies where information travels faster and reaches millions of people in real time. Reputation is, however, a contentious concept with varied interpretations and definitions. Most scholars agree that reputation is how an organization is regarded by both internal and external publics and not how it perceives itself. Accordingly, reputation has been defined as "the aggregate estimation in which a person or entity is held by individuals and the public against a criterion based on past actions and perceptual representation of future prospects when compared to other persons or entities" (Serrat, 2017, p. 481). Pires and Trez's (2018) emphasizes the composite nature of perceptions and their future implications and defines reputation as "the collective perception of the organization's past actions and expectations regarding its future actions and expectations, in view of its efficiency in relation to the main competitors" (p. 48). Corporate reputation management is thus understood as entailing managing and channelling the "thoughts, perceptions, attitudes, knowledge and feelings of internal and external" stakeholders through the dissemination of messages (Altunbas & Diker, 2015, p. 44). Fombrun (1996) argues that a corporate reputation is built in a planned manner by taking into consideration the environment in which the organization operates.

Contemporary paradigms of public relations locate corporate reputation management in the strategic functions of public relations (Adlmaier – Herbst, 2017; Lee, 2022; Serrat, 2017; Tong, 2022) whereby the primary focus of public relations is creating and maintaining beneficial relations between an organization and stakeholders (Christensen et al., 2010, p. 20). Abdullah & Aziz (2011) opine that successful corporations need to keep the support of all stakeholders by maintaining a proper balance between the interests of stakeholders and the goals of the organization.

Corporate Reputation Management in the Digital Era

There is consensus among scholars that reputation has become more fragile in the era of digital communications (Bechan, 2008; Pollak and Markovic, 2022; Slee, 2011; Van Den Berg & Struwig, 2016). However, very little is known about the impact of social media on corporate reputation in the global South, and Africa, in particular. In their study based on sentiment analysis using a sample of e-commerce representatives in Central Europe, Pollak and Markovic (2022) found that managing corporate reputation in a turbulent environment was a huge challenge as the emerging marketing continuously generated multiple variables where some of these variables create new threats while some were transformed into opportunities (Pollak & Markovic, 2022).

A study exploring the value of social media on corporate reputation based on interviews with participants from the social media realm and corporate communicators (Slee, 2011) found that social media was considered a high-value addition to corporate reputation management. Social media attributes, such as its ability to communicate with stakeholders directly, capacity to re-negotiate power relationships, enabling stakeholders to hold companies accountable through dialogue because of its facilitation of two-way communication, facilitation of relationships, maintaining and building large networks, openness and transparency, building new relationships, easy creation and distribution of content and ability to shape the news agenda, were identified as most valuable for corporate reputation (Slee, 2011). The main drawback of this study, however, was that it ignored the downside of social media in corporate reputation. Like Slee (2011), Pollak and Markovic (2022) identified cost reduction, reduced producer-consumer communication gap, availability of feedback and synergies between the consumer and the producer as some of the advantages of digital media in reputation management. However, unlike Slee's (2011) overly optimistic study, Pollak and Markovic (2022) identified the unregulated nature of the Internet and its open architecture as problematic because companies are no longer able to control their messages. Maas et al. (2020) argue that although digital communication technologies enable organizations to reach more people instantly, public relations practitioners have not fully embraced digital technologies because they were ill-equipped to do so.

Some studies have noted that although social media enables organizations to cultivate and maintain positive relationships with stakeholders, the online environment is unpredictable and spontaneous such that companies are not able to control their narratives online (Holve, 2014). Holve (2014) shows how angry customers' comments online can quickly escalate to a crisis which may draw in many social media users. This demonstrates that "electronic word-of-mouth is a dangerous factor for the reputation of an organization" (Holve, 2014, p. 2).

While this literature illuminates the opportunities created and challenges posed by the digital media to corporate reputation, these studies mainly focus on the industrialized democracies of the West, leaving a knowledge lacuna on the global South, particularly African practices. Suffice to point out that there are some snippets of literature on Africa (Bechan, 2008; Masondo, 2022; Moyo, 2022; Njuka & Phiri, 2021; Van Den Berg & Struwig, 2016; Van Den Heever & Rensburg, 2018) although none of them specifically focus on opportunities and challenges created by social media for corporate reputation management. Van Den Berg and Struwig's study based on documentary analysis and interviews (2016) examined social media policies at South African universities to shed light on existing corporate reputation management practices in the higher education sector. Deploying a descriptive survey design, Njuka and Phiri (2021) investigated factors influencing social media in managing corporate reputation of a Christian organization in Zambia, questioning whether there was a relationship between these factors. The study found that there was an impressive volume of content about the organization on social media, although its response to criticism online was unsatisfactory. Utilizing a case study research design and a combination of interviews and content analysis of social media posts and conversations, Van den Heever and Rensburg (2018) investigated the implementation of a proposed online reputation management framework for a South African Non-Profit Organization (NPO) and its effect on stakeholder engagement. However, the study did not delve into corporate reputational challenges and opportunities occasioned by social media.

There are also a few unpublished works in the form of dissertations. These include Masondo's (2022) study examining how South African hip-hop artists used social media to shape their images and reputation, and Moyo's (2022) study exploring how Twitter could be used as a blog to improve the corporate reputation of telecommunications companies operating in Zimbabwe, as well as Van den Heever's (2018) investigation on the implementation of a proposed online reputation management framework in a South African NPO. Again, these do not focus on opportunities and challenges brought by social media to corporate reputation management.

Relationship Management Theory

The relationship management theory and the agenda-setting theory provide powerful explanatory lenses for understanding how organizations manage their corporate reputations in the social media age. Recent scholarship conceptualizes public relations as a strategic management function rather than a communication activity (Grunig, 2006; Ledingham, 2003; Ledingham & Hung-Baesecke, 2015; Tong, 2022). Ledingham (2003) defines relationship management as "the ethical and efficient management of an organization-stakeholder relationship focused, over time, on common interests and shared goals in support of mutual understanding and mutual benefit" (p. 190). The relationship management theory posits that the relationship between an organization and its publics – who are viewed as "stakeholders" – must be considered the most important function of public relations. From this perspective, the fundamental role of public relations is to create and develop ongoing or long-term relationships with key stakeholders of the organization (Boie, 2012). Thus, public relations' main goal is to balance the interests of the organization and publics through management of the stakeholder relationships. Public relations is seen as most effective when stakeholders, with whom public relations practitioners communicate, are identified as part of the organization's strategic management framework and when the public relations function is managed strategically at the PR department level (Grunig & Grunig, 2000, p. 311). Public relations becomes part and parcel of the "management function that establishes and maintains mutually beneficial relationships between an organization and the publics on who whom its success or failure depends" (Cutlip et al., as cited in Ledingham, 2003, p. 181).

Relationship management theory correlates with two important theories in public relations discourse, namely the stakeholder management theory and the exchange theory postulated by Hon and Grunig (1999). Stakeholders are defined as "all those groups and individuals that can affect or are affected by the accomplishment of organizational purpose" Freeman, 1984, p. 5). The stakeholder theory posits that an organization has the responsibility to create as much value for its stakeholders, and to be able to do this, organizations must manage their relationship with stakeholders through activities such as identifying and prioritizing the interests of their stakeholders, assessing their needs, collecting ideas from them, and integrating this knowledge into the strategic management processes (Rhodes et al., as cited in Van den Heever & Rensburg, 2018, p. 59). The exchange theory links up with the relationship theory in the sense that an organization's stakeholders are perceived to be in an exchange relationship with the organization – a relationship that accrues benefits to both parties.

Agenda-Setting Theory

The theory of agenda-setting explains how public relations practitioners can use media, including social media, to influence public perceptions about corporate reputation. Although its origins are in mass communication research (Fortunato & Martin, 2016; McCombs, 2011; McCombs & Shaw, 1972), the theory has wider application in the humanities and social sciences in the contemporary world (Akpabio, 2017; Carroll, 2011; Meijer & Kleinninhuis, 2006). The theory argues that the mass media have the power to shape a nation's agenda by focusing the public's attention on a few issues or topics (Fortunato & Martin, 2016; McCombs, 2011; McCombs & Shaw, 1972). Agenda-setting means that what is prioritized by the media also tends to be prioritized by the public (McCombs, 2011). Thus, the salience of issues and objects in the mass media is linked to the formation of opinions by the public. The concept of priming reflects the way in which the mass media give attention to some issues while ignoring others. By forcing attention to certain issues, the mass media build up images of political figures and issues. The agenda-setting function is most succinctly illustrated by Cohen's statement that "the press may not be successful much of the time in telling what to think but is stunningly successful in telling its readers what to think about" (as cited in McCombs & Shaw, 1972, p. 177).

Agenda-building, an extension of the concept of agenda-setting, explains how external information resources such as public relations efforts of organizations shape public opinion and perceptions about an organization (Kim et al., 2015). For instance, it has been found that political advertising can influence issues that are prioritized by the mass media while the way an organization is portrayed in the media also influences how the public perceives the organization (Kim et al., 2015). Agenda-building relates to the notion that organizations can leverage digital communication technologies to set and frame their agendas to influence perceptions of stakeholders. By engaging in information subsidies such as press releases, statements, conferences, and commercialization, public relations practitioners can shape the media agenda by directly addressing stakeholders, thereby side-stepping gatekeepers in the mainstream media (Akpabio, 2017). Some scholars point to threats posed by digital communication technologies for corporate reputation because many people have more direct access to media which they can use to generate messages that contradict corporate narratives (Van den Heever & Rensburg, 2018). Grunig (2009) debunks the notion that digital media give public relations practitioners more control over messages. He asserts that the illusion of control comes from a paradigm of public relations that "views public relations as a messaging, publicity, information, and media relations" (p. 4).

In different ways, perceptions of Zimbabwean public relations practitioners on opportunities and challenges brought by social media in the public relations landscape mirror the ambiguities discussed above. Accordingly, the chapter addresses two key research questions: (1) What opportunities have been created by social media for corporate reputation management in Zimbabwe? (2) How does social media present challenges for corporate reputation in Zimbabwe? The next section discusses the methodology employed in the study.

Methodology

This chapter qualitatively explored Zimbabwean public relations practitioners' perceptions of opportunities created and challenges posed by social media for corporate reputation management. Data were elicited through an electronic "semi-structured" questionnaire emailed to 15 purposely selected public relations practitioners in the capital of Zimbabwe, Harare. The questionnaire comprised six open-ended questions designed to obtain information about the participants' perceptions of opportunities and challenges created by social media in corporate reputation management. The study was conducted between 21 March 2023 and 27 April 2023. An attempt was made to ensure balance by selecting participants from organizations with different levels of risk aversion encompassing civic, public, and private sectors. Incidentally, all participants were former journalists with a minimum of ten years of work experience. However, because of the qualitative, exploratory nature of this study, the idea was never to aggregate generalizations about the phenomenon under consideration, but rather, to capture the feelings, thoughts, and interpretations of meanings and processes (Vanderstoep & Johnson, 2009).

Public relations practitioners were the focal point of this study because the aim was to generate sufficient data to shed insights on the impact of social media on corporate reputation management in the Zimbabwean context. Globally, Zimbabwe being no exception, public relations practitioners are the coalface of public communication and are strategically positioned to be among innovators and early adopters of technological innovations.

Zimbabwe was suitable for this study because of two considerations. First, the country is one of the very few African countries which has experienced an accelerated growth in digitization in recent years, with 5.74 million Internet users at the beginning of 2023, which translates to an Internet penetration of 34.8% (DATAREPORTAL, 2023). Second, growth in the proportion of citizens with access to Internet and social media has the potential to disrupt the way in which information is produced, consumed, and shared, thereby posing risks to corporate reputation management.

Despite the limitations of the electronic questionnaire, linked to lack of conversation, non-existence of follow-up questions, and a limited register of communication, participants had adequate time to engage with the questionnaire and complete it from the comfort of their homes or offices and were able to think through the questions without undue pressure to provide "politically correct" responses (Opdenakker, 2006).

The textual data were transcribed, thematically coded, and analysed to explicate emerging themes. Quotations for use in the narrative report and discussion were selected, organized, and used in reporting the findings. To protect the privacy of participants, their identities were anonymized using code names such as PR1 and PR2 and were referred to only using generic titles.

Study Findings

This section discusses study findings focusing on themes that emerged from analysis of data collected using the electronic questionnaire. Emerging themes were collapsed under opportunities created by and challenges posed by social media for corporate reputation management as per the perceptions of Zimbabwean public relations practitioners.

Opportunities

With regard to opportunities created by social media for corporate reputation management, key themes were instant communication, cost-effectiveness, wider reach, feedback and interactivity, direct control of messages, networking and collaborations. Most participants mentioned how social media had made it easy to disseminate messages to their stakeholders with speed during emergency situations. They explained how social media enabled them to disseminate content instantly, "be it advertorial, promotional, or otherwise" (PR2). In this regard, social media was compared with traditional media, and it was concluded that social media had advantages because content could be "distributed and accessed faster" (RP3). One of the participants explained that instant communication meant that public relations would "improve because there is some feedback from internal and external publics" (PR8). Another participant described WhatsApp, Twitter, and Facebook as "important channels" that could be used to "quickly and timely" communicate with stakeholders (PR10). Social media is thus constructed as an enabler and a game-changer in reputation management because it makes it easy for public relations practitioners to respond to crises much faster than traditional media where they go through gatekeepers. This resonates with previous studies where new communication technologies have been framed as "competitors" to traditional media such as radio, television, newspapers, and magazines (Altunbas & Diker, 2015). However, over-emphasis on the speed with which messages are disseminated via social media accentuates an asymmetrical model of communication which resonates with the publicity paradigm of public relations. This is contrary to the strategic communication paradigm which puts premium on cementing relationships and mutual benefits between an organization and its stakeholders (Grunig, 2006, 2009; Ledingham, 2015).

Apart from speed, social media was also praised for enabling public relations practitioners to cut the costs of communication, particularly in the context of a debilitating economic crisis in Zimbabwe. One participant explained how social media reduced telephone bills and advertising in newspapers and the state-monopolized public broadcaster. Another participant described social media as a "cost-effective and efficient tool" (PR1) while another described it as "a platform where we can share our messages at minimal costs and sometimes at no cost" (PR13). The emphasis on low cost could be a reflection of the persistent economic crisis in Zimbabwe and how it is forcing organizations to adopt social media as a "cheap way of advertising compared to traditional media which has high-rate cards in a challenging economy" (PR15). One participant explained how, when you use social media, "you don't have to pay" and how "the communication department is likely to be the greatest victim of budget cuts" (PR5). The issue of cost-cutting is particularly pertinent given the persistent difficult economic environment in which companies operate in Zimbabwe – an environment in which the public relations function has always been the casualty when austerity measures must be implemented. Previous studies have noted how social media can be leveraged to promote the public relations function because it is considered cheap (Kharisma & Kurniawan, 2018). Nilasari et al. (2019) point out that social media is relatively cheaper because it makes it possible to share collaborative content with people who are geographically dispersed. Compared to traditional media, the cost of reaching customers who are geographically dispersed would be higher when using traditional than social media (Nilasari et al., 2019).

Apart from low cost, participants also explained how social media have the capacity to reach a wider audience. One participant explained how, as a "new and interesting tool", social media "opened doors to wider publics", how the medium gave organizations the opportunity to "speak to a general audience or select audiences", and to "reach different people, specific groups" (PR3). The view that social media enables public relations to reach wider audiences is echoed by Altunbas and Diker (2015) who noted that social media is a tool that helps in spreading information about an organization's products, services, and activities. However, such a view tends to accentuate an instrumentalist perspective of public relations, which emphasizes the publicity functions of public relations while downplaying its strategic communication aspect (Grunig, 2009).

Another strength of social media was that it made feedback possible because of two-way communication (Roberts, 2016). Participants lauded social media because it allowed for "interaction and real-time feedback" (PR1), enabling "instant feedback from the public" (PR9) possible, as well as the provision of tools for measuring how the messages have been received, and allowing one to "fix things quickly" (PR11) as well as "the right to reply" (PR12). However, feedback is narrowly conceived as an "intelligence" gathering exercise by organizations to promote the interests of the organization rather than a two-way process to promote mutual stakeholder benefits. Feedback is thus constructed as a way of improving "brand management" (PR15) or fixing "things quickly" (PR11). In the words of one participant, "When I think of social media, I think of .... instant feedback. Feedback from these vital stakeholders and stockholders. Unsolicited input from the public and other concerned stakeholders could help us improve brand management" (PR15).

The fact that some of the feedback is unsolicited means that feedback is not necessarily linked to the strategic communication goals of the organization, nor does it result in mutual benefits. This indicates that use of social media is not informed by a symmetrical two-way communication aimed at understanding the behaviours and attitudes of the audience to influence message strategy and creation for the ultimate benefit of the organization. Scholars argue that in corporate reputation management, two-way communication should be aimed at promoting mutual benefits, understanding, respect, and building trust between the organization and its stakeholders (Roberts, 2016).

Apart from feedback, participants also talked about how social media created opportunities for networking and collaborating with stakeholders. One participant explained how social media enabled "institutional collaborations" and how "new corporate relationships culminated in MOAs" (PR7). Another pointed out that social media had made it easier for his organization "to come closer" to its members and customers (PR10) members. Yet another described social media as a "tool for resource mobilization…and interacting with the donor community" (PR14). Others indicated opportunities of using social media as:

> Social media also helps you understand your client tell best because once you are on social media, you then know who your clients are and who are the people that can be good for you and your product.
>
> (PR8)

> People started using social media for official purposes with their brands, like really engaging with people….
>
> (PR11)

The interactive nature of social media makes it an effective platform for engaging stakeholders, building new relationships, networking, and fostering collaborations because stakeholders can produce and share content which shapes corporate agendas. This resonates with past studies which found that digital media are widely used by organizations to build and maintain organization-stakeholder relationships (Tong, 2022). Lutz and Hoffman (2013) note that social media have been a powerful tool for connecting like-minded individuals by providing an infrastructure for discursive communication, sharing information and the development of online networks for "mutual enrichment, through conversation, exchange and participation" (p. 5). Similarly, Kruger et al. (2013) argue that:

> …Social media can be used to support and increase stakeholder communication in a corporate context …. Features such as online availability, download possibilities, web forms, search engines, hyperlinks as well as feedback forms may be used to support corporate communication. Particularly the use of social media platforms such as blogs, RSS feeds, wikis, or forums offer a new form of interactivity and enables companies to address the information specifically to a variety of stakeholders.
>
> (p. 1479–1480)

Slee (2011) found that social media experts and corporate communicators believed that social media enabled organizations to build relationships with stakeholders because it allowed for more direct and real-time engagement than traditional media. Adlmaier-Herbst (2017) asserts that social media provides companies with an opportunity to engage with existing and potential customers. Organizations that engage with their stakeholders on social media can gather valuable intelligence about their stakeholders, thereby gaining a competitive advantage (Esfahan & Johnson, 2018).

However, an intriguing observation from the findings was the emphasis placed on social media's capacity to provide effective communication for the benefit of the organization at the expense of relationship building. This instrumentalist perspective of social media found expression through accentuation of the technological affordances of social media, which made organizations more effective in message delivery and public relations practitioners smarter in executing their job. Statements by a former public relations manager of a Harare-based business association and a Corporate Affairs Manager of a parastatal, respectively, are insightful in this regard –

> Social media has helped me articulate my organization's goals, objectives, and mission, and spread such to a broader public than it could have been using traditional media. It has also assisted me in reducing telephone costs when reaching out to stakeholders, say when inviting them to conferences or meetings. It has helped me contact journalists when communicating urgent issues the organization wants to share. When I hear about social media, I think of effective communication, critical communication, and feedback.
>
> (PR15)

> These tools are highly effective due to their broad reach and ability to generate feedback and debate around issues raised. Social media is very useful in enhancing corporate reputation in Zimbabwe, although it must be used carefully and considerately…The biggest opportunity is the speed at which content, be it advertorial, promotional, or otherwise gets distributed and the provision for interaction and real-time feedback. It is also a cost-effective and efficient tool.
>
> (PR1)

The above participant responses demonstrate that social media is viewed as "a tool" which empowers organizations to have more control over message production and dissemination compared to traditional media. This view echoes arguments by some scholars that public relations practitioners are still using social media in the same way they used traditional media because they use social media as "as an information dump" rather than building stakeholder relationships (Grunig, 2009, p. 4).

Grunig asserts that practitioners in this paradigm "believe that they can control what messages members of publics are exposed to" and often describe the recipient of these messages as "audiences rather than publics" which suggests an illusion of control, as Grunig (2009) states:

> These practitioners also typically believe that organisations can define, or even create their publics, and "target" them. Then they believe that publics can be persuaded – i.e.- that their cognitions, attitudes or behaviour can be

> influenced through asymmetrical communication – communication designed to promote the interests of the organization with little or no concern for the interests of publics.
>
> (p. 4)

This approach runs counter to the strategic management perspective of public relations whereby symmetrical two-way communication is deployed for the mutual benefit of all stakeholders (Grunig, 2006, p. 151).

Challenges

As much as participants talked about opportunities created by social media for reputation management, they also highlighted challenges presented by the medium. The main challenges mentioned were negative publicity, fake news, misinformation and disinformation, and difficulties in controlling corporate messages.

One of the challenges presented by social media for corporate reputation was its propensity to attract negative publicity. Thus, "an inappropriate tweet from an employee or client" could easily go viral and tarnish a company's image or brand in a matter of minutes. (PR4). It was also possible for a person to hack into the social media account of a company and post messages that countered what it was striving to achieve (PR2). Some participants explained how social media was prone to abuse through use of counterfeit materials and ghost accounts which had great potential to damage corporate brands. One participant described how some people could steal a company's name or logo and post negative messages that went viral, while competitors could "easily sponsor people to haunt your platforms and post nasty things that can damage your reputation" (PR10). Another participant lamented how some people targeted certain brands by "spreading negative vibes", thereby invalidating an organization's message (PR11). And yet another participant explained how some people created Facebook and WhatsApp accounts using the log of the organization and how "opponents can easily sponsor people to haunt your platforms and post nasty things that can damage your reputation" (PR10). Other risks included "unverified information" which could go viral because "bad news travels faster than good news" (PR12). Absence of gatekeeping and virality meant that social media was a vehicle for spreading negativity, as one participant noted, "Some social media users use social media platforms to attack our officials unnecessarily as there is no gatekeeping. Some of the attacks will be damaging without verification. That is sometimes taken as gospel truth by other social media followers" (PR13).

As audiences become empowered to post content on social media platforms, the balance of power shifts from organizations, and the definition of corporate reputation shifts from what organizations say about themselves to how customers perceive and respond to actions of organizations (Bunting, as cited in Sirzad, 2022, p. 223). Sirzad (2022) highlights how features of social media present challenges for corporate reputation management:

> Customers share their thoughts and complaints about the products and services they use with each other and company executives. However, this sharing occurs between a few individuals in the offline environment, happens very quickly between one person and thousands, and even millions of online people on social networks. Moreover, these shared experiences, complaints, and comments are searchable on wen search engines and eliminating them is very difficult and sometimes impossible. These online experiences may affect the decisions of other active or potential customers.
>
> (p. 223)

A phenomenon which aided and abated negative publicity on organizations was the "backfire effect" of social media influencers or ambassadors. This is where an organization enlists a social media celebrity to represent its products and or services to maintain brand visibility and identity. One participant explained how the use of brand ambassadors in Zimbabwe had become a bane after realizing that some brand ambassadors get involved in scandals or negative publicity which taints the brand of the organization. According to this participant, this approach "usually backfires because the person has limitations or parameters that may not necessarily associate with the brand" resulting in a lot of brand ambassadors being withdrawn because they would have failed to adhere to the brand ethos (PR11).

Negative publicity was also linked to the proliferation of fake news, misinformation, and disinformation. Some participants underscored how social media was conducive to propagating fake news. One participant explained how social media could become an "amphitheater of rumor mongering" (PR7). The tools embedded in social media allow people to share damaging information with many people. A public relations officer at a Harare-based health services organization opined that social media should be treated with caution because "not every piece of information on social media is accurate" (PR9). Fake news is a threat to corporate reputation because it diminishes public trust in the organization and its products and or services, yet the investment required to damage an organization's image is very small as it only takes a matter of minutes (VESTIGERE, 2023). One participant lamented how the "polarized political environment" in Zimbabwe played host to a plethora of corporate reputation risks due to the proliferation of counterfeit pages, which spewed vitriol against competitors or when "messages may be distorted by influencers for political reasons" (PR6). This demonstrates that some of the negative elements attributed to social media are amplified by contextual factors. It could be argued that the use of ghost accounts to attack competitors was accentuated by the intense competition in a toxic political context and suffocating economic environment forcing organizations into a reactive public relations mode. As a result, asymmetrical communication became the norm (Kharisma & Kurniawan, 2018). This is because when "countless allegations and criticisms strike an organization and put the organization into a difficult and deteriorating state" reactive public relations becomes the default strategy (Kharisma & Kurniawan, 2018, p. 15).

Aside from negativity, another challenge was that social media made it possible for organizational narratives to be "hijacked". The openness of social media made it easy for their corporate agendas to be misinterpreted or distorted by anyone who had access to them. The Corporate Affairs Manager of a Harare-based company explained how organizations exposed themselves to distortions, misinterpretations, and "brickbats and banter" the more they communicated via social media.

The multiple meanings generated from corporate messages on social media made it difficult for them to control their messages. As one participant explained power was "no longer on the communicator...Power was now everywhere" and "anyone can challenge anything" (PR9). As a result, organizations have a tough time trying to manage their narratives because whatever they say can be interpreted in different ways, sometimes to the detriment of the organization. For example, a participant noted:

> The risk is managing what you say, in the choice of words, in syntax, in diction, what do you say? The context is lost sometimes. You put a picture there, and it's interpreted in a very different manner, and the idea of responding to ghost accounts when you have senior officials, say in government, using ghost accounts to poke institutions into responding to certain situations as you see it brings risks. Huge risks that you tend to respond to non-existent people. And then you say, things that bring you into the public limelight.
>
> (PR5)

As social media democratized communication, the power of organizations to shape narratives was seriously denuded. Sirzad (2022) notes that unlike in the traditional media era where companies had a semblance of control over how events unfolded, because they would know in advance about impending customer attacks on the company's brand, this is no longer possible in the real-time communication element of social media does not give warning of "brewing" customers attacks or complaints. The open character of social media means that organizations cannot control dissemination of harmful information about them on these platforms, resulting in more reputational damage.

> ... Nowadays, when a customer launches an attack on social media companies have no control and reputation damage can be the result. Therefore, it can be claimed that social media increased reputation risk and dynamics. On social media platforms users sometimes create unapproved information – both false and accurate information about organizations. These thoughts put forward by users sometimes do not correspond to the ideals and goals that an organization would wish to share in its name. These issues lead to many problems regarding the reputation of companies.
>
> (Sirzad, 2022, p. 228)

Thus, social media has created power imbalances in the communicative equation, and by tilting the balance of power in favour of different publics, public relations is being transformed from a message production and dissemination activity to a strategic exchange communication process which must benefit all stakeholders.

Africa-Centric Trends

This chapter presents an African, particularly a Zimbabwean, perspective on opportunities and challenges presented by social media in corporate reputation management. The chapter revealed that social media plays an ambiguous role in corporate reputation management, and the new possibilities brought by social media for corporate reputation management are counterbalanced by a host of threats to corporate reputation management.

Perceptions that social media is a double-edged sword which can either build or kill brands have implications for the adoption of social media in public relations in a country where use of social media for business has been slowed down by a persistent economic meltdown. Integration of social media into corporate reputation management remains a contentious issue, particularly at executive levels, and is either resisted or not being treated as a priority. As one participant mentioned, the use of social media in brand management is more by "default" rather than company policy (PR12). That this participant's request from the company to sign up for social media training or employ a person to handle the social media aspect was turned down indicates that some organizations do not consider social media a crucial aspect of corporate reputation. As explained by this participant, decisions as to whether social media should be integrated into corporate reputation management are tied to cost factors in the context of a debilitating economic crisis, apprehensions about its potential, and propensity to taint brands. Centralization of mainstream media within the state means that organizations cannot easily access broadcast media, thereby forcing them to consider social media as an alternative channel for brand management. This means that adoption of social media for corporate reputation management in the Zimbabwe context is a function of the trade-offs between opportunities and challenges discussed above.

A fascinating aspect which emerged from the study findings was that the utility of social media in corporate reputation management was pivoted on instrumentality. As argued in this chapter, the framing of opportunities created by social media accentuated its effectiveness in disseminating messages as opposed to the building of relationships that are beneficial for all stakeholders (Grunig, 2009; Ledingham, 2015). The use of social media for corporate reputation management in Zimbabwe, and by extension Africa, does not significantly differ from how traditional media is used as it is informed by the asymmetrical model of communication whereby the media are used to generate content that seeks to buffer the organization from its publics (Grunig, 2009). Conclusively, the chapter argues that rather than accentuating control of the communication process, social media should be integrated into the strategic communication function of an organization to gather information to build relationships that are beneficial to all stakeholders.

Bibliography

Abdullah, Z. & Aziz, Y. A. (2011). Managing corporate reputation, stakeholder relations, and corporate social responsibility: A Southeast Asian perspective. *International Journal of Economics and Management*, *5*(1), 299–318.

Adlmaier-Herbst, D. G. (2017). Relationship management in a digital world. *Culture Crossroads*, *11*, 7–19. https://doi.org/10.55877/cc.vol11.128.

Akpabio, E. (2017). Towards public relations' agenda-setting theory. *Journal of Social Sciences*, *11*(3), 173–176.

Altunbas, H., & Diker, E. (2015). Corporate reputation and social media: An analysis on Facebook. *Academia*, *4*(2), 40–54.

Bechan, N. (2008). Top determinants of corporate reputation management. *Communicare*, *27*(1&2), 1–17.

Boie, C. (2012). Public relations and relationship management theory: Institutional perspectives. *Revista Trans.lvana de Stiinte ale Comunicarii, 1*(15), 13–18.

Carroll, C. E. (2011). *Corporate reputation and news media: Agenda-setting within business news coverage in developed, emerging and frontier markets*. New York: Routledge.

Christensen, J., Kent, P., & Stewart, J. (2010). Corporate governance and company performance in Australia. *Australian Accounting Review, 20*(4), 372–386.

DATAREPORTAL. (2023). *Digital 2023: Zimbabwe*. Retrieved from https://datareportal.com/reports/digital-2023-zimbabwe. Accessed 20 May 2023.

Esfahan, L. M., & Johnson, L. W. (2018). Stakeholders' engagement and strategic management of social media. *Journal of International Business Research and Marketing, 3*(6), 47–56.

Fortunato, J. A., & Martin, S. E. (2016). The intersection of agenda-setting, the media environment and election campaign laws. *Journal of Information Policy*, *6*, 129–153.

Freeman, R. E. (1984). *Strategic management: A stakeholder Ap*proach. Boston: Pitman.

Grunig, J. E. (2006). Furnishing the edifice: Ongoing research on public relations: A strategic management function. *Journal of Public Relations Research, 18*(2), 151–176.

Grunig, J. E. (2009). Paradigms of public relations in the age of digitization. *PRism*, *6*(2), 1–19.

Grunig, J. E., & Grunig, L. A. (2000). Public relations in strategic management and strategic management of public relations: Theory and evidence from the IAB Excellence Project. *Journalism Studies*, *1*(2), 303–321.

Holve, C. (2014). Online reputation management: How to reduce reputational damage in social media. Bachelor's Thesis. University of Twente, Netherlands. Retrieved from https://essay.utwente.nl/66605/. Accessed 15 May 2023.

Hon, L. C., & Grunig, J. E. (1999). Guidelines for measuring relationships. *The Institute for Public Relations Commission Public Relations Measurement and Evaluation*. Retrieved from https://www.instituteforpr.org/wp-content/uploads/Guidelines_Measuring_Relationships.pdf. Accessed 11 May 2023.

Kharisma, T., & Kurniawan, F. (2018). Public relations in the digital era: Case study of the use of social media by government public relations in ANRI. *Jurnal InterAct, 7*(1), 13–19.

Kim, J. Y., Kiousis, S., & Xiang, Z. (2015). Agenda building and agenda setting in business: Corporate reputation attributes. *Corporate reputation,* 18(1): 25-36.

Kruger, N., Schneider, A. M., Dang-Xuan, L., & Stieglitz, S. (2013). Usage of social media for external stakeholder relationship management: A study of German companies and international non-government organisations. 27th International Conference on Advanced Information Networking and Application Workshops. Retrieved from https://ieeexplore.ieee.org/document/6550605. Accessed 23 May 2023.

Ledingham, J. A. (2003). Explicating relationship management as a general theory of public relations. *Journal of Public Relations Research, 15*(2), 181–198.

Ledingham, J. A. (2015). Managing relationship management: A holistic approach. In Ki, E., Kim, J. N. & Ledingham, J. A. (Eds.). *Public relations and relationship management: A relational approach to the study and practice of public relations* (pp. 46–60). New York: Routledge.

Ledingham, J. A., & Hung-Baesecke, F. (2015). Relationship management: The core focus of public relations (unpublished manuscript). Retrieved from https://www.researchgate.net/publication/322567510_Relationship_Management_The_Core_Focus_of_Public_Relations. Accessed 25 May 2023.

Lee, J. W. (2022). Impacts of public relations on corporate reputation. *Journal of Digital Marketing*, *1*(1), 30–36.

Lutz, C., & Hoffman, C. (2013). The impact of social media on stakeholder engagement. Conference Paper. Retrieved from https://www.alexandria.unisg.ch/entities/publication/12ab2d5c-f862-4bdd-9f32-58fe271816b4/det. Accessed 23 May 2023.

Maas, P., Bieler, M., Fischer, L., & Schumacher, C. (2020). Reputation: Opportunities and threats for corporations in the age of digital opinion making. Research Report. *University of St Gallen, Institute of Insurance and Economics*. Retrieved from https://www.ivw.unisg.ch/wp-content/uploads/2020/09/20200831_Reputation-Report_ENG.pdf. Accessed 20 June 2023.

Masondo, M. R. (2022). Reputation management on social media: A case study of South African female hip-hop artists. Unpublished MTech Thesis, Cape Peninsula University of Technology.

McCombs, M. (2011). *The agenda-setting role of the mass media in the shaping of public opinion*. Retrieved from https://www.infoamerica.org/documentos_pdf/mccombs01.pdf. Accessed 10 June 2023.

McCombs, M., & Shaw, D. (1972). The agenda-setting function of mass media. *The Public Opinion Quarterly, 36*(2), 176–187.

McCorkindale, T., & Distaso, M. W. (2013). The power of social media and its influence on corporate reputation. In Carrol, C. E. (Ed.). *The handbook of communication and corporate reputation* (pp. 497–512). Oxford: Wiley-Blackwell.

Meijer, M. M., & Kleinninhuis, J. (2006). Issue news and corporate reputation: Applying the theories of agenda-setting and ownership in the field of business communication. *Journal of Communication*, *56*(3), 543–557.

Mikola, E. (2016). Managing the intangible: Role of the communications function in corporate reputation work in public business -to- business Ccmpanies. Unpublished master's Dissertation. Retrieved from https://aaltodoc.aalto.fi/handle/123456789/24533. Accessed 21 June 2022.

Moyo, T. (2022). The effect of Twitter as a social blog on corporate reputation management in the telecommunications industry in Zimbabwe. Unpublished Doctor of Business Administration. University of KwaZulu Natal, Graduate School of Business and Leadership.

Netsianda, M. (2020). Dendairy turns to court over critic. *The Chronicle*, 11 August 2020. Retrieved from https://www.chronicle.co.zw/dendairy-turns-to-court-over-critic/. Accessed 15 June 2023.

Nilasari, B. M., Jasfar, F., & Wahyndi, A. (2019). The effects of interactivity, cost effectiveness and compatibility on the use social media and its implications for organisational performance. *American Research Journal of Business and Management*, *5*(1), 1–17.

Njuka, D. A., & Phiri, J. (2021). Factors influencing social media in managing corporate reputation for a Christian organisation in developing countries based on the V14 model. *Technology and Investment*, *12*(2), 66–81.

Opdenakker, R. (2006). Advantages and disadvantages of four interview techniques in qualitative research. *Qualitative Social Research*, *7*(4). Article 11.

Pires, V., & Trez, G. (2018). Corporate reputation: A discussion on construct definition and measurement and its relation to performance. *Revista de Gestalo, 25*(1), 47–64.

Pollak, F., & Markovic, P. (2022). Challenges for corporate reputation – online reputation management in times of global pandemics. J*ournal of Risk and Financial Management, 15*, 1–18.

Roberts, J. (2016). *Writing for strategic communication industries*. Ohio: Ohio State University Press.

Serrat, O. (2017). Managing cooperate reputation. In Olivier Serrrat (eds.) *Knowledge solutions: Tools, methods, and approaches to drive organizational performance* (pp. 481–487). Singapore: Springer Nature.

Scott, D. M. (2008). *The new rules of viral marketing: How word-of-mouth spreads your ideas for free*. Retrieved from https://www.davidmeermanscott.com/hubfs/documents/Viral_Marketing.pdf. Accessed 20 June 2023.

Sirzad, N. (2022). A review of online reputation management and online reputation components. *Dogus Universitesi Dergisi*, *23*(1), 2019–242.

Slee, C. (2011). The impact of social media on corporate reputation. *Vistas Education: Economy and Community*, *1*(2), 62–70.

Stern, S. (2015). About the book. In Lloyd, J. and TooGood, L. (Eds.). *Journalism and PR: News media and public relations in the digital age* (pp. vii–viii). London: IB Tauris & Co Ltd.

Tong, S. C. (2022). Public relations in the digital era. Trust and commitment in the interplay of interactivity effects and online relational strategies. *Journal of Marketing Communications*, *28*(7), 799–819.

Van Den Berg, A., & Struwig, M. (2016). Managing organisational reputation using social media at South African Universities. *Journal of Contemporary Management*, *13*, 531–555.

Van den Heever, J. J. (2018). Investigating social media conversations: Towards designing an online reputation for NPOs. Unpublished PhD Thesis. University of Pretoria, South Africa.

Van den Heever, J. J., & Rensburg, R. (2018). Investigating social media conversations: Towards online reputation management for NPOS. *Communitas*, *23*(4), 53–70. Vanderstoep, S. W., & Johnson, D. D. (2009). *Research methods for everyday life: Blending qualitative and quantitative approaches*. San Francisco: Jossey-Bass.

Verma, N. (2015). Public relations: Scope and challenges in digital era. *Media Watch*, *6*(1), 148–152.

VESTIGERE. (2023). *Fake news: What is it and how it impacts the corporate environment*. Retrieved from https://www.vestigere.com/en/fake-news-impact-corporate-enviroment/. Accessed 25 June 2023.

Wright, D.K., & Hinson, M.D. (2008). Examining the increasing impact of social media on public relations practice. Paper presented at the 11th Annual International Public Relations Research Conference, March 9, 2008, Miami Florida. Retrieved from https://citeseerx.ist.psu.edu/document?repid=rep1&type=pdf&doi=967489627117a535f527a0285c70861cba1a67e3. Accessed 12 May 2023.

Wright, D. K., & Hinson, M. D. (2009). Examining how public relations are actually using social media. *Public Relations Journal*, *3*(3), 1–32.

4 Effect of Social Media Usage in Zimbabwe's Telecommunications Industry and Its Impact on Corporate Reputation Management

Tabani Moyo, Cecile Proches Gerwel, Emmanuel Mutambara and Upasana Gitanjali Singh

Introduction

This chapter evaluates global and regional trends in relation to a case study of the use of social media and its effects on corporate reputation management in Zimbabwe's telecommunications sector. Due to various circumstances, including economic, political, and legal factors, the trends and patterns in the usage of social media vary from country to country. This case study shows how such factors have generally affected the development of corporate reputation management in Africa, with a focus on Southern Africa. Suffice to note that the objectives of the chapter are to assess Twitter (X)'s and other social media's effectiveness in handling current issues involving corporate reputation, to compare Twitter (X) to other social media platforms on the essential components anticipated in international communication for a positive corporate reputation, and to create a framework for corporate reputation driven by social media and Twitter (X), in particular, as a tool for better reputation in the telecoms industry. Twitter (X) was selected as one of the social media platforms for examination as it is the most used platform in Zimbabwe (Statcounter, 2021).

The interaction between corporate reputation management and social media has been examined from the broad risk management perspective for specific corporations. Additionally, most research studies—where internet growth initially takes hold—have been conducted in the Americas, Europe, and Asia, whereas the African environment has received little attention (Bahia & Suardi, 2019; Economist, 2019; GSMA Intelligence, 2020; Kemp, 2019). These studies indicate that the continent of Africa is the next frontier for internet growth and usage, necessitating an investigation into how this expansion of internet use will affect the research into the effects of social media on corporate reputation management in the Zimbabwean telecommunications sector.

First, it is necessary to provide contextual background information on the telecommunications industry and social media use in Zimbabwe. This is followed by presenting concepts and theories that form the foundation of the conceptual model under investigation in this case study.

DOI: 10.4324/9781032689654-4

About the Telecommunication Sector in Zimbabwe

Five strategic categories make up Zimbabwe's telecommunications sector: postal services, fixed telephone services, courier services, mobile cellular services, and internet access providers, which have emerged as the focus of this investigation because they are closely linked to the development of social media.

The postal services, which served as the foundation for the sector's development, saw the initial growth stage of the telecommunications industry. Through Zimpost, the government established its monopoly in the industry. Fixed telephone services for fixed voice and fixed internet services were established and offered by the government's TelOne monopoly (Nyamadzawo, 2011). The establishment of courier services marked the third stage in the sector's development, with seven businesses assisting local and international stakeholders in the sector's expansion. According to Nyamadzawo (2011), the fourth stage saw the introduction of mobile cellular services offered by Econet, Telecel, and NetOne, three different players. Seven major businesses are now providing data and internet services in Zimbabwe after the last two stages of developing and expanding these internet service providers. The country now has nineteen players in the telecommunications business, as opposed to the State monopoly of the Postal and Telecommunications Company (PTC) in the early years after independence, where a single company supplied telecommunication services (POTRAZ, 2018).

Mobile subscriptions have sharply increased in Zimbabwe due to the industry's progress, particularly between 2008 and 2012, when the subscription rate curve was quite steep before increasing more gradually between 2012 and 2017 (POTRAZ, 2017). Between 2016 and 2017, subscriptions increased by 9.4%, from 12.9 to 14 million active users, while the overall number of subscriptions increased from 20.6 to 21.6 million (POTRAZ, 2017). This shows that consumers and stakeholders increasingly use online platforms, primarily through mobile phones, to communicate (Kotler, Kartajaya, & Setiawan, 2017), and marks a change in market trends since the industry's inception in the 1980s.

Global Patterns of Social Media Usage

Due to the industry's shift from traditional communication and reputation management forms, social media platforms, like Twitter (X), have become the most popular online medium. These platforms have helped shape modern perspectives on reputation management, fuelled by internal stakeholders' social capital and online engagement (Kemp, 2023). Specific to social media usage in Africa and how it affects corporate reputation management (GSMA, 2023; Moyo, 2022; Moyo et al., 2022), there is anecdotal evidence on how it affects practice and conceptual contribution to new perspectives in the management of reputation. However, there is a dearth of academic research focusing specifically on African countries. The case study presented in this chapter is a step in better understanding the connection between social media and corporate reputation management in a distinctly African context. The following sections describe the preponderance of factors contributing to the importance of this research. The number of people using the internet globally has increased significantly in recent years. Around 5.18 billion users worldwide were active in 2023, an increase of 3% overall from the year before (Kemp, 2023). The number of developing nations investing in the expansion of internet use is primarily responsible for this growth. A region like South Asia saw a surge in internet use from 31% to 41% during the same era, while India saw a sharp gain in internet use, surpassing 100 million users in a record-breaking year from 2018 to 2019. India had an internet penetration rate of over 50% as of 2023. By the end of 2022, the nation had a new high of 720 million subscribers (Kemp, 2023). Globally the number of people accessing social media on mobile devices increased by 10% to 4.5 billion people in the same period, while the overall number of social media users increased by 9% between 2020 and 2021, hitting an all-time high of 4.88 billion users. But in 2023, with a 3.2% increase from 2022 to 4.80 billion, usage achieved an all-time high.

The GSMA Intelligence (2023) predicts that by 2030, there will be more than 9.5 billion mobile connections worldwide. Smartphone penetration is anticipated to be at an all-time high—90%. With a projected 20% 5G penetration in 2024 and a projected growth to over 50% in 2030, internet connectivity speeds are also anticipated to increase significantly. The statistics show that the world is becoming more mobile, highlighting the growing significance of social media as an essential element of human conduct in the modern era. The general business community, academia, and practitioners in the communications ecosystems can learn from these trends, which point to structural alterations in global information and news consumption preferences and behaviours (GSM Intelligence, 2023).

African Trends on the Use of the Internet

Incremental investments in underwater fibre optic cables are credited for the fast development of internet usage in Africa. The South Atlantic Cable System's construction, which dismantled connectivity hurdles and established a first-ever connection between South America and Africa, is the most historic development in this regard (Madory, 2018). Cap Amilcar Cabral of Ceiba-2 (Business Ghana, 2018), METISS, and Ultramar-GE were established due to a variety of smaller businesses' actions that helped create the ecosystem of internet connectivity (Submarine Telecoms Forum, 2018). The developed world's competition to connect the global South demonstrates that the initial target market is approaching saturation and that businesses are turning their attention to the "unconnected" markets that were overlooked during the first round of connection (Song, 2019). These trends will continue as businesses invest in undersea cables to obtain a competitive edge in unexplored markets like Africa (ISOC, 2015; ITU, 2017; Lovelock, 2018).

Social Media in Zimbabwe

Statcounter (2021) determined that the following social media are the most popular in Zimbabwe: Twitter (X), pegged at 43.62%. Facebook follows this at 35.86%, while Pinterest is at 12.53%, YouTube is 4.27%, and Instagram at 2.08%. Given the proliferation and use of these platforms, these are what corporate reputation management in the telecommunications industry in Zimbabwe should focus on.

Twitter (X) usage was reported to be 25% in October 2020, compared to Pinterest's 42% usage. Still, in just a year, it gained over 18% to overtake Pinterest as Zimbabwe's most popular social media site. In general, in African trends, Facebook has a 73.88% usage rate, followed by YouTube's 10.96%, and Twitter's (X) 7.12%. On a worldwide scale, however, the patterns place Facebook at 72.22%, Twitter (X) at 8.77%, and Pinterest at 8.37%. This demonstrates how social platform behaviours in Zimbabwe differ from those in other regions and worldwide. Although Facebook usage is in second place at 35.66%, comparative research reveals that the platform has had a monopoly on use in Zimbabwe for the past ten years.

Corporate Reputation Management

Corporate reputation, from a conceptual perspective, has been viewed as an intangible or soft asset, which refers to something that cannot be measured or systematically managed (Aggerholm & Andersen, 2011; Balmer, 2017; Swoboda & Hirschmann, 2017; Thiessen & Ingenhoff, 2011). According to Deephouse (2000), an establishment's reputation involves a collective assessment of its standing from a three-tier position of affect, esteem, and knowledge. This suggests that the organisation's position is a creation of individual stakeholders' lived experience, as well as their perception of this lived experience. This is a departure point from Fombrun's (1996) definition, which brought shape and form to the concept. He defined corporate reputation as "the overall estimation in which a company is held by its constituents" (Fombrun, 1996, p. 9). However, there is not a widely accepted definition of corporate reputation management as the discipline is still developing.

The traditional approach in corporate reputation management was analysed from the traditional perspective on corporate reputation management. The six broad traditional perspectives include: (a) reputation as a derivative of signalling through information; (b) the management of an invisible (intangible) asset; (c) the micro socio-cognitive aspects of corporate reputation management; (d) the macro socio-cognitive aspects of corporate reputation; (e) cultural sociological thinking, which is founded on socio-political approaches to corporate reputation; and (f) the role of participation and communication in the formation of reputation (Barnett, Jermier & Lafferty, 2006; Johnson, Erez, Kiker, & Motowidlo, 2002; Lange, Lee & Dai, 2011; Lange & Pfarrer, 2017; Ravasi et al., 2018). These perspectives place the centrality of internal stakeholders, namely top-level operational managers and employees, at the centre of corporate reputation management through making structured and deliberate efforts towards shaping a favourable identity and image for the organisation. This led to the study of placing such stakeholders at the epicentre of inquiry, breaking them down into the three afore-stated internal stakeholders and further seeking their views on how they seek customers engaging through the new media.

Theoretical Frameworks

The contemporary study of social media use has limited research on corporate reputation management. This case study reviewed contemporary literature on how employees engage the public on social media by reviewing four main contemporary theories, while the first one (media synchronicity theory) is mainstreamed across the foundations of the conceptual framework, others are covered in more depth, namely: boundary theory (Yang, 2020); social capital theory (Cao et al., 2016; Delavari & Badizadeh, 2018); social cognitive theory (Carlson et al., 2016; Moqbela & Kock, 2018; Papadopoulos et al., 2013); and social exchange theory (SET) (Davids & Brown, 2021). These theories and their application to the conceptual framework presented in this chapter are discussed below.

The Media Synchronicity Theory

The media synchronicity theory (Chen et al., 2020) holds that all tasks must go through two fundamental communication processes, namely the conveyance process and the convergence process (Chen et al., 2020). The approach also considers how much media qualities, training, societal norms, and prior experiences might moderate behaviour on the use of public social media by the staff. This is why it is mainstreamed as anchoring the contemporary approaches and being the overall pivot upon which the study is grounded upon.

The Boundary Theory

The process and outcomes between mutually independent domains are the foundation of boundary theory, primarily focusing on the work, family, and private life domains (Yang, 2020). The theory contends that there is a distinct separation between the work and outside of work (non-work) domains, where employees at any given time establish temporal, physical, and psychological demarcations, or boundaries, to understand and apply themselves to work and outside of work roles and responsibilities (Chen et al., 2020). Whereas the traditional office serves as the physical workstation and is here referred to as "work-life", the "non-workplace" is the home and family life (van Zoonen & Banghart, 2018). As a result, academics have started investigating the effects of using public social media in relation to our work and non-work identities (van Zoonen, Verhoeven, & Vliegenthart, 2016; Yang, 2020). Regarding this case study, boundary theory contributed to the conceptual framework by noting the dichotomy of work and home domains and how they influence social media usage.

Theory of Social Capital

The institutionalisation of familial relationships, the interaction between the members of the networks and their identities that are then supported by institutional means, and the institution's dependence on those networks are all aspects of this theory that combine the current and potential. The social capital theory is based on ideas and constructs that social capital or relationships are an essential resource for organisational goals (Yang, 2020). These ideas and constructs include informal networks, trust, norms, and values. Structure, bonding, strong and weak links, and horizontal and vertical networks are all forms of social capital. According to Chen et al. (2020, p. 5), the following types of social capital are crucial for an employee's use of public social media: "bridging and bonding social capital; structural; rational and cognitive social capital; online bridging and bonding social capital and shared vision and network ties". Concerning the conceptual framework, social capital theory informs both individual and corporate relationships and how they shape the quality and quantity of social interactions through social media (Chen et al., 2020).

The Social Cognitive Theory

According to Papadopoulos, Stamati and Nopparuch (2013), social cognitive theory is based on three key variables: personal elements anchored in biological, cognitive, affective, and emotional events; environmental events; and behavioural patterns. The underlying presumptions are that each person's emotions and cognitive ability influence their behavioural patterns, which alters their environment, emotions, and cognitive processes. By extension, the three factors—a person's emotions, cognitive thinking, and environment—have a cyclical effect on one another (Chen et al., 2020). Social cognitive theory shapes the conceptual framework by grounding the study on how the environment influences the internal stakeholders' use of social media.

The Social Exchange Theory

As one of the fundamental theories used to acquire insights into the social exchange in web-based communities online, the SET has gained popularity (Gharib et al., 2017; Jahan & Kim, 2020; Kapoor et al., 2018). Homans (1958) initially developed the theory with fundamental tenets rooted in sociology, economics, and psychology. The theory aims to investigate how people behave socially in economic contexts. The idea that trade occurs through a social exchange connection is crucial to this theory.

The growth and usage of social media need to be theorised, says Li et al. (2020), particularly regarding the institutional use of social media tactics and how that affects engagement with larger stakeholders. It is sufficient to say that further funding must be put towards the creation of conceptual and theoretical frameworks to address the problems with organisational usage of social media that SET does not address (Albert & Salam, 2013; Urquhart, 2012; Vaast & Walsham, 2013). The framework presented in this chapter is a first step in addressing the dearth of social media theory. As such, social exchange grounded the conceptual framework on the practicality of utilising internal stakeholders to determine their views, basing this on how they interact with the customers. This equally influenced research design as the platforms for inquiry, where social media do not allow for experiments, as they are public platforms. The theoretical contributions to the model are illustrated in Figure 4.1.

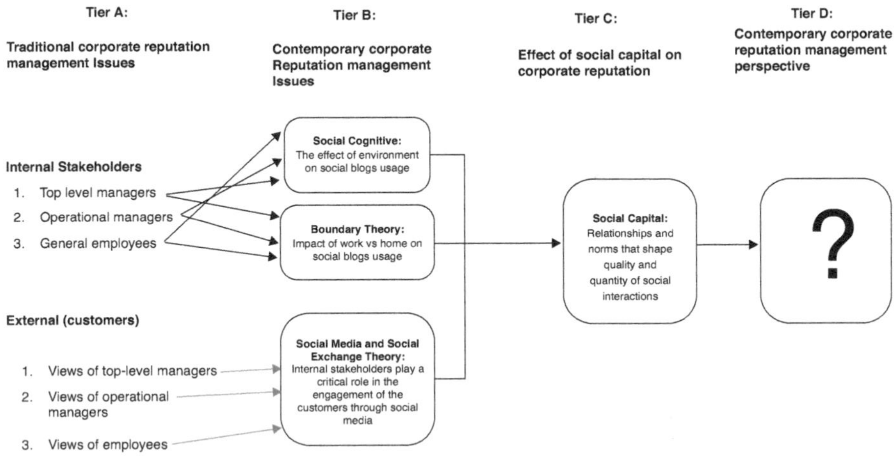

Figure 4.1 Theoretical contributions to building a conceptual framework on the effect of Twitter (X) for managing corporate reputation in Zimbabwe's telecommunications industry

Source: Researcher's own construction

Through the conceptual framework, the chapter proposes the interaction of variables emerging in the literature, which gravitates towards new approaches to corporate reputation management. This study is, therefore, guided by a conceptual framework, which seeks to assess the variables in the topic under investigation. Twitter (X) as a microblogging platform is the independent variable, while corporate reputation management is the dependent variable. The study positions Twitter (X) between the traditional corporate reputation guides (top-level managers, operation managers, general employees, and customers) and the contemporary theories (boundary theory, social cognitive theory, and SET), which became the intermediate variables for the research. In this regard, Twitter (X) usage is assumed to positively impact the shift from traditional to contemporary approaches and social capital in building corporate reputation in Zimbabwe's telecommunications Industry. Other social media (Facebook, Instagram, LinkedIn and YouTube) were used as a comparison to assess their effect on corporate reputation against Twitter (X) on how they shape corporate reputation management. These constructs are illustrated in Figure 4.2.

Hypotheses

H1: Twitter (X) usage positively affects the corporate reputation of telecommunication companies operating in Zimbabwe.
H2: Twitter (X) usage positively impacts the shift from traditional to contemporary approaches and social capital in building corporate reputation in Zimbabwe's telecommunications industry.
H3: Other social media affect how Twitter (X) and themselves shape corporate reputation management.

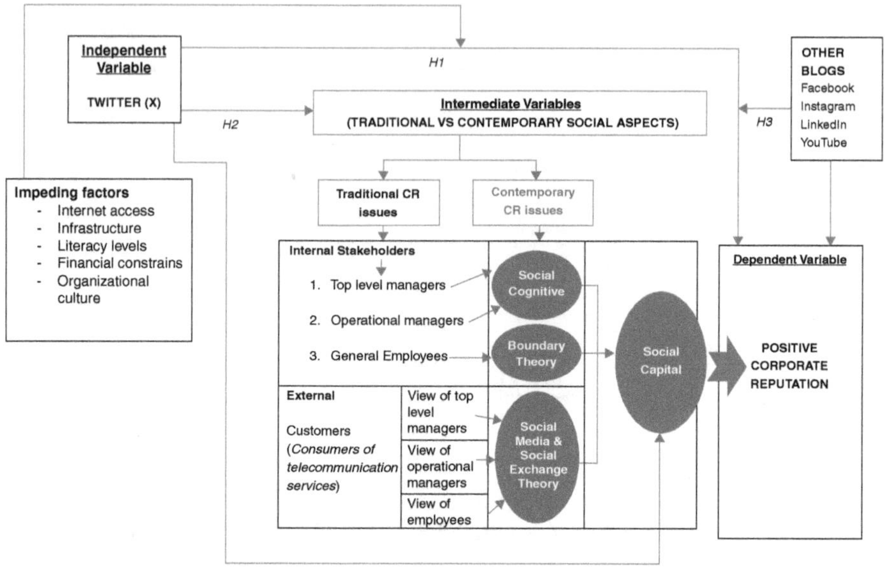

Figure 4.2 Proposed conceptual framework

Source: Researcher's own construction

Methodology

The research employed a quantitative design (Creswell, 2013; Creswell & Creswell, 2018; Creswell & Plano Clark 2011). Data for this study was acquired quantitatively, utilising survey questionnaires distributed to the targeted respondents in person and collected after completion. The survey measured the views of the internal stakeholders in management and employees on the key social media platforms they used and viewed as the most competitive in managing corporate reputation within the telecommunications industry. The questionnaires targeted the participants in marketing, call centres, front offices, customer care and public relations management. The respondents also emphasised that for the researcher to collect reliable, credible, and detailed data from the process, senior management employees are much more likely to consent to being questioned face-to-face than to complete a questionnaire.

The questionnaire was self-developed through exploration and review of the data known from the case study industry. This was intended to explain the phenomenon of the changes from traditional approaches in corporate reputation and management using new media, mainly Twitter (X), and how social capital, as a contemporary theoretical proposition, could answer the research gap on developing new perspectives on corporate reputation management. For this to happen, the instrument started by profiling the demographic, age, and educational background as it instructs the use of the platforms. Section A attempted to explore the use of Twitter (X) in the management of corporate reputation through a structured scale, probing the effectiveness of Twitter (X) in managing corporate reputation. This was based on probing the key features of Twitter that enable its communication functions and how best they facilitate the utilisation of social capital in managing corporate reputation. Section B assessed the internal stakeholder's utilisation of the platform in the furtherance of the strategic objectives of the institution around driving the vision, mission, and engagement processes. Section C was crafted to gauge the internal stakeholders' views on customers' utilisation of Twitter (X) and other social media in interacting with the company. Sections D and E were designed to facilitate internal stakeholders to rate the platforms they viewed to be strategic and critical for use towards the consolidation of social capital to develop contemporary views in corporate reputation management.

Sampling Techniques

The study employed a stratified random sampling technique. The only prerequisite is that "there is a clear theoretical rationale for assuming that the resulting groups will differ in some meaningful way" (Robinson, 2014, p. 17). Based on these requirements, the researcher used the stratification approach to determine the top five service providers in terms of the duration of operation, annual revenue generated, market share held by each organisation, and total employee count.

The targeted population was employees within the telecommunications industry in Zimbabwe, which constituted the overall target population in this study. As internal stakeholders, the employees are the critical driver of corporate reputation, revealing the need to explore how they manage corporate reputation in terms of the challenge of traditional approaches towards the new perspective driven by contemporary theories, especially social capital, in improving corporate reputation.

The decision to select the internal stakeholders in the categories of top-level operational managers and employees was settled due to the nature of the industry, which is heavily regulated, especially when it comes to handling customer information. Attempts to request information related to customers' contact details required exemptions and each customer's consent. This proved expensive and time-consuming and increased the chances that the research would be difficult to carry out within the projected time frame. A population refers to a large collection of individuals who are the focus of a scientific inquiry and from which the final sample is selected (Creswell, 2013).

The telecommunications industry is subdivided into five (5) categories: fixed telephone services, mobile cellular services, internet access providers, postal services, and courier services. A total of 6,178 full-time employees work in the 19 companies in the telecommunications industry (POTRAZ, 2019), where the overall population was deemed large enough to warrant an investigation into the operations within the industry. A proportion approach was used to calculate the number of employees that can be selected from each organization to be included in the sample of 369 from the identified five companies, namely Econet, NetOne, TelOne, Telecel and Liquid, respectively.

Research Findings

The study developed a plan for effectively applying social media to enhance the company's reputation in Zimbabwe. The suggested model's relationships between the constructs or latent variables were evaluated using structural equation modelling (SEM).

Twitter Compared to Other Social Media for Managing Corporate Reputation

This study's inclusion of additional social media sites (Facebook, LinkedIn, YouTube and Instagram) was necessary to compare the aspects determining a positive company reputation. Conversation with the intended audience, international news coverage, serving as a source for word-of-mouth, hybrid texts, a source of referrals, audio interchange and visual presentation are some of these factors. The research's conclusions are displayed in Figure 4.3.

Twitter (X) outperformed Facebook (52%), LinkedIn (10%), YouTube (4%) and Instagram (4%), especially as a conversational tool (58%). It also showed that it has greater global coverage (47%) than Facebook (46%) and other social media platforms, with LinkedIn (21%), YouTube (21%) and Instagram (12%) reporting the least from the respondents. In conclusion, three social media platforms have emerged as dominating the use of the platforms by the participants in the telecoms business. While Facebook has shown to be more popular in most areas, including as a source of word-of-mouth, supplying hybrid text, and serving as a platform for referrals and audio sharing, Twitter (X) use outpaces Facebook in conversational topics and global coverage. Regarding visual presentations for a company's reputation, YouTube is more beneficial. As a strategy for effective reputation management, it is necessary to recognise these factors: conversation, global coverage, word-of-mouth, hybrid text, referrals, audio exchange, and visual display that influence corporate reputation.

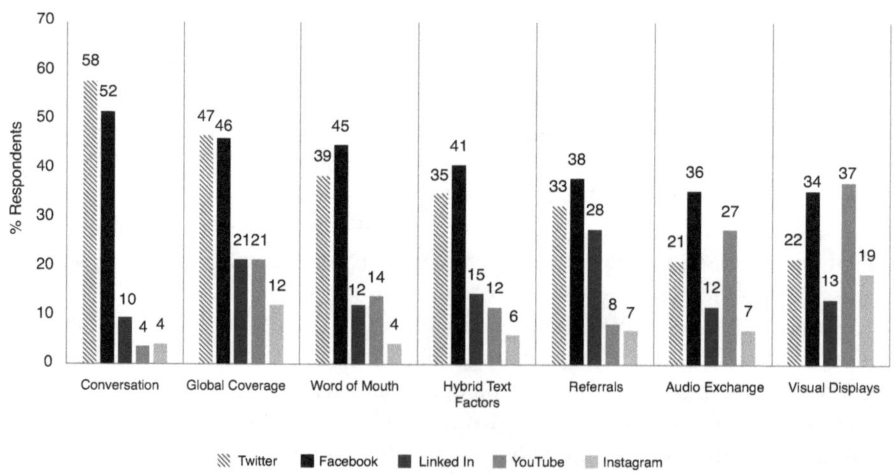

Figure 4.3 Social media's impact on corporate reputation management

Source: Research survey

As previously mentioned, social capital is at the core of current strategies for managing corporate reputation (Cao et al., 2016; Delavari & Badizadeh, 2018). Word-of-mouth, hybrid text factors, referrals, audio exchange (on Facebook), discussions, worldwide coverage (on Twitter (X)), and visual display (on YouTube) are the seven components of social capital. They are the crucial factors defining and shaping a positive company reputation in the digital age. Although Twitter (X) was the primary independent variable in the study, the results indicate that the other two social media platforms, Facebook and YouTube, are crucial in creating a good reputation. As a result, industry players must adopt a comprehensive strategy for using social media to increase their social capital and engage with their stakeholders online (Kotler et al., 2021; Statcounter, 2021; Zhou et al., 2021)

Comparison of Twitter (X) to other Social Media in Managing Modern Corporate Reputation

The study topic, which sought to compare the effectiveness of Twitter (X) to other social media in managing corporate reputation, served as the basis for creating the questionnaire. To find out if there might be another way to boost company's reputation, more investigation into Twitter (X) and other social media (Facebook, LinkedIn, Instagram, and YouTube) was required. The transformational relationship between conventional and modern foundations culminated in social capital changing a new perspective on corporate reputation. Both approaches were combined in the survey question format, focusing on the more recent concepts of boundary, social cognition, and social interaction.

Figure 4.4 presents the alternative media outlets that respondents believe to be more successful than Twitter (X) at managing brand reputation. The majority of respondents (54%) believe that Facebook is the most useful substitute for Twitter (X) when it comes to managing a company's reputation. LinkedIn (18%), Instagram (15%), and YouTube (15%) were also mentioned by respondents as superior options that might be utilised to manage business reputation. However, 17% of respondents believe that only some other social media are better than Twitter (X). This suggests

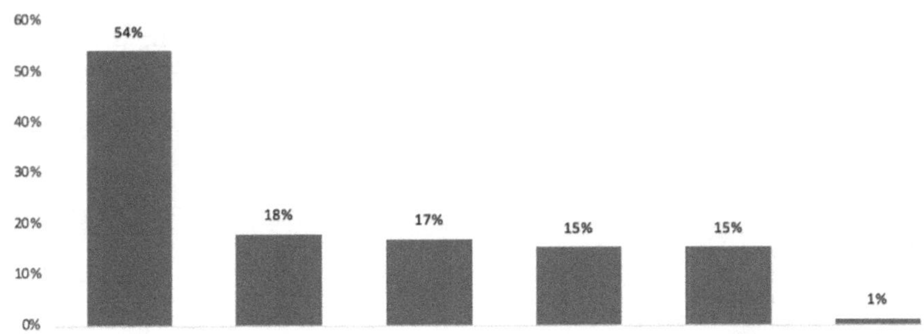

Figure 4.4 The best medium to use for managing a company's reputation

Source: Research survey

that if Twitter (X) is not complemented in enhancing its corporate reputation, all higher than 17% responses should be regarded as the next best option.

Contributing Framework for the Management of Corporate Reputation in the Age of Social Media

The study created a framework for efficient use of social media to improve company's reputation in Zimbabwe. SEM was used to assess the links between the constructs or latent variables in the proposed model.

Indexes for the Goodness of Fit

The model parameters were estimated using the maximum likelihood method in this case. Fit indices evaluate the model's goodness of fit (GFI) (Hair et al., 2017; Kline, 2005). The fit indices that assessed if there was agreement between survey data and the model included the Chi-square test (X^2), Chi-square (X^2) to degrees of freedom ratio (X^2/df), GFI, Root Mean Square Error Approximation (RMSEA), and Comparative Fit Index (CFI) (Hair et al., 2010). The test findings and inferences are presented in Table 4.1.

Except for the Chi-square, which was significant ($p<.05$), the results show that all fit indices were within a reasonable range, indicating a satisfactory fit between the survey data and the theory. The Chi-square test must not be used when evaluating model fit because it is unstable. The more stable approach is the Chi-square (X^2) to degrees of freedom ratio (X^2/df). The better metric for assessing model fit today is the CMIN/df3, which denotes a good fit. Since the calculated CMIN/df 0.03, CFI>0.9, GFI>0.9, RMSEA 0.05, and CFI>0.9 indicate a strong fit for the suggested model, the results imply a match of fit between the theory and survey data. The researcher looked into the model's proposed relationships after determining that the data were consistent. The CMIN/df shows that the hypothetical model

Table 4.1 Comparative Fit Index

Fit Index	*Recommended Value (Hair, 2010)*	*Value Obtained*	*Decision*
Chi-square (X^2)	$p>0.05$	437.234 ($p=0.000, p<0.05$)	No model fit
Chi-square (X^2) to degrees of freedom ratio (X^2/df)	< 5 preferably<3	2.789	Model fit
Goodness-of-fit Indices (GFI)	> 0.9	0.912	Model fit
Root Mean Square Error Approximation (RMSEA)	< 0.08 preferably<0.05	0.049	Model fit
Comparative Fit Index (CFI)	> 0.9	0.930	Model fit

and sample data fit together reasonably well, allowing for the modelling of the relevant variables. The route coefficients for the hypothesised relationships in the suggested model are shown in Table 4.1.

Twitter (X)

Environmental challenges were shown to be adversely connected with Twitter (X), the first association to be investigated concerning H1. The findings show a marginally negative and statistically significant link between Twitter (X) and challenges (B=-.183, $p<0.05$). The usefulness of Twitter (X) to boost a positive company reputation declines as obstacles multiply.

In relation to H2, the second relationship stated that organisational strategic possibilities including vision reputation, strategy formation, and strategic idea coordination enhance reputation through Twitter (X). The results show no evidence of a significant relationship between Twitter (X) and organisational strategic possibilities ($p>0.05$). As a result, we reject the hypothesis and conclude that Twitter (X) and organisational strategic prospects are unrelated. This is consistent with the findings of the literature research and the negative standard deviation on the issues when measuring top-level management use and roles on Twitter (X). This may be because the institution's senior management is too preoccupied with its long-term strategic objectives to effectively manage and provide content for its Twitter (X) handles. Instead, they set the agenda for those objectives' achievement.

The results also examined the connection between top-level managers and organisational strategic prospects. Results show a marginally negative correlation (B=-.247, $p<0.05$) between the two. The results indicate top-level managers are not putting organisational strategy opportunities into practice effectively, which has a detrimental impact on the corporate reputation of organisations. This reinforces the need for a structured strategy to ensure that top-level managers align with the perspectives and methods used by the other internal stakeholders to manage the company's reputation in the digital era.

The results suggested that clients utilise Twitter (X) to boost a business's reputation (H2). The findings show a marginally negative statistical relationship between consumers and Twitter (X) (B=-.247, $p<0.05$). There is an inverse relationship between public Twitter (X) use and corporate reputation. As a result, to achieve favourable results, the actors in the telecommunications business must take intentional action to mediate a positive reputation process. There is no shared understanding of how social platforms should be used. It appears that managers have a clear vision for the organisation. Still, there is no proof that this vision is shared among the organisations to maintain coherence and a sense of purpose. Based on the gaps found in the literature, a framework for the industry's players will benefit by establishing consistency on the well-known platforms and their essential components, as well as how they contribute to modern strategies for establishing a positive reputation, thereby addressing both concepts and practise (Cao et al., 2016; Delavari & Badizadeh, 2018).

Further hypothesis one (H1) was Twitter's (X) connection to conventional problems with business reputation management. Results show a somewhat negative connection between Twitter (X) and external clients (B=-.247, p<0.05). Twitter (X) and operational managers were shown to have weakly positive connections (B =.250, p >.0001), as well as Twitter (X) and general employees (B=134, p >.05). Twitter (X) does not appear to be significantly correlated with top-level management (p >.05) or SocCap (p >.05). This implies that there is no internal consensus within the telecommunications sector over how to shift away from conventional methods of reputation management or management of traditional issues that are driven by social media. This, in turn, impacts how the industry's key players use social media to manage their reputations.

Facebook

The results also outline that Facebook's relationship with respect to H3 is enhanced by organisational strategic opportunities, including vision reputation, creating strategy, strategy formulation, and strategy coordination of ideas. The results show no evidence of a significant relationship between Facebook and organisational strategic possibilities in the current industry practises (p>0.05). As a result, we reject the hypothesis and conclude that Facebook and organisational strategic prospects are unrelated.

The results also examined how operational managers and organisational strategic possibilities related to H3. The findings show an extremely strong positive correlation between the two (B=1.056, p >.001). According to research, operational managers utilise Facebook to boost their companies' favourable corporate reputations. Operational managers frequently engage in "hands-on" work. But this situation is without a predetermined framework or set of rules that promote consistency in the same direction.

The subjects of the relationship test were the utilisation of social media and general employee perceptions of the impact of business reputation in connection to H3. The findings show a highly significant positive correlation between the two (B=1.180, p>.001). According to research, regular employees use Facebook to boost their companies' favourable business reputations. Modern reputation management demands a planned method to ensure that employees' social capital contributes as much as possible to the social capital of the corporation as a whole. The industry's major players' anxieties and control-focused strategies further demonstrate how social media is crucial in reputation management, utilising classic and modern strategies.

YouTube

The results indicated that there will be a positive association between YouTube and outside users (H3). The correlation between the two is moderate to very positive and significant, according to the results (B =.630, p >.05). This is supported by research findings that demonstrate YouTube has a strong visual display, enabling users to interact with products and services using a variety of video, audio, and graphic elements.

Social Capital and Reputation Management

In addition, H2 examined the association between social capital (SocCap) and good corporate reputation (PosCopRep) as the main research relationship. According to the findings (B =.542, p >.001), social capital is a moderate-high positive predictor of favourable corporate reputation. As stated in the literature review, the interaction between social media and social capital is at the heart of the change from conventional to modern techniques in corporate reputation management. According to the research findings, this calls for a mental shift away from control-focused traditional approaches and towards a more modern approach based on teamwork, participation in dynamic online communities, engagement, and investment in employees who, in turn, drive engagement with the general public. Given that the public sphere of the compared online platforms is increasingly replacing traditional forms of communication, which increases business visibility and viability, the results demonstrate that social capital, as a driver of positive corporate reputation, is an important factor in the performance and survival of an organisation. This study's revelation of social capital powered through social media platforms lays the groundwork for future research in other industries. The literature reviewed (Cao et al., 2016; Davids & Brown, 2021; Delavari & Badizadeh, 2018; Yang, 2020) lends credence to this. The study confirmed the interactions between top-level management, operational management, general employees, and external customers to establish the mediating components in managing corporate reputation.

Final Framework for the Study

This study's framework is the technical culmination of the inquiry, which numerically illustrates the correlations between and among variables. However, the statistical display must be made simpler and more operational through interpretation. The participants in the industry and key stakeholders are depicted in Figure 4.5.

Discussion

The research study's framework suggests a dynamic interaction between corporate reputation management and social media. As discussed in the literature review, different kinds of social media can help shape and manage a positive company reputation in the Zimbabwean telecoms sector. However, the levels of influence and impacts on business reputation brought about by the numerous social media platforms vary from one platform to the next. According to the discussion in the literature review, to establish a good reputation, it is necessary to comprehend how different social media affect the development of a company's identity, personality, and strategy (Etter et al., 2018; Kaul & Chaudhri, 2019; Kotler et al., 2017). Secondly, the study demonstrates how modern viewpoints have altered a traditional approach to managing a company's reputation. In particular, internal stakeholders' use of public social media is influenced by their internal stakeholders' social capital. According to this study, Twitter (X), Facebook, and YouTube are the three

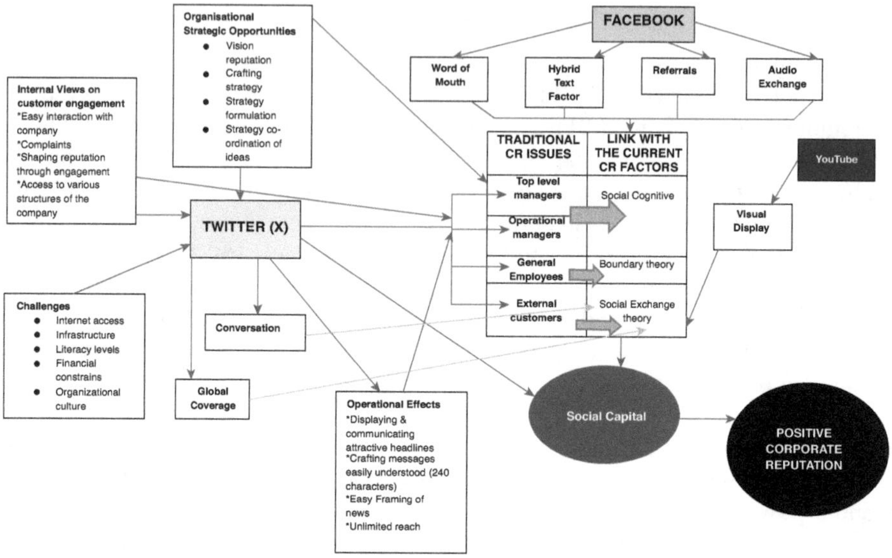

Figure 4.5 Framework for managing positive business reputations in Zimbabwe's telecommunications sector using social media platforms

Source: Researcher's construction

primary social media platforms that impact good reputation management. The management of reputation is where each of these three systems excels. According to the survey, Twitter (X) has a global audience and generates more discourse than other social media. On the other hand, compared to the other platforms, Facebook encourages word-of-mouth recommendations, offers hybrid text capabilities, and improves referrals and audio interchange. Compared to the competition, YouTube has good visual display capabilities.

These social media usage patterns have been necessitated by the multiplicity of factors as highlighted in the literature review on the general increase in global, continental, regional, and country internet connectivity, usage, and capabilities such as smartphones. In Africa, the target is to connect the population to the internet and, therefore, increase social media usage, which is shaping the new perspectives on corporate reputation (GSM Intelligence, 2023; Moyo, Proches, Mutambara, & Singh, 2022). Comparatively, though Twitter (X) is gaining traction in its usage in Zimbabwe, in other African Countries, it is declining. Yet, social media such as TikTok and Instagram are gaining traction in the Americas, and Facebook is a dominant player (GSM Intelligence, 2023; Kemp, 2023; Statcounter, 2021). It is, therefore, critical for the players in the industry to continue monitoring the social media environment to adapt and adapt as the environment changes to ensure that the new approach towards reputation management plugs in the companies in the online conversations and influences their reputations accordingly (Moyo, 2022).

Africa-Centric Trends

As located in the literature review assessing the global, continental trends in social media usage, Africa has a different trend in its usage of social media, mainly resulting from structural issues relating to the fact that it is the catchment of the next frontiers of internet growth. Further, unlike the general trend of Facebook being the main platform of social media engagement, Twitter (X) is a significant player in how internet consumption plays a major role in shaping new perspectives towards corporate reputation management.

Wherein the first wave of growth powered the global trends, it took longer to reach saturation compared to the leapfrogging powered by the sea-cabled internet infrastructure development. This has triggered an influx in the use of social media and the quality of debates that contribute to the disruptive nature within which corporate reputation is formed and shaped. This is a break from the traditional views and approaches towards new perspectives anchored by social media use and social capital. This calls for future research to invest heavily in exploring these unique dynamics. As noted in literature review, the quality of internet use and subsequent social media usage will be accelerated by 5G technology, which was at 1% coverage in 2022, at 16% in 2023, thereby increasing the internet speed significantly (GSM Intelligence, 2023). Hence, it is paramount to note that social media use trends in Africa go beyond the quantitative figures of growth and the quality of the growth, empowering the social media ecosystem to shape new perspectives of corporate reputation on the continent.

Bibliography

Aggerholm, H. K., & Andersen, S. E. (2011). Social media recruitment 3.0: Toward a new paradigm of strategic recruitment communication. *Journal of Communication Management, 22*(2), 122–137.

Albert, C. S., & Salam, A. F. (2013). Critical discourse analysis: Toward theories in social media. *International Conference on Information Systems* (pp. 1–10). https://www.researchgate.net/profile/Connie-Barber/publication/287015202_Critical_discourse_analysis_Toward_theories_in_social_media/links/57392aec08ae9f741b2be74b/Critical-discourse-analysis-Toward-theories-in-social-media.pdf

Bahia, K., & Suardi, S. (2019). *The state of mobile internet connectivity, 2019.* Global System for Mobile Communications (GSMA) Intelligence. Retrieved from: https://www.gsma.com/mobilefordevelopment/wp-content/uploads/2019/07/GSMA-State-of-Mobile-Internet-ConnectivityReport-2019.pdf [Accessed on 5 November, 2019].

Balmer, J. M. T. (2017). The corporate identity, total corporate communications, stakeholders' attributed identities, identifications and behaviours continuum. *European Journal of Marketing, 51*(9/10), 1472–1502.

Barnett, M. L., Jermier, J. M., & Lafferty, B. A. (2006). Corporate reputation: The definitional landscape. *Corporate Reputation Review, 9*(1), 26–38.

Business Ghana. (2018). *GITGE inaugurates Ceiba-2 cable.* [Online] Retrieved from: https://www.businessghana.com/site/news/business/166331/GITGE-Inaugurates-Ceiba-2-Cable [Accessed on 20 July, 2019].

Cao, X., Guo, X., Vogel, D., & Zhang, X. (2016). Exploring the influence of social media on employee work performance. *Internet Research, 26*(2), 529–554.
Carlson, J. R., Zivnuska, S., Harris, R. B., Harris, K. J., & Carlson, D. S. (2016). Social media use in the workplace: A study of dual effects. *Journal of Organizational and End User Computing, 28*(1), 15–31.
Chen, Z., Vogel, D., Yang, T., & Deng, J. (2020). The effect of social media-enabled mentoring on online tacit knowledge acquisition within sustainable organizations: A moderated mediation model. *Sustainability*, *12*(2), 616.
Creswell, J. W. (2013). *Qualitative inquiry & research design: Choosing among five approaches* (3rd ed.). Los Angeles, CA: Sage.
Creswell, J. W., & Creswell, J. D. (2018). *Research design: Qualitative, quantitative, and mixed methods approaches* (5th ed.). Los Angeles, CA: Sage.
Creswell, J. W., & Plano Clark, V. L. (2011). *Designing and conducting mixed methods research* (2nd ed.). Los Angeles, CA: Sage.
Davids, Z., & Brown, I. (2021). The collective storytelling organisational framework for social media use. *Telematics and Informatics, 62*, 1–17. https://doi.org/10.1016/j.tele.2021.101636.
Deephouse, D. L. (2000). Media reputation as a strategic resource: An integration of mass communication and resource-based theories. *Journal of Management, 26*, 1091–1112.
Delavari, M., & Badizadeh, A. (2018). The effect of social media use at work on employees' performance by considering the mediating role of trust, shared vision, network ties and knowledge transfer: An empirical case study. *Pacific Business Review International, 10*(10), 110–119.
Economist. (2019). economist.com. [Online] Retrieved from: https://www.economist.com/briefing/2019/06/08/how-the-pursuit-of-leisure-drives-internet-use [Accessed on 2 July, 2019].
Etter, M., Colleoni, E., Illia, L., Meggiorin, K., & D'Eugenio, A. (2018). Measuring organizational legitimacy in social media: Assessing citizens' judgments with sentiment analysis. *Business & Society*, *57*(1), 60–97.
Fombrun, C. J. (1996). *Reputation: Realizing value from the corporate image*. Boston, MA: Harvard Business School Press.
Gharib, R. K., Philpott, E., & Duan, Y. (2017). Factors affecting active participation in B2B online communities: an empirical investigation. *Information and Management*, *54*(4), 516–530.
Global System for Mobile Communications (GSMA) Intelligence. (2020). *The mobile economy 2020*. Retrieved from: https://www.gsma.com/mobileeconomy/wp-content/uploads/2020/03/GSMA_MobileEconomy2020_Global.pdf [Accessed on 6 June, 2020].
GSMA Intelligence. (2023). *The mobile economy 2023*. London: GSMA Intellience.
Hair, Jr, J. F., Babin, B. J., & Anderson, R. E. (2010). *A global p-erspect-ivie*. Kennesaw: Kennesaw State University.
Hair, Jr, J. F., Matthews, L. M., Matthews, R. L., & Sarstedt, M. (2017). PLS-SEM or CB-SEM: updated guidelines on which method to use. *International Journal of Multivariate Data Analysis*, *1*(2), 107–123.
Homans, G. C. (1958). Social behaviours as exchange. *American Journal of Sociology, 63*(6), 597–606.
International Telecommunications Union (ITU) (2017). *Measuring the information society report 2017, Volume 1*. International Telecommunications Union. Retrieved from: https://www.itu.int/en/ITU-D/Statistics/Documents/publications/misr2017/MISR2017_Volume1.pdf [Accessed on 28 March, 2018].

Internet Society (ISOC). (2015). *Unleashing the potential of the internet for ASEAN economies*. Retrieved from: https://www.internetsociety.org/wp-content/uploads/2017/08/ISOC_ASEAN_Digital_Economy_Report_Full_s.pdf [Accessed on 2 May, 2018].

Jahan, N., & Kim, S. W. (2020). Understanding online community participation behaviour and perceived benefits: a social exchange theory perspective. *PSU Research Review*, *5*(2), 85–100.

Johnson, D. E., Erez, A., Kiker, D. S., & Motowidlo, S. J. (2002). Liking and attributions of motives as mediators of the relationships between individuals' reputations, helpful behaviors and raters' reward decisions. *Journal of Applied Psychology, 87*(4), 808–815.

Kapoor, K. K., Tamilmani, K., Rana, N. P., Patil, P., Dwivedi, Y. K., & Nerur, S. (2018). Advances in social media research: Past, present and future. *Information Systems Frontiers, 20*, 531–558.

Kaul, A., & Chaudhri, V. (2019). Communicating CSR on Twitter: Impact on rank and reputation. In Proceedings of the 5th International CSR Communication Conference, pages 125–130, Stockholm School of Economics, Stockholm.

Kemp, S. (2019). *Digital 2019: Global digital overview*. [online] Retrieved from: https://datareportal.com/reports/digital-2019-global-digital-overview?utm_source=Reportsandutm_medium=PDFandutm_campaign=Digital_2019andutm_content=Dual_Report_Promo_Slide [Accessed on 17 June, 2019].

Kemp, S. (2023, June 20). *datareportal.com*. Retrieved from https://datareportal.com/reports/digital-2023-april-global-statshot.

Kline, T. J. (2005). *Psychological testing: A practical approach to design and evaluation*. Sage Publications. https://books.google.co.zw/books?hl=en&lr=&id=velyHqmcl2EC&oi=fnd&pg=PP15&ots=jZgF32w8-6&sig=UEeTkHIh8VVVMOZudLdk3o_fCgI&redir_esc=y#v=onepage&q&f=false

Kotler, P., Kartajaya, H., & Iwan, S. (2017). *Marketing 4.0- Moving from traditional to digital* (1st ed.). Hoboken, NJ: Wiley.

Kotler, P., Kartajaya, H., & Setiawan, I. (2021). *Marketing 5.0: Technology for humanity*. Editorial LID. https://books.google.co.zw/books?hl=en&lr=&id=S9YPEAAAQBAJ&oi=fnd&pg=PR1&dq=Kotler,+P.,+Kartajaya,+H.,+%26+Setiawan,+I.+(2021).+Marketing+5.0:+Technology+for+humanity.+Editorial+LID.&ots=QoLvjdFLMV&sig=6TJIxWHYutvqKnKMSkkTvVFh2WU&redir_esc=y#v=onepage&q&f=false

Lange, D., Lee, P. M., & Dai, Y. (2011). Organizational reputation: A review. *Journal of Management*, *37*(1), 153–184.

Lange, D., & Pfarrer, M. D. (2017). Editors' comments: Sense and structure - The core building blocks of an AMR article. *Academy of Management Review, 42*(3), 407–416.

Li, F., Larimo, J., & Leonidou, L. C. (2020). Social blogs marketing strategy: Definition, conceptualization, taxonomy, validation, and future agenda. *Journal of the Academy of Marketing Science, 49*, 51–70. https://doi.org/10.1007/s11747-020-00733-3.

Lovelock, P. (2018). *Framing policies for the digital economy: Towards policy frameworks in the Asia-Pacific*. UNDP Global Centre for Public Service Excellence. Retrieved from: https://www.undp.org/content/undp/en/home/librarypage/capacity-building/global-centre-for-public-service-excellence/DigitalEconomy.html [Accessed on 6 November, 2018].

Madory, D. (2018). *First subsea cable across South Atlantic activated*. [Online] Retrieved from: https://hub.dyn.com/dyn-research/first-subsea-cable-across-south-atlantic-activated [Accessed on 20 July, 2019].

Moqbela, M., & Kock, N. (2018). Unveiling the dark side of social networking sites: Personal and work-related consequences of social networking site addiction: *Science Direct,*

55(1), 109–119. Retrieved from: https://www.sciencedirect.com/science/article/abs/pii/S0378720617303919?via%3Dihub [Accessed on 8 June, 2020].

Moyo, T. (2022, September 30). *The effect of Twitter as a social blog on corporate reputation management in the telecommunication industry in Zimbabwe.* Retrieved from UKZN: https://ukzn-dspace.ukzn.ac.za/handle/10413/21288

Moyo, T., Proches, C. G., Mutambara, E., & Singh, U. G. (2022). The nexus between Twitter, as a social blog, and social capital in corporate reputation behaviour for the Zimbabwe Telecommunications Industry, *Gender and Behaviour, 20*(1), 1–40.

Nyamadzawo, J. (2011). *Digital opportunities for economic growth and development for Zimbabwe.* ZEPARU Working Paper Series (ZWPS 05/11). Retrieved from: http://www.zeparu.co.zw/sites/default/files/2018-03/2011%20DIGITAL% 20OPPORTUNITIES%20FOR%20ECONOMIC%20GROWTH%20AND%20 DEVELOPMENT %20FOR %20ZIMBABWE.pdf [Accessed on 7 March, 2018].

Papadopoulos, T., Stamati, T., & Nopparuch, P. (2013). Exploring the determinants of knowledge sharing via employee weblogs. *International Journal of Information Management, 33*(1), 133–146.

Postal and Telecommunications Regulatory Authority of Zimbabwe (POTRAZ). (2017). *Abridged annual postal and telecommunications sector performance report.* Retrieved from: http://www.potraz.gov.zw/wp-content/uploads/2017/03/Annual_Sector_Perfomance_Report_2017.pdf [Accessed on 22 May, 2018].

Postal and Telecommunications Regulatory Authority of Zimbabwe (POTRAZ). (2018). *Abridged postal and telecommunication sector performance report: Second quarter, 2018.* Retrieved from: https://t3n9sm.c2.acecdn.net/wp-content/uploads/2018/10/Abridged-Sector-Performance-report-Second-Quarter-2018-final.pdf [Accessed on 4 July, 2019].

Postal and Telecommunications Regulatory Authority of Zimbabwe (POTRAZ). (2019). *Abridged postal and telecommunications sector performance report: First quarter, 2019.* Retrieved from: http://www.potraz.gov.zw/wp-content/uploads/2019/07/Abridged-Sector-Performance-report-1st-Quarter-2019_final-hmed.pdf [Accessed on 16 February, 2020].

Ravasi, D., Cornelissen, J., Rindova, V. P., & Etter, M. (2018). The formation of organizational reputation. *Academy of Management Annals, 12*, 574–599.

Robinson, O. C. (2014). Sampling in interview-based qualitative research: A theoretical and practical guide. *Qualitative Research in Psychology, 11*(1), 25–41.

Song, S. (2019). *Africa telecoms infrastructure in 2018.* [Online] Retrieved from: https://manypossibilities.net/2019/01/african-telecommunications-infrastructure-in-2018/ [Accessed on 20 July, 2019].

Statcounter. (2021). *Social media Stats Zimbabwe, June 2019-July 2021.* [Online] Retrieved from: https://gs.statcounter.com/social-media-stats/all/zimbabwe [Accessed on 29 July, 2021].

Submarine Telecoms Forum. (2018). GITGE and Alcatel Submarine networks land submarine cable system linking Sao Tome to Annobon in Equatorial Guinea. *Alcatel Submarine Networks Press Release.* [Online] Retrieved from: https://subtelforum.com/gitge-asn-cable-sao-tome-annobon/ [Accessed on 20 July, 2019].

Swoboda, B., & Hirschmann, J. (2017). Perceptions and effects of cross-national corporate reputation: The role of Hofstede's cultural value approach. *International Marketing Review, 34*(6), 909–944. https://doi.org/10.1108/IMR-08-2016-0154

Thiessen, A., & Ingenhoff, D. (2011). Safeguarding reputation through strategic, integrated and situational crisis communication management: Development of the integrative model of crisis communication. *Corporate Communications: An International Journal, 16*(1), 8–26. https://doi.org/10.1108/13563281111100944

Urquhart, C. (2012). *Grounded theory for qualitative research: A practical guide.* Sage Publications. https://api.pageplace.de/preview/DT0400.9781446271582_A24016060/preview-9781446271582_A24016060.pdf

Vaast, E., & Walsham, G. (2013). Grounded theorizing for electronically-mediated social contexts. *European Journal of Information Systems, 22*, 9–25. https://doi.org/10.1057/ejis.2011.26.

van Zoonen, W., & Banghart, S. (2018). Talking engagement into being: A three-wave panel study linking boundary management preferences, work communication on social media, and employee engagement. *Journal of Computer-Mediated Communication, 23*(5), 278–293.

van Zoonen, W., Verhoeven, J. W., & Vliegenthart, R. (2016). Social media's dark side: Inducing boundary conflicts. *Journal of Managerial Psychology, 31*(8), 1297–1311.

Yang, F. X. (2020). Social media friending in building woworker guanxi: A study in the hotel industry. *International Journal of Hospitality Management, 84*, 1–13. https://doi.org/10.1016/j.ijhm.2018.10.020.

Zhou, T., Li, Z., Gan, Z., Zhang, B., Chen, Y., Niu, K., Wan, J., Liu, K., Zhao, J., Shi, Y., Chong, W., & Shngping, L. (2021). Classification, extraction, and normalization: CASIA_unisound team at the social media mining for health 2021 shared tasks. In Proceedings of the Sixth Social Media Mining for Health (#SMM4H) Workshop and Shared Task, pages 77–82, Mexico City, Mexico. Association for Computational Linguistics.

5 Twitter (X) Activism and Crisis Management

A Case Study of KFC Kenya Franchise

Anne W. Njathi and Eric Wamanji

Introduction

Within three decades, the internet has profoundly restructured the communication landscape in Kenya. Kenya's Internet Revolution began in 1997 after the Kenyan government published the Telecommunication and Postal Sector Policy Guidelines. These guidelines took cognizance of information and communication technology (ICT) as critical to national development. After the 1998 publication of the guidelines, the government passed the Kenya Information and Communication Act of 1998 (Mureithi, 2017), which introduced a multiplicity of ICT actors to the country.

The internet and social media turned a substantial population of Kenyans into producers, broadcasters, and consumers of information, a paradigm shift from the top-down communication of legacy media. The growth of Twitter (X) in Kenya was enabled by the availability of relatively affordable bandwidth, smartphones, and a liberal communication regime. The relatively easy-entry threshold to using Twitter (X), its instantaneity prowess, and as Fuchs (2013) noted, the power of messages becoming "publicly aggregated" across users means brands must engage in social listening to monitor for potential threats (p. 180).

Twitter (X) has emerged as one of Kenya's go-to platforms for news, and sharing information, and as a space to agitate for change. In early 2023, Kenya had 1.90 million Twitter (X) users (Kemp, 2023). Twitter users in Kenya have organized themselves into what is known as "Kenyans on Twitter" (KOT). This is an assemblage of virtual actors who congregate to comment on issues ranging from police brutality to racist foreigners and international news channels, such as CNN, for misrepresenting facts about the country (Nyabola, 2018). Onyango (2021) observed that Kenya has "one of Africa's loudest and most engaged internet communities known as Kenyans on Twitter (#KOT)" (para. 7). Over the past decade, Kanja (2020) argues that KOT has "built a reputation as bulldogs in their own capacity. Not only are they ferocious when mocked, but they are also sharp and fierce with their opinions, ensuring the voice of Kenyans is heard loud and clear across the globe." (para. 4)

While KOT has been "an unforgiving but a necessary force" (Nyabola, 2018, p. 114) in compelling and holding companies, the government, and individuals

DOI: 10.4324/9781032689654-5

accountable by subjecting them to public scrutiny, Twitter (X) remains a major social activism tool in Kenya; however, the public relations (PR) consequences of these practices have remained undocumented in Kenya.

Consequently, Twitter (X) in Kenya, like many other parts of the world, poses opportunities and challenges to crisis managers in relation to reputation and image management. As Austin, Liu, and Jin (2012) observed, social media use increases during a crisis as users assign a high level of credibility to social media. Online discourse, especially on Twitter (X), can degenerate into a knotty crisis of credibility and reputation. As Castells (2013) noted, self-mass communication (a characteristic of social media in the networked society) means that users set the agenda and frame the issues as they deem fit. For example, in the Kenyan context, a few researchers (Njathi, 2023; Nyabola, 2018; Mukhongo, 2020; Simon et al., 2014) have demonstrated how KOT uses the concept of self-mass communication during a crisis for social and digital activism. For example, Njathi (2023), in her study of monetization issues digital content creators are facing in Kenya, analyzed how 35 disgruntled Kenyan creators questioned the contentious and highly misunderstood digital service tax (DST). The DST debate elicited mixed reactions from influencers, especially from #KOT, who tweeted memes of all kinds on the social media platform, questioning and simultaneously ridiculing the highly misunderstood tax regime. In January 2021, KRA introduced the DST under the Finance Act. The DST is a payable income that is derived from services offered in Kenya through a digital marketplace, such as Instagram and Facebook, among others (KRA, 2021). Participants in Njathi's study expressed concern about the government's transparency regarding the launch of the DST. They accused the government of failing to engage in public consultation, as required by Article 10 of the Constitution (Kenya Law Reform Commission, n.d.), when creating policies like the DST. Despite the DST rants on Twitter, neither KRA nor the government addressed the PR crisis that was unfolding online, demonstrating a lack of empathy and mutuality, as suggested by Kent and Taylor (1998, 2002). The research in this chapter contributes to PR scholarship by focusing on online crisis management in a Kenyan context, anchored on the dialogic theory of PR (Kent & Taylor, 1998, 2002). Broadly, the study focuses on contemporary African PR, specifically crisis management on digital platforms. There is limited extant research on PR in Africa, particularly in the subfield of crisis management.

The study presented in this chapter analyzed how KFC, an American fast-food company, managed a crisis in a local Kenyan context. There has been limited scholarship in relation to the reaction and counterreaction (dialogic) from KFC and the public. Specifically for this study, it is unknown how KFC handled the pressure exerted online by the KOT to manage the crisis. First, KOT's reaction to this crisis has not been examined to fully explicate the public sentiments and how this contributed to the magnitude of the crisis. Second, KFC's actions have not been analyzed from the five principles of the dialogic theory. The objective of this study is to determine the extent to which Twitter users contributed to a cyclic crisis and to interrogate how KFC handled the crisis using dialogic communication principles. This study attempts to answer this overarching question, how did KFC engage in a dialogic engagement with its public during the boycotting crisis?

The #Boycott KFC Kenya Scandal

On January 3, 2022, at 12:10 PM, KFC posted the following notice on Twitter (X) announcing running out of potatoes for French fries:

> *Fam it was truly a Furaha December. Mlikula sherehe with your KFC faves. Ya'll loved our chips a little too much, and we've run out. Sorry! Our team is working hard to resolve the issue. In the meantime, here are some SWAP options for combo meals if you are craving our Kuku.*
> (*Furaha- Happy; Mlikula sherehe- had enjoyment; Kuku- Chicken*)
> (Source: @KFCinKenya, 2022)

KFC ran out of potatoes used to make chips (french fries). In the e-poster (Figure 5.1), KFC introduced cornmeal as a substitute. Though cornmeal is a national staple, a section of Kenyans was not amused, and in fact most Kenyans did not understand the logic of "running out of potatoes" which are plentiful in the country. Potato farming is the second largest undertaking after maize, and according to Otieno (2022), potato farming involves 800,000 small-holder farmers, employing 2.5 million people and contributing to about Sh. 50 billion to the Kenyan economy. Kenyans, and the KOT in particular, were upset that KFC would outsource its potatoes from another country when potatoes and potato farming are an important component of the Kenyan economy.

This development piqued Kenyans who took to social media, especially on Twitter (X), to fault, chastise, rebuke, and even caricature KFC. KFC's one and only tweet

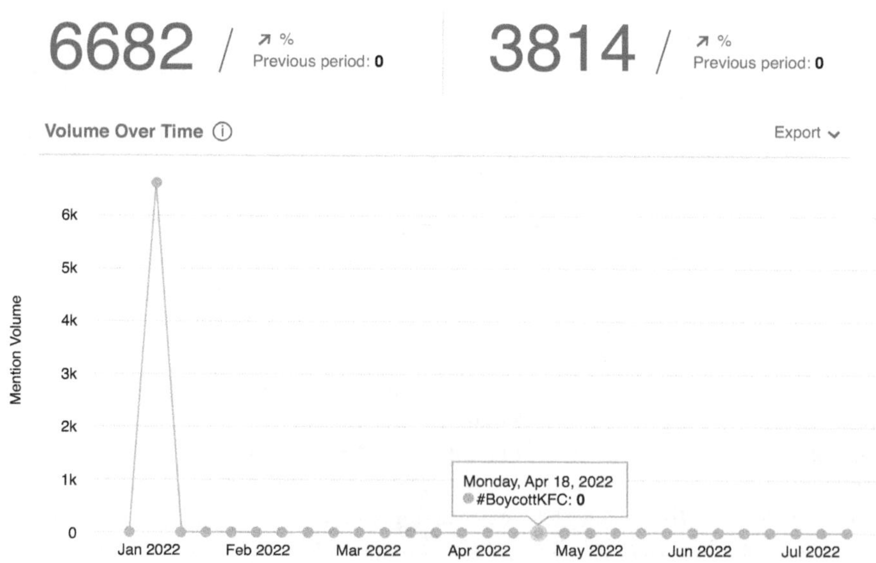

Figure 5.1 Analytics on #BoycottKFC
Source: Brandwatch, 2022

(Figure 5.1) received 669 likes and 231 retweets on the same the crisis erupted. The language used by KFC Kenya was an informal one with a mixture of English and Kiswahili. The brand lacked empathy from their tone as the tweet was met with a lot of anger and frustration. Most of this was a reaction to a tweet from Nation Africa Posted on January 4, 2022, "KFC runs out of imported potatoes for chips, snubs local farmers." That is why on Twitter (X), Kenyans called for a boycott of KFC using the hashtag #BoycottKFC, as a call to consumer activism. It was not long before the national and international media picked the reactions and pursued the story further.

The crisis moved from Twitter (X) to the legacy media. Nairobi News, an online publication of the Nation Media Group, reported a news article titled, *KOT fury at KFC over imported potatoes claim*, the same day KFC announced the lack of potatoes. In this story, Njoroge (2022) embedded screenshots of KOT's reactions against KFC including "They should also import customers"; "No wonder their fries taste terrible. Those imported potatoes must be loaded with preservatives."; and replying to a tweet by @Nationafrica (owned by Nation Media Group—Kenya's largest independent commercial media house), "KFC runs out of imported potatoes for chips, snubs local farmers" posted on January 4, 2022, at 7:48 AM, @wwashiedc reacted thus on January 4, 2022, at 8:07 AM:

> *We should boycott these idiots. They have been around for 10years and have not seen a possible local supplier?? Ama tender ya kuleta waru ni ya wenye Kenya?? Coz that is the only reason it would make sense. Kenyattas! Are you importing potatoes for KFC???(Ama tender ya kuleta waru ni ya wenye Kenya- or the tender to supply potatoes is by those who own Kenya.*
>
> (Source: Mbaabaa, 2022)

Further, Citizen Digital, an online publication of Citizen TV, which is Kenya's leading television station by viewership, reported on February 10, 2022, that Nyandarua Governor, Francis Kimemia, disclosed a deal with KFC to procure local potatoes from Nyandarua County, a leading potatoes producer region in the country. Kimemia explained "The issue was quality. We are putting the farmers together and we must prescribe the number of volumes and standards of the inputs, fertilizers, which chemicals are sprayed and how they are harvested," (as cited in Muia, 2022, para. 7). However, the case of quality contradicts what Jacques Theunissen, the Chief Executive Officer of KFC Kenya's franchise had clarified: "Ongoing potato shortage had nothing to do with the alleged poor quality of locally grown potatoes and everything to do with lack of suppliers of the semi-cooked frozen chips they use" (Tanui, 2022, para. 3).

The BBC ran the story "How KFC in Kenya got fried over its chip shortage" (Mwaura, 2022). The Standard, Kenya's second largest circulating paper wrote "Kenyans arm-twist KFC as food chain now pledges to source potatoes locally" (Kagonye, 2022). The Daily Nation, Kenya's largest circulating newspaper, wrote "Import customers as well, Kenyans retort after KFC announces potato shortage" (Njoroge, 2022) and noted that Kenyans were angered by KFC's principle of importing potatoes:

> What angered many Kenyans is the fact that Kenya is an agriculture-rich nation that produces tonnes of potatoes in its highlands, most of which go to waste due to lack of a market. By 11 a.m., #BoycottKFC was the top trending topic on Twitter in Kenya.
>
> (Njoroge, 2022, para. 3)

KFC noted that it sourced potatoes from Egypt to maintain quality and safety (Business Daily, 2022), and the shortage was caused by delays in shipment due to the COVID-19 pandemic. KFC's local business Chief Executive, Jacques Theunissen, explained to the press why potatoes are imported:

> The reason we cannot buy local at the moment is all suppliers need to go through the global QA approval process and we cannot bypass that even if we run out to ensure that our food is safe for consumption by our customers.
>
> (Business Daily, 2022, para. 6)

These revelations triggered another round of condemnation from KOT. Twitter (X) users wondered why KFC could not source potatoes locally, which are aplenty in Kenya. Others wondered why KFC did not empower local farmers to produce according to standards. Besides, local competitors, like Big Square, Burger King, and Chicken Inn, took advantage of the crisis and used Twitter (X) to remind Kenyans that the outlets had enough fries and that the potatoes were locally sourced. For instance, Chicken Inn using the handle @ChickenInnKe, on January 4, 2022, posted, "Because you love our chips a little too much, we make sure they're always there. Our potatoes are locally sourced to make fresh fries, every time." Burger King similarly tweeted a post with the text, "We have enough fries for everyone."

Government authorities also weighed in on the matter. In a press statement to newsrooms dated January 4, 2022, Francis Kimemia, the Governor of Nyandarua County (one of the 47 counties in the country) expressed his displeasure "This is very unfortunate as potato farmers across the country, more so in Nyandarua, are grappling with marketing challenges for their produce." (Maina, 2022, para. 6). In the press statement, the governor disputed the argument that Kenyan farmers were ill-trained. He outlined efforts his government, in conjunction with partners such as the German Agency for International Development (GIZ) and the International Fertilizer Development Centre (IFDC), has put into building potato farmers in the region. Tanui (2022) reported that Kenya's Ministry of Trade convened a consultative meeting with local KFC leadership ostensibly to find a solution to the potato crisis. Tanui (2022) explained, "As part of the resolutions, KFC and the ministry agreed to develop a roadmap within 2 weeks guiding the setup of a manufacturing plant to supply processing frozen chips" (para. 6). Further, according to Tuko, an online news site in Kenya, the Cabinet Secretary for Agriculture, Peter Munya was looped into the potato discourse. Wandede (2022) reported that "Agriculture Cabinet Secretary Peter Munya said his ministry had a discussion with Kentucky Fried Chicken (KFC) on reasons they were not sourcing their potatoes locally" (para. 1).

Twitter (X) and Sociopolitical Activism

Kazeem's (2016) study of Twitter (X) use in Africa demonstrated that the platform tends to be more political than in other parts of the world such as the United States and United Kingdom. According to Nyabola (2018), "In Kenya, the rise of social media has led to an expansion of the public sphere, and this is having tangible impacts on politics and public opinion across the country" (p. 48). Nyabola (2018) argues that new media like Twitter (X) in Kenya has continued to thrive as a source of information because it is a space "where narratives can be challenged, and evidence presented directly to the public to contradict officialdom" (p. 60). Campaigners have learned how to advance their interests on Twitter (X) using different tactics. Mukhongo (2020) observes that Twitter (X) has become "an online public sphere where Kenyans go to 'square it out' with their adversaries, create memes to celebrate others, shame others, and engage…" (p. 151). Hatmaker (2021) noted that in Kenya, entities pushing their agenda on Twitter (X) would hire verified account users to "promote messaging" and influence the Twitter (X) algorithm to trigger a trend. A study published by Mozilla Foundation indicated that in Kenya's general elections of 2022, politicians and political entities paid influencers between $10 and 15 a day, to push certain hashtags that not only promoted their political agenda but also exposed the thriving disinformation crisis on Twitter (X) (Madung, 2021).

Mostly, this is how KOT works. As active Twitter (X) users, they pick one issue of interest at a time, and a member comes up with a hashtag that is accompanied by short comments, mostly critical, and starts to pile pressure on either the government, public personalities, or corporations demanding for change or apology. But it's not all antagonistic. At times, KOT has rallied one another toward national unity and for charitable acts like fundraising for medical expenses. For instance, in 2015, CNN published a story claiming that "President Barack Obama is not just heading to his father's homeland, but to a region that's a hotbed of terror" (Starr, 2015, para. 1). KOTs were angered by a CNN report that branded the country as a "hotbed of terrorism." Angered KOT coined the hashtag "#SomeoneTellCNN," which they used to criticize the American news outlet for misreporting. The KOTs' reaction was so intense that

> Tony Maddox a CNN executive vice president and managing director, flew to Kenya to apologize, "It wasn't a deliberate attempt to portray Kenya negatively, it is regrettable and we shouldn't have done it. There is a world at war with extremists; we know what a hotbed of terror looks like, and Kenya isn't one".
>
> (Mutiga, 2015, para. 7)

In 2013, a social media uproar on Twitter (X) pushed renowned preacher T.D. Jakes to apologize to Kenyans for his remarks that insinuated Kenya as a poor state that only benefited from his ministry. With a viral campaign dubbed #SomeoneTell

TDJakes, #KOT's quick and furious reaction forced T.D. Jakes to apologize (Karanja, 2013, 2020; Pala, 2013).

In 2018, angry Kenyans again took to Twitter (X) to vent against the power utility firm, Kenya Power and Lighting Company Limited (KPLC), who had been accused of inflating power bills. Matters were even made worse when the management revealed that its staff engaged in fraudulent acts that led to swindling the power firm resulting in higher bills for customers. Once again KOT coined #SwitchOffKPLC, which trended for months agitating for the closure of the power firm. "The #SwitchOffKPLC campaign that started on Twitter and has since spread through wider social media spaces has unleashed an unprecedented and massive outcry against KPLC following nine consecutive months of shocking and fraudulent fleecing of electricity consumers" (Seii, 2018, para. 6).

Another popular trend with KOT is their response whenever Kenya is mentioned in a bad light. KOT engages in digital wars with "with the jokesters and meme-makers keen to overpower the other countries with insults and cruel humor" (Kanja, 2020, para. 12). KOT has engaged in an endless tirade of memes with other countries such as South Africa, Uganda, Nigeria, and Tanzania. Through bullying and online harassment, KOT puts into question even those in power such as presidents, politicians, celebrities, royalty, the wealthy, and whole countries. According to Kanja (2020), KOT bullied former Kenyan president Uhuru Kenyatta out of Twitter (X) in March 2019, where he was forced to abandon a massive following of 3.5 million followers due to the high-pressure social networking site was taking him. At other times, KOT has also advocated for sociocultural beneficial campaigns for example in 2012, a campaign dubbed #kenyans4kenyans pushed a rallying call for donations to alleviate hunger and starvation in Turkana County. In the following year, KOT launched #WeAreOne campaign following the Westgate Al Shabaab attack in September 2013.

As evidenced by the previous examples, KOT has meticulously taken advantage of hashtags to push its agenda. Hashtags operate as markers of conversations, bringing disparate comments and commenters together in an interactive space dedicated to the topic of interest (Tully & Ekdale, 2014).

As keyboard warriors, often the conversation starts and ends on Twitter, it does not translate to tangible PR results by governments and organizations beyond apologies, as seen in the cases discussed above. We argue that although digital activism creates a platform for public rants, it is far from influencing policies in Africa. A lot of digital activisms in Africa are ephemeral, whereby issues are quickly abandoned, unliked witnessed with global PR crises such as #metoo and #blacklivesmatter. Regional African online activisms such as #endsars, and #bringbackourgirls, although they went viral, did not influence change.

Social Media & Crisis Management

Like with other social media platforms, performances on Twitter (X) can also be a source of crisis. A social media crisis is an event that transpires in or is amplified by social media (Owyang, 2011). Coombs (2014) noted that because of its affordances for user-generated content, social media creates a breeding ground for crises or risks. Similar to legacy media, negative comments on social media can be damaging to corporate reputations (Distaso & McCorkindale, 2013). For instance, KFC Kenya found itself on the receiving end of a social media crisis when KOT advocated for Kenyans to boycott the franchise.

Coombs (2015) defined crisis as "an unpredictable event that threatens important expectancies of stakeholders and can seriously impact an organization's performance and generate negative outcomes" (p. 3). Further Coombs (1999) considered a crisis as "a major unpredictable event that has potentially negative results. The event and its aftermath may significantly damage an organization and its employees, products, services, financial condition, and reputation" (p. 2). Scholars have applied varied theories to studies of traditional and online crisis management. The most common theories applied to crisis management include situational crisis communication theory (SCCT), attribution theory, and image repair theory.

According to Pearson and Mitroff (1993), crises are composed of five dimensions: they are highly visible, require immediate attention, contain an element of surprise, have a need for action, and are outside the organization's complete control. Further, according to Coombs (2015), an organizational crisis is a significant threat to organizational operations or reputations that can have negative consequences for stakeholders and/or the organization if not handled properly. Thus, Allen and Caillouet (1994) noted that crisis response strategies seek to protect an organization by eliminating or reducing reputational damage. Communication is critical to the management of the crisis, as Coombs and Holladay (1996) noted, "What organizations say to their various publics during a crisis should influence the extent of the reputational and financial damage a crisis can inflict on the organizational image" (p. 292). Symbolic interaction, created through dialogue and crisis communication, between the organization and its stakeholders is critical to creating mutual understanding about the crisis. According to De Bruycker and Walgrave (2014), the practice of crisis communication begins before the crisis emerges.

Hermann (1963) noted that a crisis threatens the "high-priority values of the organization, presents a restricted amount of time in which a response can be made, and is unexpected or unanticipated by the organization" (p. 64). Though Herman is credited for pioneering research in crisis, the concept of "unexpected" and "unanticipated" has been discounted by subsequent researchers and theorists (see Coombs, Frandsen, Holladay & Johansen, 2010), Organizational crisis is not a matter of "if" but "when." It is the premise of the "when" that it is a prerequisite for organizations to anticipate and plan for a crisis. According to Heath and Millar (2004) a crisis is

> An untimely but predictable event that has actual or potential consequences for stakeholders' interests as well as the reputation of the organization...That means a crisis can harm stakeholders and damage the organization's relationship with them... Respond well and survive the crisis; respond poorly and suffer the death of the organization's reputation and perhaps itself.
>
> (p. 33)

Crisis communication involves a series of strategic communicative actions before, during, and after a crisis. The goal is to protect and restore organizational reputation. Coombs and Holladay (1996) essentially reckon that crisis strategies (using communication) are likely to affect an organization's image in the following ways: "convince stakeholders there is no crisis; have stakeholders see the crisis as less negative; and have stakeholders see the organization more positively" (p. 283).

Thus, in a crisis, it is incumbent on an organization to respond quickly and effectively in a bid to limit the harm to the organization's reputation and to its stakeholders. One such way to manage communication in a crisis is to employ the strategies outlined in SCCT.

SCCT is one of the dominant theories in crisis communication research (Avery et al., 2010), and has its origins in attribution theory. SCCT seeks to establish the most effective way of communicating during different crises. Coombs (2007) notes, "the first priority in any crisis is to protect stakeholders from harm, not to protect the reputation" (p. 165). This harm could be physical or psychological. Response to crisis is informed by a triad of denial, diminish, and rebuild strategies (Coombs, 2006). The deny strategy would involve attacking the accuser, denial of the accusations, and scapegoating and is applicable to victim-crisis types. The diminish strategy, which largely is made of excuses and justifications, is more appropriate for accident-related crises. While rebuilding strategies, like compensation and apology, work well for crises crisis that would have been preventable in the first place. Coombs and Holladay (1996) suggest that since crises vary, response strategies too must be tailored accordingly.

Although, SCCT (Avery et al., 2010) and image repair (Benoit, 2015) as theoretical frameworks are popular theories in crisis communication, the nature of Twitter (X) as a platform lends itself to dialogue. In other words, the platform is inherently designed for dialogue, which is considered a critical approach to solving crises unfolding in real time at an unprecedented pace.

Dialogic Theory

Dialogic PR and social listening are proposed as helpful approaches to tackle crises on social media platforms (Cheng, 2018; Goodman, 2018; Nierman, 2020; Valentini, Murtarelli, & Romenti, 2014). The dialogic tactical approach not only helps a brand in handling a crisis but also enhances consumer awareness and knowledge, builds confidence, and encourages two-way communication that helps to stave off social activism (Valentini, Romenti & Kruckeberg, 2018) by gaining valuable lessons in managing the future crisis with high regard for consumers' criticism. In fact, Kent (2017) explains that dialogic communicators are assumed to have a reason for coming together (to discuss issues, come to a better understanding, solve a problem, build relationships, etc.). Further, to procure social change, Kent and Taylor (2021) suggest a framework that constitutes "user expectations, engagement, content curation, and sustainment" (p. 1) as critical to dialogic engagement in the social media space.

Dialogic engagement is a meaningful interaction between an organization and its publics. Indeed, since an organization's survival is anchored on its relationship with stakeholders, engagement through communication becomes a fundamental matter. Dialogue, the exchange of concepts and meanings, has the propensity to aid parties in creating meaning and reaching a mutual understanding and has been used in negotiations, conflict resolution, and mediation. It is therefore a considered method of crisis management. As Ballantyne (2004) reckoned, "dialogue works to reconcile what seems contrary between parties, making the reconciliation of meaning possible" (p. 116). Dialogic approaches are key because they initiate and maintain contact between an organization and its publics. Pettigrew (1986) suggested that from a psychological point of view, lack of contact reinforces intergroup bias, prejudice, and dehumanization, and suggested the need to develop structured contact between disparate members of identity groups in a bid to reverse the effects of lack of contact. This contact is mainly achieved through dialogic enterprise.

Kent and Taylor (1998) introduced the concept of dialogic communication in an online context. They defined dialogic communication as "any negotiated exchange of ideas and opinions" (p. 325). Kent (2017) noted a dialogic approach to PR anchors an organization's communication on the stakeholder's needs and concerns toward mutual and genuine relationship building as opposed to turning PR into an offensive machine to suit the organization's interests. Principally, a dialogic enterprise in PR is constructivist in its approach, values people, and treats them as ends and not means to an end and is therefore ethical. Contemporary dialogic PR is credited to Pearson (1989) who considered dialogue as a two-way ethical communication aspiring for mutual benefits for organizations and their publics. Subsequently, Kent and Taylor in their 1998 article titled "Building Dialogic Relationships Through the World Wide Web" published in the *Public Relations Review*, pursued the ideal of dialogic public relations noting that it is "any negotiated exchange of ideas and opinions" (p. 325). Further, Kent and Taylor (1998, 2002) expanded the purview of dialogic PR to include online media, which has been applied extensively to social media. The two authors suggested five principles of dialogic PR listed as (1) mutuality, (2) propinquity, (3) empathy, (4) risk, and (5) commitment.

In this case, mutuality is the collaboration between an organization and its publics during engagement premised on principle of equality in a bid to construct meaningful relationships. This principle is anchored on the understanding that there is mutual benefit for both parties and, therefore, allays fear during engagement. Collaboration and the spirit of mutual equality are the two features of mutuality. Propinquity encourages consultative undertaking between the organization and its public before a decision is taken. Kent and Taylor (2002) also state that the history of parties needs to be taken into account thus informing how the engagement unfolds. Empathy is critical to constructing trust between the organization and its publics for effective dialogue to take place. Kent and Taylor (2002) regard that supportiveness, communal orientation, and confirmation are the three main features of empathy. Risk is about the vulnerability of organizations and the publics due to the unpredictability nature of dialogue especially in the wake of making disclosures. The final principle is commitment which Kent and Taylor (2002) argue that organizations and the publics should genuinely be invested in the act of dialogic communication and remain committed to mutual understanding.

Lane and Kent (2018) expanded further the scope of dialogic engagement which they noted is multifaceted and contains eleven key characteristics that are (1) treating others as valued, (2) interactions based on dialogue and turn-taking, (3) repeated interactions, (4) relationship-based, and (5) trust. Other characteristics of dialogic engagement include (6) participants given autonomy to reach a flow or engaged state, (7) activities mutually satisfying, (8) either party may initiate collaboration, (9) no agenda or manipulation, (10) coordinative, and (11) rhetorical.

According to Kent and Taylor (2002), true dialogue is complex and contains multiple concepts such as risk, trust, empathy, positive regard, propinquity, and even willingness to be changed. Since an organization's survival is anchored on its relationship with stakeholders, engagement through communication becomes fundamental. Communication engagement is the "dynamic multidimensional relational concept featuring psychological and behavioral attributes of connection, interaction, participation, and involvement, designed to achieve or elicit an outcome at the individual, organization, or social levels" (Johnston & Taylor , 2018, p. 18). Dialogic engagement is a meaningful enterprise for organizations with their online public. Dialogic engagement is multifaceted and contains eleven key characteristics that are (1) treating others as valued, (2) interactions based on dialogue and turn-taking, (3) repeated interactions, (4) relationship-based, (5) trust, (6) participants given autonomy to reach a flow or engaged state, (7) activities mutually satisfying, (8) either party may initiate collaboration, (9) no agenda or manipulation, (10) coordinative, and (11) rhetorical (Lane & Kent, 2018, p. 64).

However, on the dialogic principle of Kent and Taylor (2002), scholars (see Lane & Bartlett, 2016) are pessimistic of its practicality during a typical crisis. They suggest an improvement of the Dialogic Public Relations Theory. Lane and Bartlett (2016) also found out that PR practitioners lacked an understanding of "dialogue" and hardly engaged in the two-way communication as postulated in Dialogic PR.

Methodology

Data Selection, Extraction, and Selection

The study analyzed original tweets and replies related to #BoycottKFC by angered KOT Twitter (X) users and KFC. This was done through a Twitter sentiment analysis from the sample size of the #BoycottKFC dataset scrapped from Twitter. Research data were retrieved using a social media monitoring tool called Brandwatch. The sample size for the dataset from Brandwatch stood at 6,682 observations ($n = 6{,}682$). As Figure 1.2 indicates there was a spike in #BoycottKFC as the crisis was still fresh.

Tweets and replies with mentions of #BoycottKFC were collected, filtered, and cleaned for preparation for analysis. We used Python as the coding language for analysis with Jupyter Notebook as the tool for relevance, duplicates, and time. This resulted in a study population of 1,100 tweets and replies with #BoycottKFC mentions. The mentions of KFC, trended between January 1 and 30, 2022, were captured. The nature of online crises informs the study duration, as trending issues tend to die off quickly, and the need to standardize the time for a better comparison. In this study, tweets were selected based on the researcher's assessment and how they aligned with the purpose of the dialogic principles. To be included in this study, tweets had to include the #BoycottKFC within the time period between January 1 and 30, 2022. This approach was adopted to distinguish between older hashtags from new. To ensure a level of consistency, the unit of analysis was each individual tweet regardless of the post format and who posted it, so long as it was within the specific time period (Table 5.1).

To ensure the data were ready for analysis, we cleaned the data by removing duplicates, null rows, memes, photos, and emojis which reduced the sample size to 300 ($n = 300$) of the total data collected from Brandwatch with the said python packages.

Sentiment and Content Analysis

A sentiment analysis of the posts was conducted using the content analysis method. First, the sampled tweets and replies were analyzed sentence by sentence to construe meaning, and data were analyzed using a codebook, which included variables that were extracted from the dialogic principles. Finally, Python was used to analyze the data.

Coding Procedure

A code sheet was developed with explicitly clear content categories. Coding categories were developed, and the contents of each tweet were re-read and analyzed to identify dialogic categories that include (1) mutuality, (2) propinquity, (3) empathy, (4) risk, and (5) commitment adapted from the five dialogic principles. To make sense of the data, we adapted dialogic principles as elaborated in Table 5.2.

Table 5.1 Frequency of Tweets and Replies

	KFC
Type of tweet	*Frequency*
Original	184
Retweet	71
Reply	45
Total	300

Table 5.2 KFC Dialogic Principles Analysis

Dialogic Principle	*Enactment*
Mutuality	There was no mutual equality in KFC's engagement. Instead, it prescribed to its publics/customers what to consume in the absence of potatoes.
Dialogic Propinquity	KFC laced the principle of dialogic propinquity. It did not consult its publics on the best way out of a potato shortage.
Empathy	KFC did not seem to appreciate the needs of its audience and by understanding that cornmeal is a complete oxymoron to Kenyans in relation to French fries. Besides, the defense that potatoes could only be sourced from Egypt for quality purposes ignored Kenyans' patriotic sensibilities.
Risk	KFC did not show a sense of vulnerability. Instead, it was defensive.
Commitment	KFC's response was reactive. Cultural sensitivity lacked in KFC's interaction. KFC even deleted its tweets pertaining to this crisis. KFC downplayed socioeconomic and political dynamics—Kenyans' emotional connection to their potato produce, a sense of national pride.

For sentiment classification, we were able to create sentiment of negative, neutral, and positive from the tweets and classify them by generating the polarity of the tweets which is the overall positivity or negativity of a statement. The values range from negative to positive with 0.00 as neutral. Most of the tweets were classified as neutral. This is because most of the tweets were against KFC Kenya but were supporting local farmers. The second set of sentiments we created were sentiments of emotion which we used a package from Hugging Face. Hugging Face is a tool that enables users to build, train, and deploy Machine Learning models based on open-source (OS) code and technologies. It allowed us to classify the text into one of the following five emotions: (0), joy (1), love (2), anger (3), fear (4), and surprise (5). The most emotions shown were neutral, anger and disapproval, curiosity, caring, and realization (nationalism)

1 Anger: The frustration and disappointment that Kenyans expressed on the shortage of potatoes.
2 Surprise: The shock that KFC does not use local potatoes.
3 Curiosity: The surprise that a company as big as KFC can run out of potatoes, yet Kenya is a leading producer of potatoes.
4 Disapproval: The rejection by KOT of KFC's importation of potatoes.
5 Nationalism: Support and passion toward defending Kenya's potato industry.

Results

From our analysis, KFC only tweeted once, the original tweet (Figure 5.1) announcing the potato shortage. One significant challenge with this dataset was that KFC's tweets were not available on Twitter (X) when we scrapped the data. It is not clear whether the organization deleted all its tweets from this crisis or not.

The last time KFC posted was January 4, 2022, and their page shows a gap through February 4, 2022. In retrospect, the entire online crisis was driven by angry Kenyans, media updates, and the government response without a response from KFC. As much as the crisis was unfolding on Twitter (X), KFC did not engage online, leaving Kenyans to control the shortage of potatoes.

In essence, KFC, as illustrated in Table 5.2, ignored the five dialogic principles of PR (Kent & Taylor, 1998, 2002), bringing to question whether KFC as a brand respects Kenya's public and if it cares about its brand reputation and image in the Kenyan context. Although KFC issued statements captured by the mainstream media, it completely ignored comments and feedback provided by its online publics. The dialogic principles of PR, as espoused by Kent and Taylor (1998, 2002), are designed for internet and social media-based engagement between an organization and its publics. Even though Kent and Taylor (1998, 2002) emphasize that dialogic principles should be between an organization and its publics, it was surprising that KFC did not participate in the potato crisis Twitter (X) discourse, instead choosing to work with the mainstream media. KFC's response can arguably be attributed to KOT's ephemeral nature of online engagement and somewhat ineffective digital activism campaigns. For example, after January 10, 2022, the hashtag or scandal had died down with only 21 data points ($n=21$). This interesting finding opens a new window for further studies and interrogation about the sustainability and need to respond to online crises (Figure 5.2).

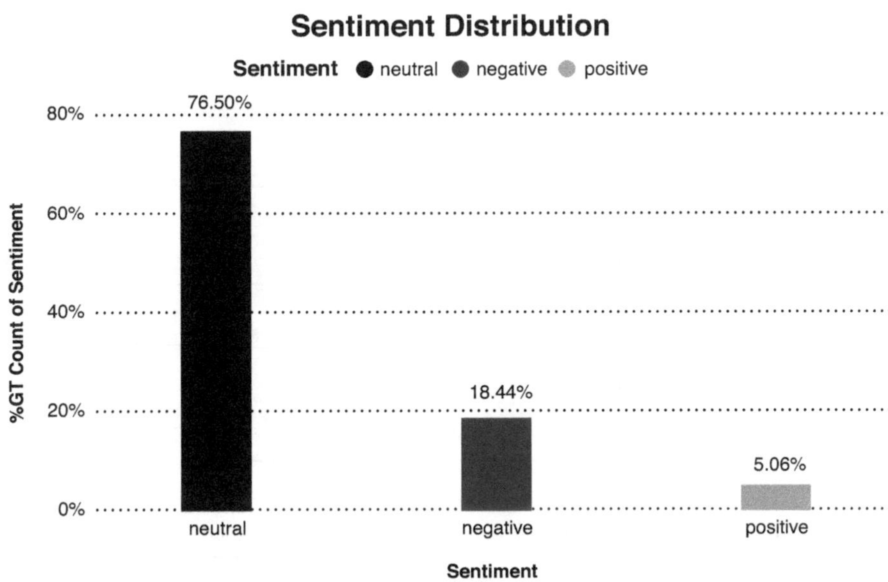

Figure 5.2 Indicates that the general tone of KFC tweets was neutral, indicating that the public did not hold any subjective opinion about the conduct of KFC but rather expressed the desire for KFC to support the local economy

Source: Author's creation.

Principles of Dialogic Theory

Communication between PR practitioners and the public is a dialogue system, which operates under the five principles of dialogic theory (Kent & Taylor, 2002, pp. 25–29). Thus, communications between organizations and its publics should be interactive and not an asymmetrical monologue. Table 5.3 shows how KFC, the online audience, held conversations on Twitter (X) in response to the crisis. Tweets and replies on KFC expressed mutuality, empathy, and commitment, a conversation exclusively held by Twitter users. However, some online audiences shared messages that posed a reputational risk to the organization, such as posts that threatened KFC to close the Kenya operation for not using local potatoes. Other posts incited the general public to stop consuming KFC products.

Online Activism

Twitter (X) Users' on Online Activism

Table 5.4 KFC's crisis escalated from retweets from opinion leaders with a large following. The leaders briefly contributed to the discussions and replied to a few tweets. Thus, there were about five to seven repeated users, while the rest of the online public engaged in the conversation were ordinary KOT. This aligns with previously discussed online activism such as #SomeoneTellCNN and #SwitchOffKPLC that have taken place in Kenya, largely driven by Twitter users with a vast following.

Table 5.3 Audience Conversations about KFC's Crisis

	KFC	
	Responses/Reactions	
Dialogic Principles	*N*	*%*
Mutuality	166	55
Empathy	23	8
Propinquity	31	10
Commitment	23	8
Risk	57	19
Total	300	100.00

Table 5.4 Twitter User Profile on KFC's Crisis

Company		*Unique users*	*Repeated users*	*Total*
KFC	Frequency	295	5	300
	%	98.3	1.7	100

African-Centric Trends on Online Crisis Management

The results indicated a couple of takeaways critical to PR and crisis management in Africa. One, African businesses do not consider crises as an existential problem, and they generally treat it with contempt until they do provide generic responses and apologies to the complaints raised as seen in the case of KPLC and #SomeoneTellCNN discussed in this study. From this study, it is evident that KFC did not apply dialogic principles to manage the reputational crises on Twitter (X) and avoid escalation of their crisis. Besides the original tweet announcing the shortage of potatoes by KFC, there were no further tweets or any other form of engagement, leading to KOT controlling the narrative. As reactionary approaches, KFC's lack of response fueled the crisis as online users felt offended after learning that potatoes are imported and that local potatoes do not meet KFC's standards.

Crisis management is not embedded in the African PR crisis management for most companies (Ochieng, 2021; PRSK, 2019; Wamanji, 2018). If anything, a study conducted on the state of PR prepared by Public Relations of Kenya (PRSK) in 2019, evidenced that crisis management is not a major PR activity in most companies and only a few private companies in Kenya factored crisis management in their PR activities. In another article titled *Why Kenya's Corporates are Hopeless in Crisis Communication*, Wamanji (2018) explains that most organizations lack structured, strategic, and coherent crisis management strategies. Lack of crisis management strategies, according to Wamanji (2018), can be attributed to the failure to hire competent crisis communication personnel and to anchor communication functions in boardrooms where strategic decisions are made. Furthermore, researchers including Nyongesa and Mwiti (2013), and Struwig, Best, and Muthwa (2017) note that consumer protection and lack of consumer rights knowledge is also common in Africa, "the concept of consumer protection is still alien in Kenya with many companies exhibiting unethical behavior in the past while the consumers and other stakeholders are unaware of actions to take" (Nyongesa & Mwiti, 2013, para. 1).

Wamanji (2014) argues that Kenyan society is ignorant of "rights and privileges" (para.12). A majority of the population in Kenya does not know their consumer rights. Only a small percentage of the elite and the #KOT know their rights but these heated online discourses end up as dead conversations online, with no proper recourse. The ignorance on the part of PR practitioners and organizations does not put much emphasis on the PR crisis to logical conclusions. Wamanji (2018) argues that the majority of the Twitter (X) discourse during a crisis is regarded as "keyword warriors" (para. 3).

We recommend more detailed studies on how African organizations are aligned to crisis communication, training programs, and education programs for consumers to understand their rights. James (2000), Middleberg (2001), Perry et al. (2003), and Nathanial and Heyden (2020) recommend instant dissemination of accurate messages via official company channels, responding to public concerns within 24 hours, continuously monitoring misinformation and prompt response to the allegation. In addition, they urge engaging with the public in discussion throughout the crisis cycle and after a crisis, using traditional media tools and products, and new media, such as press releases, memos, and press conferences, as trust and credibility are built with transparent and clear communications.

Conclusion

We found that the Twitter (X) crisis spilled over to mainstream media, and failure to engage with dialogic principles might have shown ignorance on KFC's part. KFC's behavior of ignoring the dialogic principles appears to be in line with Lane and Bartlett (2016) who observed that during the crisis the dialogic framework is impractical. In addition, we argue that online conversations can escalate to a crisis when not managed with the correct information at the time the crisis is unfolding. The online public prefers interactive communication and wants to engage companies in a dialogue. Dialogue creates trust if the company is transparent and genuine. Using multiple communication channels and products is key to educating the public and helps avert a crisis. In most cases, the public engages in online activism due to a need for more information on the issue. It would be interesting for future online crisis studies on PR to interrogate why multinational companies, in this case, KFC would choose not to engage with its publics online as the crisis is unfolding. Further, we recommend a wider study on Kenyan organizations to establish the use and practicality of the dialogic principles.

Study Limitations

This study did not interview PR representatives from KFC. Future recommendations would include gathering empirical data from PR representatives at KFC to corroborate findings collated from Twitter (X) content and sentiment analysis and, at the same time analyze the offline response KFC undertook, as opposed to engaging online. In addition, expansive data analysis could be conducted to include retweets and other comments that were driving the conversations on Twitter (X) for crises.

Twitter limitations

Although Twitter (X) is a space where Kenyans have been having a lot of social and political discourses, there are only 250,000 Twitter (X) accounts in Kenya that are regularly active and only concentrated within Nairobi—the capital city. This small fraction of active Twitter users arguably explains why KFC ignored the online conversations. In addition, this active Twitter (X) population is mainly composed of middle- and upper-class suburbs around the city (Nyabola, 2018). In other words, the active number of Twitter (X) accounts in Kenya compared to the larger Kenyan population may not significantly transform public dialogue from a national perspective.

References

Allen, M. W., & Caillouet, R. H. (1994). Legitimate endeavors: Impression management strategies used by an organization in crisis. *Communication Monographs*, 61, 44–62.

Austin, L., Liu, F. B., & Jin, Y. (2012). How audiences seek out crisis information: Exploring the social-mediated crisis communication model. *Journal of Applied Communication Research,* 40(2), 188–207. https://doi.org/10.1080/00909882.2012.654498

Avery, J. E., Lariscy, W. R., Kim, S., & Hocke, T. (2010). A quantitative review of crisis communication research in public relations from 1991 to 2009. *Public Relations Review*, 36(2), 190–192.

Ballantyne, D. (2004). Relationship specific knowledge. *Journal of Business & Industrial Marketing*, 19(2), 114–123.

Benoit, W. (2015). Image repair theory in the context of strategic communication. In D. Holtzhausen & A. Zerfass (Eds.), *The Routledge handbook of strategic communicatio*n (pp. 303–311). London: Routledge.

Business Daily. (2011, August 11). *Kentucky fried chicken opens in Nairobi on Friday.* Business Daily. https://www.businessdailyafrica.com/bd/corporate/companies/kentucky-fried-chicken-opens-in-nairobi-on-friday-1989898

Brandwatch. (2022). *Analytics on #BoycottKFC. Extracted on April 2022.*

Castels, M. (2013). Communication Power. New York., Oxford University Press.

Cheng, Y. (2018). How social media is changing crisis communication strategies: Evidence from the updated literature. *Journal of Contingencies and Crisis Management*, 26(1), 58–68.

Coombs, W.T. (2006). The protective powers of crisis response strategies: Managing reputational assets during a crisis. Journal of Promotion Management, 12, 241-260.

Coombs, W. T. (1999). *Ongoing crisis communication: Planning, managing and responding*. Thousand Oaks, CA: Sage.

Coombs, W. T. (2014). *Applied crisis communication and crisis management: Cases and exercises.* Thousand Oaks, CA: Sage.

Coombs, W. T. (2015). *Ongoing crisis communication: Planning, managing and responding* (4th edn). Thousand Oaks, CA: Sage.

Coombs, W. T., Frandsen, F., Holladay, S. J., & Johansen, W. (2010). Why a concern for apologia and crisis communication? *Corporate Communications: An International Journal*, 15(4), 227–349.

Coombs, W. T., & Holladay, J. S. (1996). Crisis communication and attribution in a crisis: An experimental study in crisis communication. *Journal of Public Relations Research*, 8(4), 279–295.

De Bruycker, I., & Walgrave, S. (2014). How a new issue becomes an owned issue. Media coverage and the financial crisis in Belgium (2008–2009). *International Journal of Public Opinion Research*, 26(1), 86–97.

Distaso, W. M., & Mccorkindale, T. (2013). A benchmark analysis of the strategic use of social media for Fortune's most admired U.S. companies on Facebook, Twitter and YouTube. *Public Relations Journal*, 7, 1–33.

Fuchs, C. (2013). *Social media a critical introduction*. Los Angeles, CA: Sage.

Google Scholar Pion, M. (1975). On the meaning of the notion of conflict and its study in social psychology. *European Journal of Social Psychology*, 4, 389–436.

Hatmaker, T. (2021, November 3). *On Twitter, political disinformation clouds Kenya's trending topics*. TechCrunch. https://techcrunch.com/2021/11/03/kenya-twitter-political-disinformation-trends/

Goodman, T. (2018 August 21). *Listen to the Tweets*. LinkedIn. https://www.linkedin.com/pulse/listen-tweets-taylor-goodman/?trk=read_related_article-card_title

Heath, R. L., & Millar, D. P. (2004). A rhetorical approach to crisis communication: Management, communication processes, and strategic responses. In D. P. Millar & R. L. Heath (Eds.), *Responding to crisis: A rhetorical approach to crisis communication* (pp. 1–18). Mahwah, NJ: Lawrence Erlbaum Associates.

Hermann, C. F. (1963). Some consequences of crisis which limit the viability of organizations. *Administrative Science Quarterly*, 8, 61–82.

James, D. (2000, June 11). When your company goes code blue. *Marketing News*, 34(23), 1.

Johnston, K. & Taylor, M. (2018). Engagement as communication: Pathways, possibilities, and future directions. In Johnston, K. & Taylor, M. (Eds.) *The Handbook of Communication Engagement* (pp. pp. 1–15). Hoboken, NJ: Wiley-Blackwell.

Kagonye, F., & Kerubo, Brenda. (2022, January 5). *Kenyans arm-twist KFC as food chain now pledges to source potatoes locally*. Standard Media. https://www.standardmedia.co.ke/national/article/2001433428/kfc-pledges-to-source-potatoes-locally-following-online-furore

Kanja, K. (2020, November 11). *KOT: Kenya's humour wall that tickles and silences the world*. Standard Media. https://www.standardmedia.co.ke/entertainment/news/article/2001393553/kot-kenyas-humour-wall-that-tickles-and-silences-the-world

Karanja, A. (2013, October 18). *US pastor TD Jakes apologises over Kenya comments*. Daily Nation. https://nation.africa/kenya/news/us-pastor-td-jakes-apologises-over-kenya-comments-905700

Kazeem, Y. (2016, April 6). *Politics and activism are driving Africa's Twitter conversations to new highs*. Quartz. https://qz.com/africa/654958/politics-and-activism-are-driving-africas-twitter-conversations-to-new-highs

Kemp, S. (2023, February 13). *Digital 2023: Kenya*. Datareportal. https://datareportal.com/reports/digital-2023-kenya#:~:text=Twitter%20users%20in%20Kenya%20in,total%20population%20at%20the%20time.

Kent, M., & Taylor, M. (1998). Building dialogic relationships through the world wide web. *Public Relations Review*, 24(3), 324–334.

M. L. Kent (2017). Principles of dialogue and the history of dialogic theory in public relations. Chapter prepared for Xianhong Chen (Ed.), *Prospects of public relations science* (pp. 2–51) Beijing, China: Peking University Press.

M .L. Kent, & Taylor, M. (2002). Toward a dialogic theory of public relations. *Public Relations Review*, 28, 21–37. https://doi.org/20.1016/S0363-8111(02)00108-X.

M. L. Kent, & Taylor, M. (2018). Understanding the rhetoric of dialogue and the dialogue of rhetoric . In Ø. Ihlen & R. L. Heath (Eds.), *Handbook of organizational rhetoric and communication: Foundations of dialogue, discourse, narrative, and engagement* (pp. 315–327). Nj: Wiley-Blackwell.

KFC. [@KFCinKenya]. (2022, January 03). *Fam it was truly a Furaha December....* https://twitter.com/KFCinKenya/status/1477930454036594769

Lane, B. A., & Bartlett, J. (2016). Why dialogic principles don't make it in practice— and what we can do about it. *International Journal of Communication,* 10(2016), 4074–4094.

Lane A., & M. L. Kent (2018). Engagement as dialogue, dialogue as engagement. In Johnston K., Taylor, M. (Eds.), *Handbook of Communication Engagement* (pp. 61–72). NJ: Wiley-Blackwell.

Madung, O., & Obilo, B. (2021, September 2). *Fellow research: Inside the Shadowy World of disinformation-for-hire in Kenya*. Mozilla. https://foundation.mozilla.org/en/blog/fellow-research-inside-the-shadowy-world-of-disinformation-for-hire-in-kenya/

Maina, W. (2022, January 5). *Why potato farmers are vulnerable to broker exploitation*. Daily Nation. https://nation.africa/kenya/news/why-potato-farmers-are-vulnerable-to-broker-exploitation-3689450

Mbaabaa [@wwashiedc] (2022, January 3). *We should boycott these idiots...* https://twitter.com/wwashiedc/status/1478231523270795266

Middleberg, D. (2001). *Winning PR in the wired world: Powerful communications strategies for the noisy digital space*. New York: McGraw-Hill.

Muia, J. (2022, February 10). *Nyandarua Governor Francis Kimemia discloses deal with KFC on local potatoes*. Citizen Digital. https://www.citizen.digital/news/nyandarua-governor-francis-kimemia-discloses-deal-with-kfc-on-local-potatoes-n292228

Mukhongo, L. L. (2020). Participatory media cultures: Virality, humor and online political contestations in Kenya. *Sage*, 55(2), 148–169.

Mureithi, M. (2017). The Internet journey for Kenya: the interplay of disruptive innovation and entrepreneurship in fueling rapid growth. In B. Ndemo & T. Weiss (Eds.), *Digital Kenya* (pp. 27–43). London: Palgrave Macmillan.

Mutiga, M. (2015, August 14). *CNN executive flies to Kenya to apologise for 'hotbed of terror' claim*. The Guardian. https://www.theguardian.com/world/2015/aug/14/cnn-kenya-apologise-obama

Mwaura, W. (2022, January 8). *How KFC in Kenya got fried over its chip shortage*. BBC. https://www.bbc.com/news/world-africa-59898362

Nathanial, P., & van der Heyden, L. (2020). Crisis management: Framework and principles with applications to CoVid-19 [working paper]. Insead Working Paper No. 2020/17/FIN/TOM. https://doi.org/10.2139/ssrn.3560259

Nierman, E. (2020, March 25). *Five steps to effectively use social media for crisis management*. Forbes. https://www.forbes.com/sites/theyec/2020/03/25/five-steps-to-effectively-use-social-media-for-crisis-management/?sh=e9f07b557b81

Njathi, A. W. (2023). *The glitz and glamour platform economy: Issues for Instagram monetization for influencers in Nairobi, Kenya* [Doctoral dissertation, North Carolina State University]. NC State University Libraries. https://repository.lib.ncsu.edu/handle/1840.20/40891

Njoroge, J. (2022, January 4). *Import customers as well, Kenyans retort after KFC announces potato shortage*. Nation. Africa. https://nation.africa/kenya/business/import-customers-as-well-kenyans-retort-after-kfc-announces-potato-shortage-3671730

Nyabola, N. (2018). *Digital democracy, analogue politics: How the Internet era is transforming politics in Kenya*. London: Zed Books Ltd.

Nyongesa, S., & Mwiti, F. (2013, February 18). *Consumer rights protection in Kenya: Towards a regulatory framework*. Candid. https://search.issuelab.org/resource/consumer-rights-protection-in-kenya-towards-a-regulatory-framework.html

Ochieng, F. (2021, January 21). *Crisis management is an art that Magoha should learn*. PR. Review. https://rococo.co.ke/prreview/2021/01/21/crisis-management-is-an-art-that-magoha-should-learn/

Onyango, E. (2021, September 13). *Kenyan influencers paid to take "guerrilla warfare" online*. BBC. https://www.bbc.com/news/world-africa-58474936

Otieno, B. (2022, January 5). *KFC Opens doors for local potato suppliers who meet standards*. Business Daily. https://www.businessdailyafrica.com/bd/corporate/companies/kfc-opens-doors-potato-suppliers-who-meet-standards-3672476

Owyang, J. (2011, August 31). *(Report) Social media crises on rise: Be prepared by climbing the social business hierarchy of needs*. Webstrategist. https://web-strategist.com/blog/2011/08/31/report-social-media-crises-on-rise-be-prepared-by-climbing-the-social-business-hierarchy-of-needs

Pala, O. (2013, October 20). *Who are you calling natives, Mr Jakes?* Standard Media. https://www.standardmedia.co.ke/article/2000096360/who-are-you-calling-natives-mr-jakes

Pearson, R. (1989). *A theory of public relations ethics*. Unpublished doctoral dissertation, Ohio University.

Pearson, C., & Mitroff, I. (1993). From crisis prone to crisis prepared: A framework for crisis management. *Academy of Management Executive*, 7(1), 48–59.

Perry, D. C., Taylor, M., & Doerfel, M. L. (2003). Internet-based communication in crisis management. *Management Communication Quarterly*, 17(2), 206–232. https://doi.org/10.1177/0893318903256227

Pettigrew, T. F. (1986). The intergroup contact hypothesis reconsidered. In M. Hewstone & R. J. Brown (Eds.), *Contact and conflict in intergroup encounters* (pp. 169–195). Oxford: Basil Blackwell.

PRSK. (2019, April 6). *State of PR in Kenya Report November 2019*. Public Relations Society of Kenya. https://www.prsk.co.ke/state-of-pr-in-kenya-report/

Seii, J. (2018, May 31). *Power struggles: Unmasking the Thieves behind the KPLC Heist*. The Elephant. https://www.theelephant.info/features/2018/05/31/power-struggles-unmasking-the-thieves-behind-the-kplc-heist/

Simon, T., Goldberg, A., Aharonson-Daniel, L., Leykin, D., & Adini, B. (2014). Twitter in the cross Fire—The use of social media in the westgate mall terror attack in Kenya. *PLoS ONE,* 9(8), e104136. https://doi.org/10.1371/journal.pone.0104136

Starr, B. (2015, July 23). *Obama's trip raises security concerns*. CNN. https://edition.cnn.com/2015/07/22/politics/obama-kenya-visit-al-shabaab-threat/

Struwig, M., Best, L., & Muthwa, S. (2017, August 14) *There's still a gap between consumer protection and sustainability in Africa*. The Conversation. https://theconversation.com/theres-still-a-gap-between-consumer-protection-and-sustainability-in-africa-81641

Tully, M., & Ekdale, B. (2014). Sites of playful engagement: Twitter hashtags as spaces of leisure and development in Kenya [ICTs for Leisure in Development Special Issue]. *Information Technologies & International Development*, 10(3), 67–82.

Tanui, C. (2022, January 24). *KFC clarifies why it could not source local potatoes*. Capital Business. https://www.capitalfm.co.ke/business/2022/01/kfc-clarifies-why-it-could-not-source-local-potatoes/

Wamanji, E. (2018, June 10). *Why Kenya's corporates are hopeless in crisis communication*. PR. Review. https://rococo.co.ke/prreview/2018/06/10/why-kenyas-corporates-are-hopeless-in-crisis-communication/

Wamanji, E. (2014, February 2). *We thrive in mediocrity as our collective psyche shuns the noble and civil*. Nation. Africa. https://nation.africa/kenya/life-and-style/we-thrive-in-mediocrity-as-our-collective-psyche-shuns-the-noble-and-civil-944980

Wandede, N. (2022, January 18). *Kenya to start producing waru variety preferred by KFC to end importation, CS Peter Munya*. Tuko. https://www.tuko.co.ke/kenya/440343-kenya-start-producing-waru-variety-preferred-by-kfc-end-importation-cs-peter-munya/

Valentine, C., Romenti, S., and Kruckerberg, D. (2018). Handling crises in social media. In L. Austin, and Y. Jin (Eds.), *From stakeholder crisis awareness and sense making to organizational crisis preparedness in social media and crisis communication*. New York: Routledge.

Valentini, C., Murtarelli, G., & Romenti, S. (2014). Organisations' conversations in social media: Applying dialogue strategies in times of crisis. *Corporate Communications: An International Journal,* 19(1), 10–33.

6 Digital Beef or Digital Bluff? An SMCC-based Analysis of General Muhoozi's Provocative Tweets and Contentious Kenya-Uganda Twitter (X) Discourse

Teresia Nzau and Luke Capizzo

Digital marketing and public relations in Africa take place in and for a wide variety of organizations, purposes, and contexts. Many organizations use social media as a listening tool (Ballestar et al., 2020) as well as a significant avenue for disseminating essential news due to the increase in social media usage (Apuke & Omar, 2021). The number of African social media users has risen continuously, amounting to over 384 million as of 2022 (Galal, 2022). Social media has been used to cultivate relationships between the government and the individual—essentially democratizing government communications (Cogburn & Espinoza-Vasquez, 2011). The political nature of many issues and crises creates a naturally convergent space where there is value in understanding the issues, risks, and crises that organizations face (e.g., Heath & Waymer, 2011). Government organizations—be they agencies, municipalities, or nations—are no exception. Social media use can add to the policy-making process, as its tools can provide a platform for symmetrical communication (Ociepka, 2012). Using social media has enabled those involved in public diplomacy to engage in branding and promoting a specific persona to their audiences (Zaharna & Uysal, 2016). These platforms also deliver accounts that shape narratives and impact perceptions—for better or for worse (Golan et al., 2019).

The deeply divisive history of conflict between Kenya and Uganda provides the backdrop for this case study. Uganda has previously had border conflict, with Kenya stationing troops at the border and Kenya pledging to retaliate against any Ugandan attempt to cross the frontier in pursuit of rebels. Another row was witnessed in 2021 and it encompassed succession politics engulfing Kenya ahead of its general election the following year. Broadly, we situate this chapter as an East African contribution/context toward a more holistic and globally enriched understanding of digital crisis communication or "the collection, processing and dissemination of information required to address a crisis situation triggered, mediated, and/or aggravated by digital social media" (Liu et al., 2023, p. 192). Following recent advances integrating African cultural knowledge and cases into public relations theory (e.g., Ngondo & Klyueva, 2023; Pompper & Adae, 2022), the purpose of this chapter is to augment social-mediated crisis communication (SMCC) and paracrisis knowledge, extending theory by centering the Kenyan-Ugandan conflict, the particular actions of Ugandan General Muhoozi, and the swift, robust, and often hilariously caustic responses of

DOI: 10.4324/9781032689654-6

what has come to be called "Kenyans on Twitter (X)" (KOT)—not an organization in any sense, but digital community of like-minded, aggressive, vocal, and politically savvy users who flock to respond to emerging issues, reflecting the principles of connective action (Bennett & Segerberg, 2012). The chapter begins with background information on the case, followed by the literature review, method section, results, and discussion, concluding with practical implications and future directions.

Case Background

Despite previous productive bilateral relations, Uganda and Kenya have experienced many decades of conflict. The chapter looks at the recent conflict between Uganda and Kenya involving Uganda's defense minister, General Muhoozi Kainerugaba. In October 2022, Muhoozi sparked a diplomatic row with neighboring Kenya over a series of provocative, taunting tweets about invading the country. The tweets angered hundreds of Kenyans on social media, forcing the Ugandan government to apologize to Kenya (Makong, 2022). But this is not the only reported recent conflict between these neighboring countries. Uganda has previously had border conflict with Kenya stationing troops at the border and Kenya pledging to retaliate against any Ugandan attempt to cross the frontier in pursuit of rebels. Another row began in 2021, encompassing the succession politics engulfing Kenya ahead of its 2022 general election. This conflict spilled beyond its borders, pulling in its western neighbor, Uganda, and threatening to rock the cordial relations that the two East African countries have enjoyed for decades. As much as other kinds of conflicts were reported before, the recent social media conflict created by General Muhoozi threatened to harm Uganda's reputation.

Following this tweet, thousands of KOT flocked to the platform and responded harshly to Muhoozi. KOT have been known to aggressively attack anybody who gets in their way on Twitter (X). A poll conducted by the United Nations Office on Drugs and Crime ranked Kenyans as the worst bullies on Twitter (X) (Ndonye, 2021; Tennydelp, 2021). They are well known for their capacity to band together and battle shared opponents, as well as dismantle both actual and perceived adversaries. South Africa, Nigeria, Tanzania, and, most lately, Uganda have all been the targets of Kenyan fury on Twitter (X). Among the primary victims of Kenya's social media bullying are important individuals, corporations, politicians, and even countries. For example, in 2015, members of KOT demanded an apology from Cable News Network (CNN) for referring to Kenya as a "hotbed of terror" (Jerotich, 2022; Kaigwa, 2017). This became a worldwide trending issue with the hashtag #SomeonetellCNN (Anyangwe, 2016; Jerotich, 2022; Kaigwa, 2017; Nothias & Cheruiyot, 2018). In another instance, a Nigerian journalist drew the wrath of the KOT sometime in 2019 when she stated that she would not visit Kenya due to a terror attack (Jerotich, 2022). This message sparked a Twitter (X) fight between Kenyans and Nigerians in which the Kenyans did not hold back. The case of Muhoozi's provocative tweets and responses from KOT, the Ugandan government, and mainstream media provides a window into the management of potential crises in an East African context.

Literature Review

Social Media Proliferation and Research in Africa

Social media is a central means of communication for a large population across Africa. Social media usage is growing throughout Africa as mobile internet access becomes more widespread and smartphones become more affordable (Bornman, 2012). Many Africans' lives are now surrounded and impacted by social media. For many people, social media has made obtaining information much simpler. Social media, because of the communicative affordances they offer, such as immediacy and wide dissemination, have given the public the democratic agency to generate conversations across various platforms in the current context of the global COVID-19 pandemic and people's need for information (Madziva et al., 2022). Public relations scholarship has examined many aspects of communication management on the African continent (e.g., Ngondo & Klyueva, 2023; Pompper & Adae, 2022; Pratt, 2003), but little research has focused directly on public relations and social media in Africa beyond this edited volume, with several notable exceptions (Mersham et al., 2011; Ngondo, 2019; Ngondo & Klyueva, 2020).

According to Galal (2022), the number of African social media users across all platforms increased to 384 million, with the Northern and Southern Africa blocks having 56 and 45% of their populations using social media, respectively. These numbers were confirmed by Ndlela (2020) when he conducted an analysis and found that Facebook, WhatsApp, YouTube, and Twitter (X) were the most widely used social media platforms. According to Statcounter (2023), the most popular social media sites in Africa as of August 2023 were Facebook (81.26%), YouTube (6.55%), Instagram (4.94%), Twitter (X) (4.6%), Pinterest (2.22%), and LinkedIn (0.23%). Celebrities and politicians have also contributed to the increase of social media users in Africa, with Mo Salar, Davido, and Yemi Alade leading the followership charts with 42.1, 20.1, and 13.8 million followers, respectively (Knowafrica, 2024). Despite its relatively low popularity, Twitter (X) has become a primary space for African political discourse and agenda setting.

Additionally, social media is transforming Africa's political environment, with more politicians embracing it. According to statistics obtained by Africa No Filter between 2020 and 2021, the top ten most prominent African politicians have a combined Twitter (X) following of slightly over 24 million. However, according to statistics acquired by Africanews in January 2022, the figure has risen to 27 million, demonstrating a general growth in social media usage. According to the survey, Egyptian President Abdelfattah Elsisi is the most followed African politician on Twitter (X)– (5.5 million followers), with Kenyan President, William Ruto (4.4 million), and Nigerian President, Muhammadu Buhari (4 million) close behind. General Muhoozi who is key in this study joined Twitter (X) in 2014 and has a following of 809.3k followers, as per the counter on his account as of October 2023.

Social Media and Crisis Communication in Public Relations

Social media and social media tools have swiftly evolved and begun to affect society, particularly in recent years, and compelled enterprises to modernize their connection with the outside world. The study of social media in the field of public relations is also reported to have risen, becoming one of the discipline's most important subjects of study (Li & Kent, 2021). There is evidence that issues related to social media have garnered a growing body of literature, with a significant number of studies assessing the function of social media in crisis management. Simultaneously, public relations scholars have focused on Twitter (X)'s potential for crisis communication. In the realm of social media, specifically Twitter (X), there is a network of actors who have a following. Some of these accounts are well known, and their fan base has significant influence over the public perception of specific events. According to Zhao et al. (2019), these influential users are crucial during a crisis and may assist in spreading official statements quickly. Many studies on the usage of social media and crises have also been undertaken. Coombs and Holladay (2008) believe that issues that develop on social media may be quite unpredictable in terms of how they evolve and how the public reacts to them; as a result, organizations should be aware of information involving them and what their audience says online. Each crisis requires information, explanations, or replies (Coombs & Holladay, 2008, 2010, 2022; Coombs et al., 2020), but the reactions produced determine the outcome of a crisis. These social-mediated crises have been heavily studied in Asian, European, and North American contexts but less so in Africa.

Paracrisis

To understand paracrisis, it is important first to understand what crisis means. The term "crisis" has been used in a variety of contexts to refer to a range of events, both man-made and natural, that either cause harm or interrupt daily activity (Reynolds & Seeger, 2005; Seeger, 2006). Coombs (2007) defines a crisis as any occurrence or course of action that damages an organization's reputation and causes operational disruption (p. 164). In his most recent works, he broadens the concept to cover any disruptive behavior that jeopardizes the interests of stakeholders or the organization (Coombs & Holladay, 2022). Crisis perceptions are impacted by emotions (Xiao et al., 2018), an organization's crisis history (Eaddy, 2023; Eaddy & Jin, 2018), and message factors such as humor (Fraustino & Ma, 2015; Kuhnhenn, 2021; Yu et al., 2022). Members of affected communities make meaning of crises by synthesizing multiple narratives around the event (M.F. Perreault & G. Perreault, 2019). Yet, due to their urgency and emergent nature, acute crises tend not to be situations conducive to genuine dialogic engagement among organizations and their stakeholders (Kent & Lane, 2021).

Therefore, according to Coombs and Holladay (2012), a paracrisis is not yet a full-fledged crisis, but it is a warning sign that might evolve to a crisis level if enough stakeholders pay attention to it. These scholars used the word paracrisis to describe a risk or crisis threat (threatening issue) that arises via social media and is viewed by the public as irresponsible or unethical behavior on the part of the organization (e.g., Chen & Holladay, 2023; Honisch & Más Manchón, 2020; Roh, 2017; S.B. Smith & B.G. Smith, 2022). Paracrisis, according to Coombs and Holladay (2012), is not a crisis in and of itself. Rather, it is a circumstance that resembles a crisis (potential crisis) and, if not properly handled, can evolve into a crisis, and undermine the organization's reputation. In the domain of crisis management, a paracrisis occurs before a crisis and arises in the preventative stage.

Another useful lens for understanding crises/potential crises on social media is the SMCC model, which focuses on the ecological network of crisis actors rather than solely prioritizing the organization at the center of the issue.

Social-Mediated Crisis Communication (SMCC) Model

To address the impact of social media on crisis communication, Liu et al. (2011) developed SMCC (Austin et al., 2012). This model describes interactions among a crisis-affected organization and several publics that produce and consume information prior to, during, and shortly after crises (Jin & Liu 2010; Zhao et al., 2019). It goes on to illustrate how social media distributes information both directly and indirectly. Crisis information, for example, is transferred directly from prominent social media producers to "social media followers," but it may also be transmitted indirectly from "influential social media followers" to "social media inactive" (Austin et al., 2012). During a crisis, the SMCC model describes and forecasts how information spreads among the public. To learn how and why consumers seek crisis-related information on social media vs conventional media sources, scholars have integrated concepts such as information vetting (Lu & Jin, 2020). Jin et al. (2014) tested three major components of the SMCC model in a field study—crisis information form, crisis information source, and crisis origin—to find the role of social media in effective crisis management. The theory has also been applied in several distinct cultural/national contexts, such as in China (Kong & Chen, 2022) and Europe (Honisch & Más Manchón, 2020). For example, in China, the theory was used to test how social media characteristics affect dialogue between organizations and their publics. Such potential cultural differences have not yet been explored for SMCC in an African context.

The SMCC model (Austin et al., 2012), which suggests that crises start primarily on social media via prominent social media producers who disseminate information with their following, is often discussed in relation to paracrisis. As word spreads, this crisis information reaches individuals who may not be on social media, as it spills over into conventional media or other access points. Though useful for analyzing social media-promoted crises, models such as the SMCC see social media primarily as platforms for information dissemination, and research shows that organizations primarily use social media for information dissemination during a crisis (Einwiller & Steilen, 2015; Lovari & Bowen, 2020). Additionally, these social media crisis models also have the potential to investigate how societal and community value is generated (or destroyed) through engagement.

Research Question

How, if at all, does the public discourse around General Muhoozi's provocative tweets reflect SMCC in an East African context?

Methods

This study focuses on the recent conflict between Uganda and Kenya involving Uganda's defense minister General Muhoozi Kainerugaba and investigates how Muhoozi's tweets reflect or contradict best practices in the SMCC model. This case has multiple actors (the originator of the crisis, Kenyan government officials, influencers, and social media followers who drive the conversation on Twitter (X)). Given the complex, layered meaning embedded in this discourse, we utilized a case study approach to provide a rich overview of the situation from multiple vantage points (Yin, 2014). To do so, we collected 150 tweets as well as 10 press releases and public statements from the Ugandan government, and 30 news articles about the situation. Textual analysis (e.g., Tracy, 2013) was used to examine relevant tweets (General Muhoozi, Kenyan and Ugandan Ministries of Foreign Affairs, etc.), hashtags used, government statements made, and online news articles published in response to these research topics. Textual analysis has been used in prior global and transnational public relations studies to allow for researcher analysis of complex, multifaceted cultural themes (e.g., Taylor & Yang, 2015).

All data were collected from Twitter (X) and news sources at the height of the conflict: October 2–31, 2022. To draw news articles related to this study, the following search terms were put in Nexis Uni database; "Muhoozi Kainerugaba," "Muhoozi capture Nairobi," "Capture Nairobi in two weeks," "Tweeting General," "two weeks to capture Nairobi," "Muhoozi controversial tweet," and "KOT attack Muhoozi." The search yielded 113 news articles referencing Muhoozi during the time period in question. These were narrowed to the most reputable sources utilizing the BBC Media Guide (April 25, 2023) which notes that Kenya has eight major press/online newspapers and websites. Some of these include *The Daily Nation*, *The Standard*, *The Star*, *The East African*, *Taifa Leo*, *Business Today*, *Kenyans.co.ke,* and *Tuko News*. Apart from the major news sites in Kenya, we incorporated most read international online sites such as British Broadcasting Corporation (BBC), CNN, Agence France-Presse (AFP), and Bloomberg News among others.

Twitter (X) posts were found through Twitter (X) search using the codes "mini_retweets" and "mini_faves" and use of Twitter (X) hashtag. We started by creating a list of hashtags that were relevant to the case study: We utilized the hashtag #Muhoozi and added the username @mkainerugaba, which yielded 3,801 tweets, 2,590 quotes, and 17,800 likes for the period in question. The 150 posts (which include more than 300 comments) were then selected by ensuring they were not duplicates, were related to the controversial online discourse, were in English language, and included both text and picture.

Results

The authors created a data collection that included the date of each tweet, the account's Twitter (X) handle, the account's name, and the content of the tweets, and then evaluated the data to answer the study's research question. The tweets were classified according to message form, channel, and strategy. The textual analysis across multiple data sources and media channels revealed four central themes to address the research question: (1) conflicting understandings of crisis type and severity among the central stakeholders, (2) multivocal humor (3) lack of genuine stakeholder engagement, and (4) a bullying culture among KOT.

Conflicting Understandings of Crisis Type and Severity Among the Central Stakeholders

From the findings, we see that there are multiple actors, all of whom have a stake in advocating for distinct understandings of the situation. Some actors emphasize the scenario's seriousness, while others find it nonthreatening and humorous—in the end, the situation becomes a potential crisis for Ugandan leaders not because of the threat of armed conflict, but because of reputation damage from the humorous attacks. The actors' approach to the Twitter (X) post leaves one wondering whether Muhoozi's tweet caused a crisis or something that resembled a crisis (paracrisis). For example, Ugandan leader Bobi Wine asked Kenyans not to assume Muhoozi's post was meaningless, "Sadly, beneath the senseless tweets lies a monster who brutalizes and tortures our people for fun!" (Wine, 2022). His sentiments are seen to resonate with those of another Kenyan leader, Samson Cheralgei, "I expect the ministry of foreign affairs to summon the Ugandan ambassador to shed light on Muhoozi's social media outbursts and subsequent apology. This is undermining the spirit of unity of EAC" (Cherargei, 2022). By contrast, KOT made a joke about the whole situation and taking Muhoozi's threats lightly. For example, one KOT member shared, "It will just take 10 luhyas from shimakhokho and nyaribare chache to eat the whole of Uganda" (Liquor, 2022). Luhya is a tribe in Kenya and in this case, the person who tweeted wanted to show how tiny Uganda is compared to Kenya.

Most of the tweets that employed sarcasm and humor can be concluded to show that Muhoozi's post was not meant to be serious, while of the 150 selected Twitter (X) posts, less than 2% indicate seriousness in the post. Instead of being angry at Muhoozi, the KOT made fun/jokes about him and his country. In addition, the KOT participants were less likely to be angry about Muhoozi when the Twitter (X) response messages were framed as a joke.

Multivocal Humor

The theme of "humor" was found in the expression of responses across the network of actors in the discussion. Within the humor theme, expressive non-discrete categories were identified: ironic expression, aggressive humor, self-enhancing humor, wordplay humor or puns, juvenile humor, affiliative humor, sarcasm, parody or satire humor, and topical humor. There was a strategic use of humor from multiple sides, which was used for individual benefit. For example, at first, Kenyans were seen to take the issue with seriousness of Muhoozi's provocations, but when they incorporated humor and started responding to humor with humor, it created the potential for embarrassment and a paracrisis for the Ugandan government. Collectively, KOT regarded Muhoozi's threat as a joke: hilarious and 'humorous' in other comments. Even Muhoozi later tweeted, sarcastically, "I am glad that I have scared you Kenyans a bit!" (Kainerugaba, 2022) in an attempt to downplay the seriousness of his threats.

The following are examples of some of the humor-related data points: KOT responded in a hilarious and sarcastic manner, suggesting that the Ugandan army is no match for Kenya's modernized military. KOT employed aggressive, humorous expressions. This type of humor often relied on belittling others or making fun of another person. One commenter said, "The only thing Ugandans can capture from Nairobi is the fake certificate they gave our Governor" (Oguda, 2022), "It will take the Kenyan military a day to seize your father's toilet," (Sakwah, 2022) while another "A country whose past, present and future president is one and the same should not threaten countries like Kenya" (Mohamed, 2022) and "You first need to capture your dad's tailor" (Mwangi, 2022). Ironic expressions also captured the feeling of Kenyans on Uganda's military capability in capturing Kenya. This consists of [laughter] ("It would take these 5 KDF soldiers less than 3 days to capture the whole of Uganda" (Gichuri, 2022) similar irony was captured in another tweet "How long has it taken you to capture Joseph Kony [laughter]. Only thing you can capture are Bobi Wine Riots in Kampala" (Akillah, 2022) "Even if you come with the whole of Uganda you can't even capture Kariobangi, Try Tanzania not Kenya" (Gideon, 2022) (Figures 6.1 and 6.2).

Additionally, many Kenyan government officials also used humor in responding to Muhoozi, though many of the tweets have since been deleted.

Kenyan Twitter (X) users focused on the absurdity of the Muhoozi threat, turning the potentially dangerous geopolitical conflict into a meme contest. They took to their accounts to make fun of their Ugandan counterparts. The memes ran from currency, politics, education, infrastructure, economy, and lifestyle; they were also making fun of who is superior to the other. Some of these read, "Man thinks Nairobi is a village like Uganda where he can use Capture and recapture method ☺" (Right, 2022). "You also need basic English lessons… 'my army and I' (Mungai, 2022) and" "Kenya ranks higher than Uganda in terms of military strength ranking. Kenya also spends more on the military than Uganda" (Capital, 2022) (Figures 6.3 and 6.4).

In terms of a positive attitude, humor was constructed as something that Kenyans used interactionally to minimize the threats of Muhoozi. Humor assisted respondents in making light of Muhoozi's post, which allowed Kenyans to laugh at the post's repercussions (laughing about Uganda and Ugandans) and develop rapport and relationships with Ugandans in general. Kenyans' use of humor was more essential than Muhoozi's threat to capture part of their nation, and it brought the topic to ridicule Ugandans because of Muhoozi. Here, we conclude that at times, humor can be useful to diffuse and ease difficult situations and crises on social media.

Figure 6.1 Examples of humorous memes used #KOT under #Muhoozi (Author illustration)
Source: Ndaire, 2022

Figure 6.2 Examples of humorous meme used #KOT under #Muhoozi (Author illustration)
Source: Sakwa, 2022

Figure 6.3 Example of tweet displaying humorous meme contest as a result of Muhoozi tweet

Source: Mwangi, 2022

Figure 6.4 Example of tweet displaying humorous meme contest as a result of Muhoozi tweet

Source: Mundeke, 2022

Lack of Genuine Stakeholder Engagement

The study also shows that KOT, who are a more vocal group relative to Ugandans, responded to Muhoozi, but Muhoozi ignored them and avoided having conversations with them. It is evident that the communication was one way, in that Kenyans started talking amongst themselves in response to Muhoozi, while Muhoozi never responded to them. While Muhoozi had significant influence on the discourse, his communication was one way. These findings suggest that it was not a back-and-forth kind of communication where Muhoozi could respond but a unidirectional communication.

From the tweets, we see Muhoozi's initial post saying it would take him and his army only two weeks to capture Kenya. As many Kenyans flocked to Twitter (X) to respond to him, he remained silent and did not respond. This shows a lack of dialogic communication or engagement. Several days later after Kenyans ranted and belittled his provocations, he tweeted that "I would never beat up the Kenyan army because my father (President Museveni) told me never to attempt it. So, our people in Kenya should relax" (Kainerugaba, 2022). His comment was clearly affected by the groundswell of antagonism and bullying humor directed at him but did not engage with the KOT conversation.

From our analysis, there was no reciprocation between Muhoozi and KOT. We found that a larger number of tweets were noninteractive as opposed to interactive. For example, Muhoozi's initial post then disappears and lets Kenyans engage. We also note that some of the government actors involved in the network, such as the Ugandan government, distanced itself from Muhoozi's post when the Ministry of Foreign Affairs issued a statement that was published on its Twitter account implying that Ugandan government does not communicate official matters on social media,

> The Ministry of Foreign Affairs wishes to clarify that the Government of the Republic of Uganda does not conduct its Foreign Policy and other official business through social media, nor does it depend on social media sources in dealing with other sovereign Governments.

Uganda's president, Yoweri Museveni through a press conference also issued an apology to Kenyan over his son's provocative tweet. On the other hand, most Kenyan government and influential actors remained silent. Some of them, even though they joined the conversation, did not directly respond to Muhoozi's tweet or address Muhoozi. In public communications, silence is deemed as a form of communication, and in this case, we can conclude that the network of actors in the discussion did not talk to each other, they lacked genuine engagement. For example, when President Yoweri Museveni apologized to Kenya, the Kenyan government or president did not respond to him, signaling a lack of value in their statement and a dismissive attitude toward the situation and Muhoozi's threats. Another example is when Muhoozi apologized to Kenya's President, William Ruto, with no statement or tweet was sent to acknowledge the same "I have never had any problem with Afande Ruto. If I made a mistake anywhere, I ask him to forgive me as his young brother. God bless East Africa!" (Kainerugaba, 2022).

There was no interaction between the message source/originator and social media followers/users and the affected government. Another example is when Muhoozi apologized after the incident on Twitter (X) to the Kenyan president, "I have never had any problem with Afande Ruto. If I made a mistake anywhere, I ask him to forgive me as his young brother. God bless East Africa!" (Kainerugaba, 2022). No one from the Kenyan government, including the president, bothered to respond back.

Bullying Culture Among KOT

Our findings show that, as the #Muhoozi tweet was trending on Twitter (X), Ugandans were relatively quiet. The findings indicate that KOT acted through trolling, tweeting, retweeting, and liking to present a unified perspective. Some of the tweets that we saw were "Remember our force's don't use Kalashnikov Soviet made like the Ugandans, ours is modern" (Nick, 2022), "Nairobi budget almost equals your GDP, think. It could be a better idea in the previous regime. But for now men in power don't slumber nor drink" (Meru, 2022), "With which English? Anjument? Sit down Uganda aka East Africa Village" (Ndanu, 2022).

Kenyans did not change their attitude toward bullying in their responses, instead, they made fun of the situation. Their creativity and humor did not demonstrate any sympathy for Muhoozi, but the connections they made with Ugandan citizens reflected the focus of their ire on national leaders. The conceptualization of the bullying act on Twitter (X) revolved around four key themes. These included repetition, power, emotional effects, abuse, and intimidation.

Discussion

This examination of social media-centered paracrisis discourse around a Kenyan-Ugandan conflict provides an opportunity to reexamine and learn from an East African context to extend public relations theory. While paracrisis and SMCC inform this analysis of Twitter (X), this case explores facets with the potential to provide additional insights for crisis management in digital and political conflicts. These include insights drawn from the central themes of the case analysis: (1) the conflicting understandings of crisis type and severity among the central stakeholders, (2) the lack of genuine engagement and conversation among stakeholders, (3) the reflection of a bullying culture within Kenya, and (4) the central role of humor in escalation and de-escalation, as well as unexpected relationship building. Each of these represents aspects of the crucial nuances of a cross-national and cross-cultural crisis or paracrisis.

Theoretical Implications

Prior SMCC research has examined information vetting (Lu & Jin, 2020), terrorism (Zhao et al., 2019), public diplomacy contexts (Boatwright & Pyle, 2023), and looked within a variety of cultures (e.g., Kong & Chen, 2022) but has not examined in detail the cross-cultural and crisis type-conflict scenarios evident in this case. In this case, the cultural and political differences among actors in this transnational discourse contributed to conflicting interpretations of crisis type and exacerbated historical dissension that contributed to the potential for crisis (e.g., Eaddy, 2023; Eaddy & Jin, 2018). There is additional space for theorizing crisis history as a component of the updated SMCC model (Liu et al., 2023).

Humor, while a not uncommon approach in risk and crisis communication (e.g., Fraustino & Ma, 2015; M.F. Perreault & G. Perreault, 2019; Yu et al., 2022), has rarely been examined in the public relations literature on crisis communication. When it has, it is often to demonstrate its limits and potential for backlash (Kuhnhenn, 2021; Xiao et al., 2018) rather than its positive potential as an organizational tactic or in its intra-stakeholder relationship-building potential. In an SMCC context, this case study provided an additional factor of complexity related to humor: The interactive (and strategic) choices among actors to be humorous, to rely on humor, or to explain that they had been joking when taken to task for their language. Thus, we posit that humor can act as (1) a weapon—in this case, one of the causes of the paracrisis, (2) a minimization tactic—in this case, to avoid taking full responsibility for prior statements, and (3) as a unifying or coalescing force as part of the development of publics themselves or across publics (i.e., points of shared humor between Kenyan and Ugandan Twitter (X) users).

Finally, despite the significant literature on engagement and dialogue as well as digitally enabled opportunities for conversation, crises and paracrises continue to reflect (both theoretically and in this case study) a negative dialogic space (Kent & Lane, 2021). In this case study, actors were unable or unwilling to listen or work to further understand each other's perspectives—and it was not strategically valuable for many actors to do so. Thus, while the influence networks of SMCC (e.g., Liu et al., 2023; Zhao et al., 2019) were reflected, actors missed opportunities to better understand each other amid the contention.

Practical Implications

Public relations and digital marketing professionals, particularly those in governmental or public diplomacy roles, must be aware of the potential for digital paracrisis situations to occur on their watch. In our scenario, a rogue actor (Muhoozi) stirred up conflict in a delicate political situation, causing challenges for a national government (Uganda) that needed to be addressed through both traditional media relations outreach as well as public diplomacy. The response from Kenyan citizens showcased the power and collective strength of a humorous, sarcastic response that carried weight in the international politics of East Africa without any formal intervention from the Kenyan government. This is also reflective of the complexity of transnational public spheres: an entire discourse and paracrisis occurred via digital media that had significant influence over public diplomacy but was not addressed by official government actors directly within these digital spaces.

Limitations and Future Directions

This case study reflects the specific East African context and the nations involved but provides useful theoretical findings as well as directions and questions for subsequent scholarship. Given the textual analysis approach, the dataset reflected a focus on central actors rather than a broad, computational gathering and analysis of the full scope of community and citizen engagement, which would provide a useful corollary to this study. More research should investigate the cross-national and cross-cultural dimensions of digitally enabled crises, including through the lens of public diplomacy (Boatwright & Pyle, 2023), providing insights for different types of organizations, and reflecting the true complexity of global public spheres for digital crisis and paracrisis discourse. Humor, both as a stakeholder response and as an organizational minimization tactic, invites additional inquiry and theory building as part of crisis communication. Finally, the opportunities for dialogue, engagement, and organizational listening amid paracrisis and crisis situations—even as they may have significant limits—are valuable areas for investigation and synthesis. Public relations and digital marketing theorize the importance of such deep engagement and relationship building but tend to prioritize reputation during crisis (Liu & Fraustino, 2014). This case, while not challenging that narrative, provides a potentially useful explanation of the natural limits of conversation within a cross-national conflict, which may be helpful in finding productive spaces for future scholars and practitioners.

Africa-Centric Trends

This paper and, broadly, this volume, contribute to the growth of Africa-generated public relations and digital marketing theories (e.g., Holtzhausen, 2005; Ngondo & Klyueva, 2023; Pompper & Adae, 2022; Pratt, 2003), rather than only seeing Africa as a case or application of global or Western theorizing. The diversity of communities, governmental structures, technological affordances (Song et al., 2021), and cultural contexts ensure that Africa will continue to be verdant ground for the development of theories with global reach and impact.

This case confirms the assertion that Twitter (X) has been utilized as a political discourse medium to mobilize, create good change, and channel popular anger (Gitonga, 2015; Kaigwa, 2017; Nyabola, 2018). This implies that Twitter (X) is utilized as a forum for political conversation, where individuals express how they feel about certain problems and political information, shaping how they look and focus politically. From our findings, we found four main themes which include and are not limited to humor and bullying culture. We can conclude by saying the use of humor and memes helps citizens to articulate their issues and is similar to what

Nyabola (2018) and Kaigwa (2017) observed, which is that mockery and humor have always been part of political practice in Kenya and in Africa. They allow the citizens to use wit to highlight sensitive issues or condemn without being seen to overtly challenge the current government. However, it is important to note that sometimes what is presented as humor could also double up as bullying, which occasionally deteriorates into threats of physical harm and hate.

Bibliography

Africanews. (January 28, 2022). *Most followed African politicians on Twitter (X)*. https://www.africanews.com/2022/01/28/most-followed-african-politicians-on-Twitter (X)//

Akillah, W. [@Walter_Akillah]. (2022, October 3). ☺☺☺ *how long has it taken you to capture Joseph Kony. Only thing you can capture are Bobi Wine Riots in Kampala*. Twitter (X). https://twitter.com/Walter_Akillah/status/1576921172150669313

Anyangwe, E. (2016). Media perspectives: Is Africa's development story still stuck on aid? In M. Bunce, S. Franks & C. Paterson (Eds.), *Africa's media image in the 21st century* (pp. 128–131). Routledge.

Apuke, O. D., & Omar, B. (2021). Fake news and COVID-19: Modeling the predictors of fake news sharing among social media users. *Telematics and Informatics, 56*, 101475. https://doi.org/10.1016/j.tele.2020.101475

Austin, L., Fisher Liu, B., & Jin, Y. (2012). How audiences seek out crisis information: Exploring the social-mediated crisis communication model. *Journal of Applied Communication Research, 40*(2), 188–207. https://doi.org/10.1080/00909882.2012.654498

Ballestar, M. T., Cuerdo-Mir, M., & Freire-Rubio, M. T. (2020). The concept of sustainability on social media: A social listening approach. *Sustainability, 12*(5), 21. https://doi.org/10.3390/su12052122

Bennett, W. L., & Segerberg, A. (2012). The logic of connective action: Digital media and the personalization of contentious politics. *Information, Communication & Society, 15*(5), 739–768. https://doi.org/10.1080/1369118X.2012.670661

Boatwright, B. C., & Pyle, A. S. (2023). "Don't Mess with Ukrainian Farmers": An examination of Ukraine and Kyiv's official Twitter (X) accounts as crisis communication, public diplomacy, and nation building during Russian invasion. *Public Relations Review, 49*(3), 102338. https://doi.org/10.1016/j.pubrev.2023.102338

Bornman, E. (2012). The mobile phone in Africa: has it become a highway to the information society or not? *Contemporary Educational Technology, 3*(4), 278–292. https://doi.org/10.30935/cedtech/6084

British Broadcasting Corporation (BBC). (2023, April 25). *Kenya media guide*. https://www.bbc.com/news/world-africa-13681344

Capital, M. [@MwangoCapital]. (2022, October 3). *Kenya ranks higher than Uganda in terms of military strength ranking. Kenya also spends more on the military than Uganda*. Twitter (X). https://twitter.com/MwangoCapital/status/1576930951917015040

Chen, F., & Holladay, S. J. (2023). Identifying and responding to social media risks: Towards an organizational paracrisis communication framework. *Corporate Communications: An International Journal, 28*(1), 103–117. https://doi.org/10.1108/CCIJ-11-2021-0124

Cherargei, S. [@scherargei]. (2022, October 3). *I expect by morning the ministry of foreign affairs to summon Ugandan ambassador to shed light on Gen. Muhoozi social media outbursts & subsequent apology. This is undermining the spirit of unity of EAC*. Twitter (X). https://twitter.com/scherargei/status/1576987723969110016

Cogburn, D. L., & Espinoza-Vasquez, F. K. (2011). From networked nominee to networked nation: Examining the impact of Web 2.0 and social media on political participation and civic engagement in the 2008 Obama campaign. *Journal of Political Marketing, 10*(1–2), 189–213. https://doi.org/10.1080/15377857.2011.540224

Coombs, W. T. (2007). Protecting organization reputations during a crisis: The development and application of situational crisis communication theory. *Corporate Reputation Review, 10*(3), 163–177. https://doi.org/10.1057/palgrave.crr.1550049

Coombs, W. T., & Holladay, S. J. (2008). Comparing apology to equivalent crisis response strategies: Clarifying apology's role and value in crisis communication. *Public Relations Review, 34*(3), 252–257.

Coombs, W. T., & Holladay, S. J. (2010). Examining the effects of mutability and framing on perceptions of human error and technical error crises: Implications for situational crisis communication theory. In W. T. Coombs & S. J. Holladay (Eds.), *The Handbook of Crisis Communication* (pp. 181–204). Wiley-Blackwell.

Coombs, W. T., & Holladay, S. J. (2012). The paracrisis: The challenges created by publicly managing crisis prevention. *Public Relations Review, 38*(3), 408–415. https://doi.org/10.1016/j.pubrev.2012.04.004

Coombs, W. T., Holladay, S. J., & White, K. L. (2020). Situational crisis communication theory (SCCT) and application in dealing with complex, challenging, and recurring crises. In Y. Jin, B. H. Reber & G. J. Nowak (Eds.), *Advancing crisis communication effectiveness: Integrating public relations scholarship with practice* (pp. 15–17). Routledge.

Coombs, W. T., & Holladay, S. J. (2022). Orientation to the second edition. In W. T. Coombs & S. J. Holladay (Eds.), *The handbook of crisis communication* (pp. xxvii–xxix). John Wiley & Sons.

Eaddy, L. L. (2023). Unearthing the facets of crisis history in crisis communication: A conceptual framework and introduction of the crisis history salience scale. *International Journal of Business Communication, 60*(4), 1177–1196. https://doi.org/10.1177/2329488420988769

Eaddy, L. L., & Jin, Y. (2018). Crisis history tellers matter: The effects of crisis history and crisis information source on publics' cognitive and affective responses to organizational crisis. *Corporate Communications: An International Journal, 23*(2), 226–241. https://doi.org/10.1108/CCIJ-04-2017-0039.

Einwiller, S. A., & Steilen, S. (2015). Handling complaints on social network sites: An analysis of complaints and complaint responses on Facebook and Twitter (X) pages of large US companies. *Public Relations Review, 41*(2), 195–204. https://doi.org/10.1016/j.pubrev.2014.11.012

Fraustino, J. D., & Ma, L. (2015). CDC's use of social media and humor in a risk campaign—"Preparedness 101: Zombie Apocalypse". *Journal of Applied Communication Research, 43*(2), 222–241. https://doi.org/10.1080/00909882.2015.1019544

Galal, S. (2022, November 17). Social media in Africa – statistics & facts. *Statista.* https://www.statista.com/topics/9922/social-media-in-africa/#topicHeader__wrapper

Gichuri, M. [@MuchiriGichuri]. (2022, October 3). *It would take these 5 KDF soldiers less than 3days to capture the whole of Uganda*. Twitter (X). https://twitter.com/MuchiriGichuri/status/1576922793270472704

Gideon, B. [@bosco_gideon]. (2022, October 3). *Even if you come with the whole of Uganda you can't even capture Kariobangi, Try Tanzania not Kenya.* Twitter (X). https://twitter.com/bosco_gideon/status/1576921650591064065

Gitonga, P. N. (2015). *A relevance-theoretic analysis of political discourse in Kenyan social media: A case study of the 2013 presidential campaigns* (Doctoral dissertation, University of Nairobi).

Golan, G. J., Manor, I., & Arceneaux, P. (2019). Mediated public diplomacy redefined: Foreign stakeholder engagement via paid, earned, shared, and owned media. *American Behavioral Scientist, 63*(12), 1665–1683. https://doi.org/10.1177/0002764219835279

Heath, R. L., & Waymer, D. (2011). Corporate issues management and political public relations. In J. Stromback & S. Kiousis (Eds.), *Political public relations* (pp. 147–165). Routledge.

Holtzhausen, D. R. (2005). Public relations practice and political change in South Africa. *Public Relations Review*, *31*(3), 407–416. https://doi.org/10.1016/j.pubrev.2005.05.011

Honisch, S. V., & Más Manchón, L. (2020). The effects of paracrisis origin and response strategy on Facebook audience's perceived organizational reputation and behavioural intentions. *Corporate Reputation Review*, *23*(3), 133–144. https://doi.org/10.1057/s41299-019-00070-4

Jerotich, S. (2022, March 20). *6 times when the wrath of #KOT united Kenyans*. Citizen Digital. https://www.citizen.digital/entertainment/6-times-when-the-wrath-of-kot-united-kenyans-n294675

Jin, Y., Liu, B. F., & Austin, L. L. (2014). Examining the role of social media in effective crisis management: The effects of crisis origin, information form, and source on publics' crisis responses. *Communication Research, 41*(1), 74–94.

Jin, Y., & Liu, B. F. (2010). The blog-mediated crisis communication model: Recommendations for responding to influential external blogs. *Journal of Public Relations Research, 22*(4), 429–455.

Kaigwa, M. (2017). From cyber cafe to smartphone: Kenya's social media's lens zooms in on the country and out to the world. In B. Ndemo & T. Weiss (Eds.), *Digital Kenya: An entrepreneurial revolution in the making* (pp. 187–222). Palgrave Macmillan.

Kainerugaba, M. [mkainerugaba]. (2022a, October 3). *I'm glad that I have scared you Kenyans a bit! Two weeks is long. Nairobi in one week for sure! Aided by my brothers from Carnival!*. Twitter (X); https://twitter.com/mkainerugaba/status/1576971390162325509?lang=en

Kainerugaba, M. [mkainerugaba]. (2022b, October 3). *I would never beat up the Kenyan army because my father told me never to attempt it! So our people in Kenya should relax*! Twitter (X). https://twitter.com/mkainerugaba/status/1576983135526432769?lang=en

Kainerugaba, M. [mkainerugaba]. (2022, October 13). *I have never had any problem with Afande Ruto. If I made a mistake anywhere, I ask him to forgive me as his young brother. God bless East Africa!" he tweeted.* Twitter (X). https://twitter.com/mkainerugaba/status/1580584931553443842

Kent, M. L., & Lane, A. (2021). Two-way communication, symmetry, negative spaces, and dialogue. *Public Relations Review*, *47*(2), 102014. https://doi.org/10.1016/j.pubrev.2021.102014

Knowafrica. (2024, January). *Top 10 African celebrities with most social media followers.* https://knowafrika.com/top-10-african-celebrities-with-the-most-social-media-followers/

Kong, S., & Chen, H. (2022). Revisiting the SMCC model: How Chinese public relations practitioners handle social-mediated crises. *Public Relations Review, 48*(5), 102259.

Kuhnhenn, M. (2021). Gift im Bier: A context-sensitive analysis of culturally-rooted messages and humor in risk communication on glyphosate in Germany. *Journal of International Crisis and Risk Communication Research*, *4*(3), 579–604. https://doi.org/10.30658/jicrcr.4.3.5

Li, C., & Kent, M. L. (2021). Explorations on mediated communication and beyond: Toward a theory of social media. *Public Relations Review, 47*(5), 102112. https://doi.org/10.1016/j.pubrev.2021.102112

Liquor, S. [@styles_liquor]. (2022, October 3). *It will just take 10 luhyas from shimakhokho and nyaribare chache to eat the whole of Uganda.* Twitter (X). https://twitter.com/styles_liquor/status/1576933319928729600

Liu, B. F., Austin, L., & Jin, Y. (2011). How publics respond to crisis communication strategies: The interplay of information form and source. *Public Relations Review, 37*(4), 345–353. https://doi.org/10.1016/j.pubrev.2011.08.004

Liu, B. F., & Fraustino, J. D. (2014). Beyond image repair: Suggestions for crisis communication theory development. *Public Relations Review, 40*(3), 543–546.

Liu, B. F., Jin, Y., & Austin, L. L. (2013). The tendency to tell: Understanding publics' communicative responses to crisis information form and source. *Journal of Public Relations Research, 25*(1), 51–67. https://doi.org/10.1080/1062726x.2013.739101

Liu, B. F., Jin, Y., & Austin, L. (2023). Digital crisis communication theory: Current landscape and future trajectories. In C. H. Botan & E. J. Sommerfeldt (Eds.), *Public relations theory III: In the age of publics* (pp. 191–212). Routledge.

Lovari, A., & Bowen, S. A. (2020). Social media in disaster communication: A case study of strategies, barriers, and ethical implications. *Journal of Public Affairs, 20*(1), e1967.

Lu, X., & Jin, Y. (2020). Information vetting as a key component in social-mediated crisis communication: An exploratory study to examine the initial conceptualization. *Public Relations Review, 46*(2), 101891. https://doi.org/10.1016/j.pubrev.2020.101891

Madziva, R., Nachipo, B., Musuka, G., Chitungo, I., Murewanhema, G., Phiri, B., & Dzinamarira, T. (2022). The role of social media during the COVID-19 pandemic: Salvaging its 'power' for positive social behaviour change in Africa. *Health Promotion Perspectives, 12*(1), 22. https://doi.org/10.34172/hpp.2022.03

Makong, B. (2022, October 4). KoT attacks Muhoozi after Controversial Tweet on Capturing Nairobi. *Capital FM.* https://www.capitalfm.co.ke/news/2022/10/kot-attacks-muhoozi-after-controversial-tweet-on-capturing-nairobi/

Mersham, G., Skinner, C., & Rensburg, R. (2011). Approaches to African communication management and public relations: a case for theory-building on the continent. *Journal of Public Affairs, 11*(4), 195–207. https://doi.org/10.1002/pa.413

Meru, D. [@Commoner98]. (2022, October 3). *Nairobi budget almost equals your GDP, think. It could be a better idea in the previous regime. But for now men in power don't slumber nor drink.* Twitter (X). https://twitter.com/Commoner98/status/1577137559079071744

Mohamed, A. [@AlinurMohamed_] (2022, October 3). *A country whose past, present and future president is one and the same should not threaten countries like Kenya.* Twitter(X); https://twitter.com/AlinurMohamed_/status/1576950222059499520

Mundeke, M. [@MundekeM]. (2022, October 3). *First secure Turkana Eastern of part of Kenya from Bandits then come back and comment nonsense. Uganda no longer fight Bandits, we fight terrorists and win them. Mogadishu can confess* Tweet. https://Twitter (X).com/MundekeM/status/1576931752492224512?s=20]. Twitter (X).

Mungai, A. [@Andychuho]. (2022, October 3). *You also need basic English lessons... "my army and I".* Twitter (X). https://twitter.com/Andychuho/status/1577706241782054913

Mwangi, S. [@Mwangisimon]. (2022, October 3). *You first need to capture your Dad's tailor.* Twitter (X). https://twitter.com/MwangiSimon/status/1576931506471456768

Ndaire, S. [@Ndaire_]. (2022, October 3). *The commander of the Ugandan armed forces.* Twitter (X). https://Twitter (X).com/Ndaire_/status/1576928699223375872?s=20].

Ndanu, J. [@JacqueNdanu]. (2022, October 3). *With which English? Anjument? Sit down Uganda aka East Africa Village.* Twitter (X). https://twitter.com/JacqueNdanu/status/1577173846980820992

Ndlela, M. N. (2020). Social media algorithms, bots and elections in Africa. In M. N. Ndlela & W. Mano (Eds.), *Social media and elections in Africa, Volume 1: Theoretical perspectives and election campaigns* (pp. 13–37). Springer International Publishing.

Ndonye, M. (2021). Kenyans on Twitter (X) undisputed world bullying champions. *The Standard*. https://www.standardmedia.co.ke/commentary/article/2001394518/why-kenyans-on-Twitter (X)-are-the-most-vicious-global-bullies.1

Ngondo, P. S. (2019). An exploratory study: digital and social media use by Zimbabwean public relations practitioners. *Public Relations Journal, 12*(3), 55. https://prjournal.instituteforpr.org/wp-content/uploads/NGONDO_PR_Journal.pdf

Ngondo, P. S., & Klyueva, A. (2020). Exploratory study of public relations roles in Zimbabwe. *Public Relations Review, 46*(5), 101961. https://doi.org/10.1016/j.pubrev.2020.101961

Ngondo, P. S., & Klyueva, A. (2023). Inviting an Ubuntu-based approach to public relations theory building in sub-Saharan Africa. In C. H. Botan & E. J. Sommerfeldt (Eds.), *Public relations theory III: In the age of publics* (pp. 374–392). Routledge.

Nick. [@azdaknick]. (2022, October, 3). *Remember our force's don't use Kalashnikov Soviet made like the Ugandans ,ours is modern*. Twitter(X). https://twitter.com/azdaknick/status/1576928745528913920

Nothias, T., & Cheruiyot, D. (2018). A'Hotbed'of digital empowerment? Media criticism in Kenya: Between playful engagement and co-option (Stuart Hall Award 2018 Winner). In *The International Association for Media and Communications Research (IAMCR)*, June 20–24, 2018, Eugene, Oregon.

Nyabola, N. (2018). *Digital democracy, analogue politics: How the Internet era is transforming politics in Kenya*. Bloomsbury Publishing.

Ociepka, B. (2012). The impact of new technologies on international communication: The case of public diplomacy. *Information Sciences, 59*, 24–36. https://www.ceeol.com/search/article-detail?id=13979

Oguda, G. [@gabrieloguda]. (2022, October 3). *The only thing Ugandans can capture from Nairobi is the fake certificate they gave our Governor*. Twitter (X). https://twitter.com/gabrieloguda/status/1576927495131045888

Perreault, M. F., & Perreault, G. (2019). Symbolic convergence in the 2015 Duggar scandal crisis communication. *Journal of Media and Religion, 18*(3), 85–97. https://doi.org/10.1080/15348423.2019.1678945

Pompper, D., & Adae, E. K. (2022). Public relations and sustainability across the African continent: Using Afro-centric philosophies to remember what's been "forgotten or lost". In D. Pompper, K. R. Place, & C. K. Weaver (Eds.), *The Routledge companion to public relations* (pp. 276–288). Routledge.

Pratt, C. B. (2003). Managing sustainable development in sub-Saharan Africa: A communication ethic for the global corporation. In K. Sriramesh & D. Verčič (Eds.), *The Global public relations handbook* (pp. 477–494). Routledge.

Reynolds, B., & Seeger, M. W. (2005). Crisis and emergency risk communication as an integrative model. *Journal of Health Communication, 10*(1), 43–55. https://doi.org/10.1080/10810730590904571

Right, M. [@MrRightKe]. (2022, October 3). *Man thinks Nairobi is a village like Uganda where he can use capture and recapture method*☺. Twitter (X). https://twitter.com/MrRightke/status/1576931059060551681

Roh, S. (2017). Examining the paracrisis online: The effects of message source, response strategies and social vigilantism on public responses. *Public Relations Review, 43*(3), 587–596. https://doi.org/10.1016/j.pubrev.2017.03.004

Sakwa, C. [@Csakwah_]. (2022, October 3). *It will take the Kenyan military a day to seize your father's toilet. Once we have the control of his toilet, we can colonize Uganda. He runs Uganda from his toilet, that is why the country's democracy stinks to high heavens.*

Twitter (X). https://twitter.com/CSakwah/status/1576935704227368962]Seeger, M. W. (2006). Best practices in crisis communication: An expert panel process. *Journal of Applied Communication Research, 34*(3), 232–244. https://doi.org/10.1080/00909880600769944

Smith, S. B., & Smith, B. G. (2022). What amounts to a paracrisis? Interactivity as a lens for evaluating social media-propagated crises. *Journal of Contingencies and Crisis Management, 30*(2), 204–216. https://doi.org/10.1111/1468-5973.12374

Song, S., Zhao, Y. C., Yao, X., Ba, Z., & Zhu, Q. (2021). Short video apps as a health information source: an investigation of affordances, user experience and users' intention to continue the use of TikTok. *Internet Research, 31*(6), 2120–2142. https://doi.org/10.1108/INTR-10-2020-0593

StatCounter Global Stats. (2023, August). *Social media Stats Africa*. https://gs.statcounter.com/social-media-stats/all/africa

Taylor, M., & Yang, A. (2015). Have global ethical values emerged in the public relations industry? Evidence from national and international professional public relations associations. *Journal of Business Ethics, 130*, 543–555. https://doi.org/10.1007/s10551-014-2226-4

Tennydelp. (2021). Kenya Reignites Online War on Twitter (X) with Uganda - African Bullies Sent Ugandans Back to Kabaka. *Opera News*. https://ke.opera.news/ke/en/entertainment/700e78e6e218f6b6b72f37b1669cdf41

Tracy, S. J. (2013). *Qualitative research methods* (2nd ed.). Sage.

Wine, B. [@HEBobiwine]. (2022, 0ctober 3). *Dear KENYANS, you now understand what it means to live in Uganda under Gen. Museveni and his son, whom he gifted the highest military ranks and put him in charge of our land forces! Sadly, beneath the senseless tweets lies a monster who brutalises and tortures our people for fun*! Twitter (X). https://twitter.com/HEBobiwine/status/1577003965769666560

Xiao, Y., Hudders, L., Claeys, A. S., & Cauberghe, V. (2018). The impact of expressing mixed valence emotions in organizational crisis communication on consumer's negative word-of-mouth intention. *Public Relations Review, 44*(5), 794–806. https://doi.org/10.1016/j.pubrev.2018.10.007

Yin, R. K. (2014). *Case Study Research Design and Methods* (5th ed.). Sage.

Yu, Y., Huang, L., Qing, P., & Chen, T. (2022). How humor reduces the impact of negative feedback on social media. *Journal of Interactive Marketing, 57*(4), 601–613. https://doi.org/10.1177/10949968221123771

Zaharna, R. S., & amp; Uysal, N. (2016). Going for the jugular in public diplomacy: How adversarial publics using social media are challenging state legitimacy. *Public Relations Review, 42*(1), 109–119. https://doi.org/10.1016/j.pubrev.2015.07.006

Zhao, X., Zhan, M. M., & Liu, B. F. (2019). Understanding motivated publics during disasters: Examining message functions, frames, and styles of social media influentials and followers. *Journal of Contingencies and Crisis Management, 27*(4), 387–399. https://doi.org/10.1111/1468-5973.12279

7 Digital Marketing and Public Relations in Egypt

Amany Bassyouny

Introduction

In the past decade, Egypt witnessed tremendous growth in digital marketing (DM) activities. With a population of over 111 million Egyptians and over 80 million internet users in Egypt (Kemp, 2023), it has become one of the largest markets for e-commerce and DM activities in Africa and the Middle East. On the one hand, DM has been replacing many traditional marketing activities in Egypt on so many levels (Marketing, 2021); namely in budget allocations by major clients, in strategic planning and execution of campaigns (Fareed & Tantawi, 2022), in the spread of DM agencies that forced some old-fashioned marketing agencies out of business. On the other hand, Egypt is suffering from vast digital divide since World Bank reports of 2022 indicated that over 27% of the Egyptian population were under poverty line and illiterate, which insinuated that they are deprived of basic needs for honorable living, suitable infrastructure, and access to the internet (WorldBank, 2022). AlHady (2022) highlighted the negative effects of such digital divide on slowing economic growth and underdevelopment of technology adoption in industry, agriculture, production, commerce, and all related DM activities (AlHady, 2022).

Egypt introduced the internet infrastructure in 1993 and has been vastly expanding the accessibility and use of the internet and social media (SM) since the early years of the 21st century. Statistics indicated that there are over 80.75 million Egyptian internet users in 2023, with internet penetration rate of 72.2%. The SM users reached 46.25 million users, which equals 41.4% of Egypt's total population (Kemp, 2023). According to global statistics, Egypt is the number one country in Facebook accounts in the Middle East and North Africa (MENA) region and second after Saudi Arabia in YouTube accounts. The internet boom coincided with the introduction of mobile services in Egypt in 1996, with huge investments and development of the telecommunication services and infrastructure, so that the number of mobile users reached 93.9% of Egypt's population in 2023 (Kemp, 2023).

Country statistics indicate that the Egyptian digital market is very dynamic and continuously changing. The number of Facebook users decreased by 6% (2.8 million) in the first quarter of 2023, although it remained the number one SM platform in Egypt with 43 million Egyptian users in 2022. Instagram and YouTube also

DOI: 10.4324/9781032689654-7

suffered decreases in the numbers of Egyptian users during the same period. Akin to global statistics (Wong, 2023) Egyptians' mood shifted towards TikTok that increased by 17% and LinkedIn that increased by 23.4% in the first quarter of 2023 (Kemp, 2023).

There are many factors that contributed to such unexpected dependency on DM activities by international and local organizations in Egypt. Some of these factors include the adoption of free economic market policies in Egypt since the eighties, the development of a strong internet infrastructure, the realization of the power of SM that was crystallized in the 2011 Egyptian revolution and its aftermaths as well as the current economic, political, and media environment in Egypt (Ahmad, 2018). To meet the needs of the booming digital market in Egypt, the number of DM agencies exceeded 500 agencies (Guide, 2023), which had a negative effect on the specialized public relations (PR) agencies in Egypt, so that it decreased from twenty-five agencies in 2019 to thirteen agencies in 2023 (kompass, 2023).

The internet and interactive SM platforms offered an outstanding opportunity for marketers and PR professionals in Egypt. Just like the rest of the world, SM has influenced all aspects and directions of communication and changed the lives of individuals and communities. This study analyzed the opportunities and challenges of SMPR in Egypt and aimed to explore the digital communication business environment in Egypt. To provide an up-to-date overview of how professionals practice DM and SM PR in Egypt, the researcher conducted a systematic qualitative study using in-depth interviews (IDIs) with ten Egyptian professionals. The literature review will explore the studies of the more general discipline of DM in Egypt before scanning the studies related to the specific discipline of SM PR.

Literature Review

Digital Marketing in Egypt

According to the American Marketing Association, digital marketing refers to 'any marketing methods conducted through electronic devices which utilize some form of a computer, including online marketing efforts conducted on the internet' (AMA, 2022). Researchers associated the introduction of DM in Egypt with the expanding use of the internet twenty years ago (Fareed & Tantawi, 2022). The beginnings of DM in Egypt were characterized by randomness, nonstrategic communication, and ad hoc reliance on imitation of global DM techniques. A study of DM activities of ten small businesses in Egypt concluded that they relied on generic use of Facebook and Instagram, with no mention of paid online advertising, mobile applications or online stores. The limited use of proper DM in Egypt was referred to the tight budgets and the managers' lack of understanding of DM potentials and techniques (Fareed & Tantawi, 2022). By time, clients' awareness of the value of DM grew and they started requesting effective performance marketing, not buzz-creating campaigns. In 2020, certain trends of growth and importance of DM revealed in Egypt; like the massive numbers of e-commerce websites, the growing search for DM courses, and the increasing number of clients who changed their usual traditional marketing and were seeking serious DM services (Marketing, 2021). The government also pushed large investments that reached US$375m to fulfill Egypt's vision of digitalization and sponsor the training of one hundred thousand young Egyptians in areas of website design and DM (Marketing, 2021).

Egypt's main sources of economy are the gas exports, Suez Canal revenues, and tourism. The studies of Badr (2019), Kotb (2016), and Mkwizu (2020) discussed the use of DM campaigns to support tourism. Most of these studies suggested the poor, nonstrategic use of DM activities to support tourism in Egypt. For example, a study discussed the underutilization of e-marketing potentials in the promotion of cultural tourism in Egypt as well as in the preservation of UNESCO World Heritage sites and destinations in Egypt (Kotb, 2016). Another study measured the search engine optimization efficiency of nine official tourism websites in Egypt and concluded that all websites were facing difficulties which had a negative impact on their efficiency (Badr, 2019). Reports highlighted how Egypt's expensive DM campaign to boost tourism in 2015 backlashed with negative outcomes:

> The campaign encouraged people to use the hashtag #ThisisEgypt when posting their experiences on social media. The campaign has suffered from negativity, with several people using the hashtag to highlight terror acts and human rights issues.
>
> (Report, 2021, p. 11)

The efficient utilization of DM strategies was evident in the telecommunication and nongovernmental business sectors in Egypt. Al Gindy (2019) depicted strategic, successful integrated marketing communication campaigns by telecommunication companies which properly manipulated the features of SM platforms, especially Twitter (Al Gindy, 2019). Ibraheem and Abdelsalam (2021) confirmed that e-commerce applications and online shopping have become a booming source of income for millions of Egyptians in the past few years, especially with the COVID-19 lockdown and the associated job loss, downsizing, and economic recession. A study on 30 women entrepreneurs in Egypt concluded that SM was the main factor that increased their social capital and their self-efficacy (Beninger, Ajjan, Mostafa, & Crittenden, 2016).

On the business level, a unique study, conducted in 2018 on 425 companies in Egypt, indicated that organic activities, which are any free content shared on SM profiles, were the most used techniques by 97% of companies surveyed, and 50% of marketing budgets were dedicated to DM activities, especially SM advertising. The astonishing result was that most companies in Egypt were running SM marketing in house and only 9% of them are outsourcing (Insights, 2019).

Public Relations and SMPR in Egypt

PR is defined as 'the management of communication to build and maintain a mutual, two-way relationship between an organization and its internal and external publics to achieve mutual understanding and acceptance' (Tench, 2017). Egypt was the first country in the Arab world to adopt the modern science of PR and develop it academically and professionally, but it lost its pioneer status and witnessed slow-down of growth and creativity (Agwa & Youssef, 2005).

Globally, SMPR research had been mounting in the past decade and it covered the various techniques of practicing PR on SM (Wang & Yang Cheng, 2021) The researcher found twenty published studies in the Arabic library associated with SMPR in Egypt, covering topics related to the use of SMPR activities in governmental organizations (Albert, 2016; Al Gindy, 2019; Bekhit, 2009; Othman, 2019), in civil-society organizations (CSOs) (Al Awadly, 2015; Bassyouny, 2016), and in crisis communication management (Abdallah, 2017; Bassyouny, 2013; Khalil, 2017). Other studies focused on the SMPR practices, benefits, challenges, ethics, and future trends in Egypt (Atteya, 2018; Ghobashy, 2021; Khaleel, 2022; Montasir, 2022; Taher, 2021).

The studies that analyzed SMPR of the governmental institutions in Egypt concluded that the government's main models of online communication were the press agentry and the public information one-way PR models. A study depicted lack of running a variety of online content and messages, focusing on providing organizational news and beneficial awareness information rather than activating dialogic features of SM (El Deeb, 2021b). Al Gindy described the tweets of the Egyptian military spokesperson as press releases with no response to the comments, nor engagement with the page followers (Al Gindy, 2019). Analysis of the Ministry of Interior SMPR strategies and their effect on impression management indicated that the intensive self-promotion and exemplification messages of the ministry on SM did not generate public's positive impressions about the ministry, rather a majority of neutral and negative impressions were depicted (Albert, 2016). An 'average' score describes the Egyptian public's trust, mutual control, satisfaction, and commitment in relation to governmental SM pages (El Deeb O., 2021a). Positive indicators showed the relationship between the public's increasing trust in the SM pages of the government and those pages' proactive disclosure of official reports and timely refutation of rumors (Othman, 2019).

Scholars agreed that SMPR in CSOs in Egypt was extremely important to create credibility with volunteers and donors for fundraising (Al Awadly, 2015). According to Bassyouny (2016), there was a shift in donors' philanthropy behavior based on positive or negative electronic word-of-mouth on Egyptian SM platforms. The study concluded that the CSO's inability and inefficacy to conduct strategic SMPR to defend its reputation drove them to lose credibility and donation money consequently.

As 'crises' had been the title of the period in Egypt since 2011 till today, the role of SMPR in crisis management received massive academic attention in conferences and studies. Researchers (Abdallah, 2017; Atteya, 2018; Khalil, 2017) agreed that SMPR was not professionally used in crisis communication management in Egypt, either by private companies or by the governmental bodies. A study that analyzed the communication strategies related to the Russian plane crash in 2015 described the online crisis communication as inefficient and restricted to routine informative roles, while facing the challenges of wrong information, inexperienced people talking in media about the Russian plane crisis, international pressure, political manipulation of the crisis and rumors (Atteya, 2018). Khalil (2017) revealed practitioners' fear of using SMPR during crisis situations and concluded that SM makes them unable to control the user-generated content of the public, which is usually negative during the crisis, often causing recurrent and escalating crisis situations. A similar study confirmed that most of the study samples of PR and marketing managers in Egypt stated that the use of SM in crisis management weakens the image and reputation of the organization and escalates the crisis beyond control (Abdallah, 2017).

A study revealed that PR professionals in Egypt use SM to improve company image, promote company activities, and create online sales (Ghobashy, 2021). They use SMPR for controlling internal communication, management of issues, and setting organizational communication policies (Taher, 2021). Unethical practices of DM and SMPR were detected by researchers, like fake content or accounts, spreading rumors, leaking information, bribes to influencers, and use of AI in digital PR (Khaleel, 2022; Montasir, 2022).

The review of literature provided an overview of the most relevant academic studies and reports related to DM and SMPR in Egypt. Nevertheless, since the author's specialization is PR, the focus of the primary study is on SMPR professional practices, opportunities, and challenges. The purpose of the current study is to help both professionals and scholars better understand the opportunities and challenges of SMPR professional practices in Egypt from the perspective of experienced professionals in the Egyptian market.

Conceptual Framework and Methodology

The primary study will employ the notions of the Excellence Theory to explore the professional practices of SMPR in Egypt. The theory suggested benchmarks for excellence in PR practices and functions to realize effectiveness for organizations. The two-way symmetrical communication system, empowerment and independence of the PR managers, and strategic PR practices in addition to professional applications are some of the factors to fulfill the requirements of excellence and achieve mutually beneficial quality relationships between the organization and its public (Grunig, L., Grunig, J., & Dozier, 2002). A country's environment and infrastructure, its media atmosphere and societal culture were factors depicted by scholars to affect the excellence in PR practices (Tench, 2017). The presentation of this research results will align with the principles and affecting circumstances of the Excellence Theory with application to the PR and SMPR practices in Egypt. Through IDIs with ten experienced marketing, PR, and media professionals to gain deep insights about the opportunities and challenges of SMPR practices in Egypt and the nature of digital business environment in Egypt.

The research questions are:

RQ1: What are the opportunities for SMPR in Egypt?
RQ2: What are the main challenges of the use of SMPR in Egypt?
RQ3: What are the key features of the PR profession and the digital business environment in Egypt?

This study adopts the qualitative IDI method as data collection tool to gain deeper understanding of the professional practices (Mears, 2012) of SMPR and DM in Egypt. Through semi-structured personal interviews with a purposive sample of ten professionals, who have been working in the Egyptian market for at least ten years (Table 7.1), the researcher aimed at exploring their firsthand experiences with the SMPR practices in Egypt. Of the ten interviewees, there were six females and four males representing the PR profession, DM, and media professions in Egypt. The sample was divided as follows: four PR consultants, four digital media experts, and two newspaper editors. Each of the respondents had from ten to twenty years' of professional experience in the corresponding field and they are all communication consultants working in the Egyptian communication industry and well-acquainted with the Egyptian PR, DM, digital media, and media environment. The study was conducted during Fall 2020 and Spring 2021, which was a significant period for the increasing dependence on DM and PR activities, following the total COVID-19 lockdown from March to June 2020, and witnessing a cautious easing of restrictions. As Egypt was witnessing the third wave of the pandemic during the time of the study, data were collected either through face-to-face meetings or SM. The researcher recorded the responses for later transcription and thematic analysis according to the research questions.

Table 7.1 List of Egyptian Experts Interviewed

Participant	*Gender*	*Title*	*Specialization*
Interviewee (1)	Male	Founder and CEO of *Afqar Studio Digital Media Agency*	Digital marketing
Interviewee (2)	Female	Research & Marketing communication consultant	Marketing & PR
Interviewee (3)	Male	Social Media consultant and adjunct faculty at AUC (Independent)	Digital marketing
Interviewee (4)	Female	Editor in *Egypt Independent* Newspaper and communication consultant	Media
Interviewee (5)	Male	Communication consultant at *Rada Research PR Agency* and lecturer of IMC	Public Relations
Interviewee (6)	Male	Digital Consultant at *Regional Digital Lead*	Digital marketing
Interviewee (7)	Female	Marketing communication and PR consultant (Independent)	Marketing communication and PR
Interviewee (8)	Female	Digital media manager at *IQVIA*	Digital marketing
Interviewee (9)	Female	Deputy Editor-in-Chief of *Al Ahram Weekly* Newspaper	Media
Interviewee (10)	Female	CEO of *Rada Research PR Agency* and lecturer of public relations	Public Relations

Research Results

This study aimed at generating a comprehensive picture of how the PR and DM professionals perceive SMPR, how they utilize it, and the challenges they face with this booming new practice in the PR profession in Egypt. Results will be analyzed in alliance with the variables of the Excellence Theory of PR.

RQ1: The Opportunities of SMPR in Egypt

Eight respondents agreed that SM facilitated the interactivity between companies and stakeholders, intensified direct engagement with target publics, and diversified the channels of communication between the organization and its internal and external publics. Interviewee (2), research and marketing communication consultant, highlighted that more than one-half of Egyptian population is connected to the internet. The findings of the opportunities of SMPR were categorized according to the most vital functions of SMPR, namely in brand communication, corporate communication management, crisis communication, media relations, public affairs, and SMPR functions for the PR profession in Egypt.

SMPR in Brand Communication

As for the use of SMPR in brand communication, all respondents highlighted the increasing power of SM as the farthest-reaching media nowadays used in the PR and DM activities for brands in Egypt. Interviewee (4), editor and communication consultant, said that brand communities are formed on Facebook. All respondents agreed that influencer marketing is an innovation of SMPR and that the influencers' endorsements for brands are currently the most trending PR activity that contributes tremendously to the positioning of brands in Egypt.[1]

The respondents emphasized the role of SM in ensuring bigger customer base and brand recognition through curated and seeded electronic word-of-mouth (EWOM) to boost brands and companies. Interviewee (5), a communication and PR consultant, seconded that opinion and stated that PR professionals prefer SM to announce events of product launches, competitions, and awards to reach a much wider audience via SM compared to traditional media.

Interviewee (6), a regional digital consultant, stated that brand communication and marketing is better, easier, and more efficiently performed digitally than through traditional means. He explained that SM supports monitoring activities and audience behavior, necessary for targeting in DM. Interviewee (7) added that SM is also contributing to the experts' understanding of audience interests, so PR can effectively address these interests directly and incorporate social sharing into strategic PR programs.

SMPR in Corporate Communication Management and Crisis Communication

Interviewees (6) and (10), CEO of a leading PR agency, highlighted that renowned businesspeople in Egypt use their SM personal accounts as official channels to manage their companies,[2] communicate with the publics and engage in public discussions. She added that SM redefined corporate reputation management programs in Egypt as indicated by numerous social responsibility (CSR) programs and challenges that occur only on SM. Interviewee (10), stated:

> An example of a successful non-strategic campaign on SM is the ice-bucket campaign[3] for awareness for ALS[4] disease. It was amazing. Now we see many other initiatives to interact with stakeholders & publics.

She added that SM hosted the interactive trends of food bank challenge during the COVID-19 pandemic in Egypt. She explained that companies of the same industry challenged each other online to donate more food boxes to the needy people. There were examples from the companies of the dairy industry in Egypt as well as from within the agencies' sphere. Interviewee (10) said:

> Beauty of these online challenges is that competitive companies of the same industry join their forces to show responsibility towards the society during crisis, like the PR agencies' online challenge to see which agency will donate more food boxes during the pandemic, thus reflecting the role of SMPR in community service.

Interviewee (3), a DM consultant, said that SMPR has evolved into proactively engaging in reputation management activities and identifying potential problems in a business relationship with the public, thus adding the need for PR professionals to fully understand and master SM. Interviewee (2) echoed the role of SMPR in relationship marketing. She said that corporations and private businesses, like real estate and steel companies in Egypt, have huge budgets allocated for relationship marketing and PR activities to form lasting relationships with their internal and external stakeholders and those corporations dedicate a large chunk of this budget to DM and digital PR.

There were two opposing views regarding the role of SM in crisis management. Interviewee (1), CEO of a digital media agency, praised the positive role of SM in the early detection of a crisis, real-time crisis management that allows dissemination of proactive communication messages and preventing escalation of a crisis when the PR team is fast, prepared, and wisely responsive. Interviewee (10) highlighted the exclusive role of SMPR to enhance the relationship between the organization and its internal publics, who are usually forgotten. SMPR advanced internal communication in Egypt in all types of organizations.

Some respondents contradict this position as they argue that SM is considered an obstacle during crisis situations, as the negative word-of-mouth on SM is louder than the strategic messages of the PR experts, who suffer to get their messages through on SM during crisis situations. Interviewee (5) said that the clutter, spam, and false information of SM challenges the companies' PR and crisis communication efforts and messages. Interviewee (7) mentioned that having a good and timely crisis management team is a challenge in Egypt, especially when SMPR is utilized in crisis communication. She added that most cases of SMPR show reactive crisis responses rather than proactive ones.

SMPR in Media Relations

Experts highlighted that SM strengthen the relationship between traditional media people and PR professionals. Interviewee (1), a digital media consultant and CEO of a digital media agency, said:

> When a topic arises, journalists often check SM to see what people are saying. PR professionals join that online discussion to influence journalists to present a certain angle.

Interviewee (9), a deputy editor-in-chief, said:

> SM allowed PR professionals to communicate directly with media people, respond to their inquiries and feed them with updated, real news. This equation facilitated by SM strengthened PR professionals' relationship with editors and traditional media, hence creating a recognized value for both entities to enjoy mutual gains.

Interviewee (4) added that most desired projects are activities that attract free media coverage and those events suit SM content perfectly.

SMPR in Public Affairs

Respondents agreed that the Egyptian government expanded their use of SM and improved many of the strategic communication deficiencies that marked its early digital existence. Interviewee (3) and Interviewee (10) emphasized the recognized developments in the digital strategic communication of the different governmental organizations as part of the national project of 'digital Egypt'. The interviewees agreed that SM enabled the Egyptian government to communicate directly with Egyptian youth. Many ministries and governmental officials are giving statements, announcements on the official SM pages and engaging in dialogues with the public through SM platforms. Interviewee (3), SM consultant, stated:

> The Egyptian President, Prime Minister and Minister of Health have communicated directly with the Egyptian public through their Facebook pages, especially during the COVID-19.

Nine respondents indicated that SMPR is growing rapidly in Egypt and the Egyptian government has been allocating significant funding for PR to regain its image on the national and international levels. They stated that since 2018 every Egyptian cabinet member had one or more PR and marketing communication consultants in his team in addition to official spokespeople for every ministry and public organization. Those consultants are managing the communication activities through both traditional and digital media including SM platforms. Many studies (Albert 2016; Al Gindy 2019; El Deeb 2021; Othman 2019) traced the increasing use of SMPR by the Egyptian government in the past few years and confirmed recognizable positive impacts like providing exclusive news and correcting false ones, yet the governmental budgets allocated for PR and SMPR are not publicly announced.

SM Opportunity for the PR Profession

Regarding the benefits of SM to the PR profession, interviewee (4) believed that SM facilitated conducting a live PR messaging workshop with the company/client, highlighting the main target audience and unique selling points, and then using these messages to plan various DM activities. She added that SM enhanced the client/agency relationship, facilitated dialogues with all concerned parties, thus reducing misunderstanding and chains of approvals. Interviewee (7) mentioned the value of SMPR in providing clients with reliable, quantitative measures of the effectiveness of PR programs.

Interviewee (2) highlighted the added value of SMPR by describing SM as 'places of culture' offering a rich educational and social experience for both the communicators and users. She also called the 'SM community' a vital relationship-building tool rather than a 'marketplace'.

RQ 2: Challenges of the Use of SMPR in Egypt

Tench (2017) identified three main factors that directly affect excellence in PR, namely a country's infrastructure (composed of political, economic, and legal systems as well as social activism), media environment (control, diffusion, and accessibility) and societal culture. Accordingly, the Egyptian professionals listed numerous challenges for the adoption of SMPR in Egypt.

Key Variables Related to Egypt's Infrastructure

All respondents agreed that the complex structure and nature of the Egyptian environment add to the challenges of SMPR in Egypt. Interviewee (2) highlighted the fact that almost 60% of the Egyptians live in rural areas, which was a challenge to the use of SMPR in Egypt. Respondents emphasized that a large segment of the poorly educated Egyptians are unable to differentiate between fake news and real news. The high illiteracy rate in Egypt with the low media literacy misled lots of Egyptian people to believe trends, even if they were rumors or fake news. Interviewee (9) stated that most Egyptian people resorted to SM sources for information and news more than traditional media. Six interviewees mentioned the technology adoption dilemma in Egypt as an obstacle to the manipulation of the full potential of SMPR. Studies in both DM and PR fields confirmed this stance concluding that the DM managers lack the full understanding of the technology adoption model, its stages, and proper functions (Fareed & Tantawi, 2022). The Egyptian organizations' weak use of dialogic features of SMPR and conversational marketing were highlighted by PR scholars (El Deeb, 2021b). Interviewee (7) stated:

> I believe the rapid technological growth with the lack of best practices of how to use it in PR is an issue in Egypt.

Most respondents argued that the economic crisis, the unjust socioeconomic structure of the Egyptian society, and the wide gap between the few rich and the many poor constitute challenges to the efforts of PR in Egypt, especially SMPR. She said that SM users often attacked the business companies, people, as well as their marketing campaigns as a way of purging out of their daily frustrations.

Interviewee (8) agreed with that opinion and added that the economic crisis was highly reflected in all marketing and PR efforts, as Interviewee (7) said:

> Budgets remain a big concern, especially in times of financial challenges. Also, how this budget is spent on which PR tactics is still a concern at the top managerial level.

Interviewee (4) seconded her opinion and added that SMPR has become more expensive than before, especially in influencer marketing. All interviewees highlighted the challenge of lack of specialization and skilled PR calibers in Egypt, let alone skilled SMPR employees. Interviewee (2) confirmed that qualified talents were hard to find in Egypt, as digital communication is a recent endeavor, and the dynamics of the digital media industry are changing rapidly. Most respondents agreed that there are no university programs in Egypt yet to provide the starving market with skilled digital communication technicians and specialists.

Key Variables Related to Media Environment in Egypt

Respondents highlighted that the complex system of traditional media ownership, management and control-imposed challenges for the PR campaigns and activities in Egypt, while the uncontrolled, chaotic nature of digital media added to their challenges and limitations.

Interviewee (4) stated that the media landscape in Egypt today is segmented into semi-independent or government-owned media. She argued:

> Even if the medium is not owned by the government, it is usually sponsored by or partially owned by organizations that are affiliated with the government. Hence, it may be difficult sometimes to get the media's attention, if there is no clear direction from the government that the proposed topic is relevant.

She added that this pattern of control limited PR professionals' accessibility to traditional media and thus to its audience. Interviewee (3) added that traditional media use of digital platforms was stagnant as journalists practiced old, traditional one-way communication on digital platforms, with no real dialogue or comprehension of SM's potential to initiate conversations and build relationships for PR purposes. He explained:

> All traditional media were forced to go online after the revolution of 2011. Today, the Egyptian media could not capitalize on SM. SM is used only to put content and to increase traffic, with minimal interactivity.

The 2011 revolution was considered a direct result of the increasing power of activist groups and their ability to use SM to mobilize public opinion. Younis and Akram (2017) suggested that SM was a unique source that enabled the activists to communicate directly and quickly with other activists as well as with Egyptian citizens.

Respondents called traditional media a challenge due to the immature business model of newspapers and TV channels. Interviewee (4) stated that official news sites disseminated inaccurate information quickly without verification to increase traffic. Respondents mentioned some unethical practices by some media people like expecting free giveaways in exchange for publishing an article or broadcasting a segment about the clients. Experts agreed that the most important challenge for SMPR practices was the clutter of digital content and mechanism of disseminating news. Interviewee (2) said:

> There are unlimited sources of content online in addition to enormous user-generated content. This avalanche of information makes it very difficult for the PR professional to power-through with strategic PR messages.

Interviewee (3) mentioned unethical challenges related to digital media in Egypt, like some sites' use of click-baiting to deceive the netizens. He also stated the challenge of the substantial number of fake accounts and fraud SM pages that resemble companies' official sites and pages, which were responsible for tons of fake news that destroyed the credibility of companies, officials, and non-profit organizations. Interviewees (8) and (5) stated that false information and rumors spread quickly, negative word-of-mouth on brands and companies found their way on SM and created trends that destroyed companies.

Key Variables Related to Societal Culture

The most uncontrolled challenge that PR professionals faced when using SMPR in Egypt was the audience's aggressive negative response to many PR and other DM communication messages. Audience's negative reactions and the sarcastic nature of Egyptian people in general, who ridiculed and often scolded marketing communication messages, represented a major challenge to communication and PR professionals in Egypt, according to Interviewees (1), (3), and (5). They mentioned that the socioeconomic structure of the Egyptian society, and the wide gap between the haves and have-nots, was the main reason PR messages of companies and businesspeople are met with negative reactions from the SM users. Interviewee (10) articulated that PR was considered the voice of rich, privileged business sector of Egypt. Most interviewees agreed with that opinion and added that many digitally publicized CSR initiatives were called 'hypocrisy' and were discredited by the Egyptian public on SM platforms. News reports depicted the rage of Egyptian SM users towards the multimillion pounds' advertising campaigns publicizing the CSR projects of banks, telecommunication, and construction companies every Ramadan. The SM users attacked the extravagant PR advertisements of those companies and doubted the actual execution of those CSR initiatives (AlJazeera, 2022).

Language, as a vital component in any culture, formed a challenge to professionals in Egypt. [5]Three interviewees explained that traditional PR in Egypt depended on formal classic Arabic language to provide news releases to newspapers. Now, as SM platforms have become the most important channel for PR, experts differed among themselves on the suitable language to be used in SMPR in Egypt. Interviewee (9) believed that SM solved the problem of language, as it carried simple short messages and posts in both Arabic and English with more visuals and graphic materials. Digital media experts added that sophisticated classic Arabic is no longer needed, and SM has given space for written colloquial Egyptian Arabic to take over. Two interviewees disagreed with this opinion and considered language of communication on SMPR in Egypt as a major challenge to the practice of PR, because Egyptian governmental entities still required formal classic Arabic statements and news on their Facebook pages and many clients believed that maintaining the use of formal language was a core variable associated with the image and personality of the organization.

RQ3: Features of the PR Profession and the Digital Business Environment in Egypt

The analysis of the current scene in Egypt showed a considerable degree of professional practice of PR, increasing appreciation of PR, growing dependence on SMPR coinciding with deteriorating traditional media, and a shocking dispute between PR agencies and DM agencies.

Five respondents confirmed that both PR professionals and many clients enjoyed a good understanding of SM's nature and potential and an appreciation of the power of SMPR. Yet, there were still clients in Egypt, who do not understand the difference between marketing, advertising, and PR.

Interviewees (4) and (10) accused media convergence of eliminating the clear-cut lines between the PR functions and the marketing functions, thus leading to the loss of credibility of PR messages, especially during crisis situations. The interviewees indicated that Egypt is currently witnessing a major quarrel between all types of agencies because of SM. Most respondents confirmed that DM agencies are gradually replacing PR agencies in Egypt. This notion is supported by formal statistics. In 2019, there were 25 local and international specialized PR agencies operating in Egypt.[6] The online guide this year listed only thirteen specialized PR companies in Egypt (kompass, 2023). There were no formal reports available online regarding the number of DM firms in Egypt, yet various sources estimated them to be over 500 small, medium-size, and large DM firms in 2023 (Guide, 2023). Six respondents pointed to the state-ownership of many DM entities that enjoyed vast financial and logistical privileges in the market, thus crushing private agencies and driving many of them out of business. Interviewee (8) argued that although all PR agencies in Egypt had SM arms, more clients nowadays resort to the much cheaper digital media agencies.

On the other hand, Interviewees (1) and (3) believed that PR professionals in Egypt did not really understand the interactive nature of SM platforms and their content strategies. They confirmed that some PR firms used traditional and old-fashioned strategies for digital media, and this was the reason for the failure of some PR campaigns in Egypt. Interviewee (6) added:

> Now in one agency I can execute all communication functions. I can do research with analysis of target audience, their insights and behavior through digital channels. I can collect statistics regarding my audience quantitatively and qualitatively. PR is also done digitally with novel offers, communication with stakeholders, and even apologies. Advertising is efficiently executed online and much cheaper.

Interviewees (5) and (10) acknowledged that, like the rest of the world, communication industry in Egypt experienced a shift from strategic thinkers represented by counsellors and relationship managers to young technical SM experts. All interviewees agreed that qualified, professional calibers in DM and SMPR are rare to find in Egypt.

Summary

In conclusion, the ten interviewed experts confirmed that modern, advanced PR was being practiced in Egypt with proven success indicators in specialized areas. All interviewees agreed that SM has offered vast abilities to measure public opinion, defend the reputation of companies and brands, highlight the corporate social responsibility functions, and provide measurable KPIs for the success of communication campaigns. Strategic PR communication, whether through traditional or digital media presented a unique model that allowed engagement and active interaction between organizations and their publics in Egypt.

Nevertheless, they listed multiple challenges that they encountered while practicing SMPR in Egypt, like the underdeveloped, tightly controlled traditional media, scarcity of professional digital PR calibers, and Egyptian SM users' fierce attacks on companies and their PR campaigns. They agreed that SM have tremendous potential to become the most used media to carry PR messages in Egypt, but the fierce competition between PR agencies and DM agencies was hindering the maturity of strategic DM and online PR in Egypt.

Africa-Centric Trends

The results of research indicated that if compared to other African countries, Egypt hosted both tremendous opportunities as well as numerous challenges regarding the future of DM and SMPR.

The opportunities were evident in the significant percentage of internet penetration (over 73%), the accelerating adoption of new SM platforms, like TikTok and LinkedIn as well as the government's huge investments in this sector to support the digitalization of Egypt. Some scholars believe that Egypt's population is a blessing, because over 60% of this population is under 30, which makes Egyptian society a young one (Khamis, 2017). I second this opinion in relation to opportunities for growth of the Egyptian digital market based on the number of internet users (80 million), second after Nigeria, and number of SM users in Egypt (over 46 million) according to 2023 statistics (Kemp, 2023).

Egypt came first in spending on programmatic advertising among African countries with a total spending of 557.57 million dollars in 2021. Egypt, South Africa, Morocco, and Nigeria are the leading markets in Africa spending on programmatic advertising with expenditures surpassing 100 million dollars in 2021 (Statistica, 2023).

A recent study endorsed the enormous advantage of Egypt in using DM to boost its tourism industry, which is a major contributor to Egypt's GDP. According to World Travel and Tourism Council (WTTC), the top African countries that led the world for travel and tourism GDP growth in 2018 were Ethiopia (+48.6%) and Egypt (+16.5%). The author said:

> Egypt has the Facebook subscriber competitive advantage over other African countries; hence, it has a better opportunity in digital marketing in terms of the capacity to utilize social media marketing through social media to boost tourism.
>
> (Mkwizu, 2020)

On the other hand, Egypt is encountering many limitations in relation to technology adoption, digital divide, economic performance, development of talented calibers, and lack of a fair, professional competitive environment. This study concluded that despite the rapid digital adoption growth rate in Egypt, the strategic planning and execution of DM and SMPR activities was still very primitive. Many DM and SMPR activities of governmental institutions used the one-way communication model of posting press releases or news, without the employment of the dialogic feature and two-way engagement with the public. Even though Egypt had 90 universities serving 3.6 million students in 2023 (EgyptToday, 2023), the outdated underdeveloped educational programs in Egypt failed to produce sufficient professional calibers who properly understand and employ the functions and potentials of the digital technology. With over 500 DM companies operating in Egypt, the right talents are still scarce to find. The increase in the number of DM companies that coincided with the decrease in the number of professional PR agencies in Egypt added to the challenges of the strategic planning and execution of professional SMPR campaigns. The digital divide that deprived 30 million (27%) Egyptians from access to the internet was also an obstacle to the development of DM and SMPR in Egypt.

The digital market in Egypt is dynamic and progressing on many levels. The current qualitative study offered insights from Egyptian professionals regarding the opportunities and challenges of strategic SMPR in the Egyptian market. The interviewed professionals anticipated a dispute between traditional PR agencies and modern, young digital media and DM agencies in Egypt. The field of DM and online PR deserves more research and analysis to draw a comprehensive picture that will be beneficial for both professionals and academics.

Notes

1 https://www.facebook.com/MountainViewEgypt/videos/marwan-younis-at-mountain-view/507203533232707/ Egyptian real estate mogul used a famous influencer to take a tour in the headquarters, highlighting what a great place to work in. The influencer was very successful with this sarcastic viral video that reached millions.
2 Like Hisham Ezz El Arab, Ex-CEO of CIB Bank and the Egyptian billionaire, Naguib Sawiris.
3 Ice-bucket Campaign, Egypt. http://cairogossip.com/gossip/life-style/als-ice-bucket-challenge-takes-over-egypt/
4 Amyotrophic lateral sclerosis (ALS) is a neurodegenerative disease that attacks nerve cells and causes paralysis before ultimately killing the individual with it.
5 Classic Arabic is taught in schools and universities and used in news of traditional media, while colloquial Egyptian Arabic is the language of citizens, songs, and drama. Egyptian young netizens created a totally different written chat language on SM, where they write Egyptian Spoken Arabic in English letters, and it became so popular that Google recognized it in English Arabic translations and named it *Arabizi*. Arabizi has been considered the new language of Egyptian youth on SM and forced some companies to adopt this language to communicate with their publics (Abu-Liel, Eviatar, & Nir, 2020).
6 Courtesy of Dr. Sherine Zaklama, CEO of Rada Research Agency, extracted from IPRA data on Egypt.

Bibliography

Abdallah, D. (2017). Egyptian Organizations Use of Social Media in Crisis Communication (in Arabic). *Scientific Journal for Public Relations and Advertising Research, 2017*(9):51–108.

Abu-Liel, A., Eviatar, Z., & Nir, B. (2020). Arabic Teenagers' Attitudes to Electronic Writing in Arabizi. *Journal of Cultural Cognitive Science, 5*:20–57.

Agwa, A., & Youssef, M. (2005). *Planning and Management and Public Relations (in Arabic).* Cairo, Egypt: Cairo University Print House.

Ahmad, F. (2018, 7, 1). *Public Relations from Pen and Paper to the Fourth Generation of the Technological Revolution (in Arabic).* Retrieved from Alborsanews: https://alborsaanews.com/tag

Albert, A. (2016). Ministry of Interior Impression Management strategies on Social Media and its relationship to the Public Image of Ministry (in Arabic). *Scientific Journal for Public Relations and Advertising Research, 2016*(5):75–141.

Al Awadly, S. (2015). Non-Profit Organizations' Use of Social Media (in Arabic). *Scientific Journal for Public Relations and Advertising Research, 2015*(2):1–40.

Al Gindy, S. (2019). Egyptian organizations use of Twitter as a modern Marketing and PR Tool (in Arabic). *Scientific Journal of Public Relations and Advertising Research, 2019*(17):1–46.

AlHady, M. (2022, 12, 1). Towards a Sustainable Digital Society (in Arabic). *Al Magala Al Masreya lel Maaloumat*, pp. 5–10.

AlJazeera. (2022, 3, 22). *Ramadan Charity Advertising, Annual Controversy in Egypt.* Retrieved from www.Al Jazeera.net: https://1-a1072.azureedge.net/politics/2022/3/22/

AMA. (2022, 14 1). *What Is Digital Marketing.* Retrieved from American Marketing Association: https://www.ama.org/what-is-digital-marketing/.

Atteya, R. (2018, 1, 1). *Public Relations and the Management of Tourism Crisis in Egypt.* Retrieved from Ain Shams University: http://srv4.eulc.edu.eg/eulc_v5/Libraries/Thesis/BrowseThesisPages.aspx?fn=PublicDrawThesis&BibID=12551496.

Badr, R. (2019). Evaluating Governmental Tourism Websites in Egypt Using Search Engine Optimization Tools. *International Journal of Heritage, Tourism and Hospitality, 13*(2):286–298.

Bassyouny, A. (2013). Effective Crisis Communication Strategies in Egypt. *The Arab Journal for Media and Communication Research, 1*(1): E2–11.

Bassyouny, A. (2016). Effects of Word-of-mouth WOM on Donators' Relationship with CSOs in Egypt after 2013. *Scientific Journal for Public Relations and Advertising Research, 2016*(7): 1–23.

Bekhit, E. (2009). Online Public Relations in the Arab Governmental Websites. *Journal of Arab & Muslim Media Research, 2*(1):53–80.

Beninger, S., Ajjan, H., Mostafa, R., & Crittenden, V. (2016). A Road to Empowerment: Social Media Use by Women Entrepreneurs in Egypt. *International Journal of Entrepreneurship and Small Businesses 27*(2/3):308.

EgyptToday. (2023, 1, 11). *Egypt has 90 Universities Serving 3.6 M Students, Higher Education Minister.* Retrieved from www.Egypttoday.com: https://www.egypttoday.com/Article/1/121838/Egypt-has-90-universities-serving-3-6M-students-Higher-Education

El Deeb, O. (2021a). Communication Strategies of the Egyptian Government and its Role in Managing the relationship with the Public (in Arabic). *Scientific Journal of Public Relations and Advertising Research, 2021*(21):465–493.

El Deeb, O. (2021b). Effect of Use of Communication Technology on the Government Relationship Management with the Publics (in Arabic). *Scientific Journal of Public Relations and Advertising Research, 2021*(22):547–576.

Fareed, G., & Tantawi, P. (2022). Digital Marketing Adoption Framework for Small Businesses in Egypt: A Grounded Theory Approach. In M. D. Bilgin (ed.), *Eurasian Business and Economics Perspectives. Eurasian Studies in Business and Economics* (pp. 251–268). Springer.

Ghobashy, N. (2021). Effect of Public Relations Practitioners' Use of Social Media in the effective Management of the Organization Reputation (in Arabic). *Scientific Journal of Public Relations and Advertising Research, 2021*(21):341–410.

Grunig, L., Grunig, J., & Dozier, D. (2002). *Excellent Public Relations and Effective Organizations.* New Jersy: Lawrence Erlbaum Associates.

Guide, E. (2023, 8, 1). *Digital Marketing Companies in Egypt.* Retrieved from www.sortlist.com: https://www.sortlist.com/digital-marketing/egypt

Ibraheem, A., & Abdelsalam, R. (2021). E-Commerce Adoption in Egypt Insights from COVID-19 and Beyond. *Scientific Journal of commercial and Environmental Studies, 12*(2), 37–55.

Insights, D. M. (2019, 8, 9). *Digital Marketing Insights*. Retrieved from Digital marketing community: Digital Marketing Insights (2019). www.digitalmarketingcommunity.com/articles/digital-marketing-insights-in-egypt-2019-25-stats-will-make-you-nervous/
Kemp, S. (2023, 2, 13). *Digital 2023 Egypt*. Retrieved from Datareportal: https://datareportal.com/reports/digital-2023-egypt
Khaleel, I. (2022, 1, 1). Ethics of Public Relations Practices in the Digital Transformation Age. *Scientific Journal for Public Relations and Advertising Research*, *2022*(23):209–177.
Khalil, I. (2017). Use of Social Media in Crisis Management (in Arabic). *Scientific Journal for Public Relations and Advertising Research*, *2017*(11):305–385.
Khamis, S. (2017, 11, 20). *Egypt's Population Growth, a Blessing or a Curse*. Retrieved from Arab Center Washington, DC: https://arabcenterdc.org/resource/is-egypts-population-growth-a-blessing-or-a-curse/.
Kirat, M. (2016). Public Relations Professionalism and Excellence in the Arab World. *Revue Albahit Al ijtima'i*. https://www.researchgate.net/publication/308414690.
Kompass. (2023, 8, 1). *Public Relations Agencies in Egypt*. Cairo, Egypt. Retrieved from eg.kompass.com: https://eg.kompass.com/a/
Kotb, N. (2016, 2, 14). *Developing Sustainable Cultural Tourism at UNESCO World Heritage Destination through E- marketing*. Retrieved from Academia Edu: https://www.academia.edu/30735161/DEVELOPING_SUSTAINABLE_CULTURAL_TOURISM_AT_UNESCO_WORLD_HERITAGE_DESTINATIONS_THROUGH_E_MARKETING_THE_CASE_.
Marketing, D. (2021, 9, 6). A Review of Digital Marketing in Egypt. *A Review of Digital Marketing in Egypt*. Cairo, Egypt: Egypt Ripplemark.
Mears, C. (2012). In-Depth Interviews. In J. W. Arthur (ed.), *Research Methods and Methodology in Education* (pp. 170–176). California: Sage Publications.
Mkwizu, K. (2020). Digital Marketing and Tourism: Opportunities for Africa. *International Hospitality Review, 34*(1):5–12.
Montasir, A. (2022). Modern Trends of the Use of Digital Networks in Public Relations, Comparative Analytical Review (in Arabic). *Scientific Journal for Public Relations and Advertising Research*, *2022*(23):177–209.
Othman, S. (2019). Credibility of Social Media Pages of the Governmental Institutions in the Proactive Disclosure of Official Data. *Egyptian Journal of Studies of Communication*, *2019*(68): 263–308.
Report, E. T. (2021). *Egypt Tourism Report (5-Year Forecast)*. Fitch Solutions. Retrieved from: https://store.fitchsolutions.com/tourism/egypt-tourism-report.
Statistica. (2023, 7,3). *Top African Countries in Programmatic Advertising Spending in 2021*. Retrieved from Statica: https://www.statista.com/statistics/1310922/programmatic-ad-spend-africa/
Taher, I. (2021). Employment of Social Media Tools in the Professional Practice of Public Relations (in Arabic). *Egyptian Journal For Communication Studies*, *2021*(76):383–422.
Tench, R. (2017). *Exploring Public Relations. Global Strategic Communication* (4th ed.). London: Pearson Education.
Wang, Yuan & Cheng, Yang & Sun, Jie. (2021). When public relations meets social media: A systematic review of social media related public relations research from 2006 to 2020. *Public Relations Review, 47*,102081. 10.1016/j.pubrev.2021.102081.
Wong, B. (2023, 5, 18). *Top Social Media Statistics and Trends of 2023*. Retrieved from Forbes Advisor: https://www.forbes.com/advisor/business/social-media-statistics/#source.
WorldBank. (2022). *Egypt, Arab Republic*. World Bank.
Younis, M., & Akram, M. J. (2017). Social Media Fostering the Revolutions: Case Study of the Arab Spring. *International Journal of Advanced Research (IJAR)*, *5*(2):1558–1570.

8 Social Media Marketing of Public Universities in Ghana

The Use of Facebook

Akwasi Bosompem Boateng

Introduction

Marketing activities have transformed due to the emergence of digital and social network environments. Like other industries, higher education institutions have recognized the usefulness of digital marketing via the internet as compared to traditional ways of marketing their brands (Constantinides & Stagno, 2012). Many universities are using communication technologies especially new (social) media to market, reach and engage their students, attract new students, relate with their alumni, or increase donations, among others. Higher education institutions are taking advantage of digital marketing campaigns and social media because many of their potential and current students and other stakeholders have become more aware of online platforms, making it easy for engagements (Constantinides & Stagno, 2012). Therefore, marketing and communication departments in universities are exploring digital marketing techniques and user-friendly ways of providing easy access to information and messages about their brands on social media platforms.

Social media describes a wide range of applications that are supported by the internet whose impact on higher education institution has been an issue of debate in marketing communication. Social media platforms influence the behaviours of individuals and educational environments making them potential instruments for marketing universities (Ameyaw, 2021; Boateng, 2022; Kolan & Dzandza, 2018; Manu et al., 2021). As of 2023, there was an estimated number of 4.9 billion people who use social media globally, which is expected to rise to approximately 5.85 billion users by 2027 (Wong, 2023). One of the popular social media platforms is Facebook (thefacebook.com), which is a social networking site where individuals provide information about them to the public that allows them to communicate with their groups, friends and colleagues, among others (Jothi, Neelamalar & Prasad, 2011). As of February 2022, there were over 8.6 million registered users of Facebook, which is expected to reach 16.46 million users in 2027 (Degenhard, 2023).

Research on higher education institutions has highlighted the potentials of marketing and communication when employed by universities to attract students and other stakeholders (Boateng, 2015; Times Higher Education, 2023). According to Hemsley-Brown and Oplatka (2006), an important research theme in this field is

DOI: 10.4324/9781032689654-8

marketing communication, where there are gaps between information that audiences, students and prospective students are looking for and the information that universities provide in their traditional communication activities. The gap indicates the need for improvement in marketing communication especially through social media by higher education institutions including public universities in Ghana. Discussions of issues regarding the subject are increasing globally; however, little attention has been given to the impact of these social media platforms in higher education in Africa, particularly Ghana. Social media usage as a marketing tool by universities is necessary given the growing rate of adoption by young people who form the large number of potential students in institutions (Boyd & Ellison 2007; Constantinides & Stagno, 2012). While the advent of social media is a relatively recent phenomenon, the adoption rate is staggering. As of January 2022, there were over 8.8 million registered users of social media in Ghana (Sasu, 2022), out of which 5.65 million of them are Facebook users (Datareportal, 2023). In the beginning of 2023, the advertising audience of Facebook in Ghana was made up of 59.8% males and 40.2% females (Datareportal, 2023).

Ghana and Social Media Use in Ghana

Ghana is a developing country in West Africa and the first nation on the continent to gain independence in March 1957. Ghana has a young age structure with approximately 57% of its 33.8 million population under 25 years (Datareportal, 2023). At the beginning of 2023, Ghana had an internet penetration rate of 68.2% with about 23.1 million internet users of the country's total population (Datareportal, 2023). With over 39 812 171 mobile network subscribers, and 22 756 215 data subscribers in January 2023 (National Communication Authority, 2023), coupled with mobile internet connection speed of 7.90 Mbps and fixed internet connection speed of 27.70 Mbps, social media use is becoming widespread in Ghana (Datareportal, 2023).

This study argues that the use of social media platforms in promoting higher education institutions including public universities does not only attract students, but also helps potential students and other stakeholders to choose particular brands of institutions. Several studies (Clark et al., 2017; Nazeeer, 2017) have been conducted on how digital marketing through social media has been used to promote the brands of higher education in different contexts. For example, Clark et al. (2017) have studied the role of social media engagement and relationship in higher education marketing in European context. Nazeeer (2017) also explored the impact of social media on university marketing and advertisements on students. Most of these studies conducted on social media marketing of higher education have focused on Western countries, with relatively little work done in Africa especially Ghana. Little is known about how public universities in Ghana use social media and what influence these platforms have in reaching and engaging their students, attracting new students and academics, and relating with their alumni and stakeholders, among others. The few studies in Ghana that have been conducted on higher education marketing have explored different aspects such as branding and advertising (Boateng, 2015; Gyasi, Wang, Owusu-Ampomah & Kusi, 2017), whose findings established that strategic advertising activities promote university brands to attract global audiences; with little attention to how social media marketing is transforming the brands of public universities in the competitive global environment. Inasmuch as there have been initiatives undertaken in Ghana by public universities on social media platforms, there is little published research on the issue of social media marketing. It has become imperative to examine how the phenomenon is enabling public universities to attract many audiences, students and other stakeholders for patronage. This study contributes to the body of knowledge by investigating how the University of Cape Coast as one of the best universities in Africa (Times Higher Education, 2023) utilize social media marketing to promote its brand. The transformation of the University of Cape Coast into the fourth best in Africa and first in West Africa and Ghana makes it a suitable case to provide empirical evidence of how social media have contributed to the position of its brand in the competitive higher education industry. This article sought the following research objectives.

Research Objectives

1 To discuss the usefulness of social media to the University of Cape Coast in marketing its brand to attract stakeholder audiences to the institution.
2 To identify social media strategies employed by the University of Cape Coast in marketing its brand to attract stakeholder audiences to the institution.
3 To analyse the nature of documents posted on the Facebook page of the University of Cape Coast in marketing its brand to attract stakeholder audiences to the institution.

Research Questions

1 What is the usefulness of social media to the University of Cape Coast in marketing its brand to attract stakeholder audiences to the institution?
2 What social media strategies are employed by the University of Cape Coast in marketing its brand to attract stakeholder audiences to the institution?
3 What is the nature of documents posted on the Facebook page of the University of Cape Coast in marketing its brand to attract stakeholder audiences to the institution?

Literature Review

Higher Education Marketing

Marketing in higher education provides opportunity for institutions to liberalize the high level of control, which enables them to brand and campaign to attract many audiences and stakeholders (Boateng, 2015; Hemsley-Brown & Goonawardana, 2007). The reputation of brands of universities is built not only on their quality of activities, product, services and achievements, but also on the marketing, communication and engagements with stakeholders to create and promote distinctive identities through compelling narratives for their institutions (Times Higher Education, 2023). This implies that higher education institutions, especially public universities, need to respond to the dynamics by taking advantage of the benefits of marketing, especially via digital and social media channels and platforms to gain a competitive edge over others. Scholars, for example, Donkor and Kyei (2020) and Fosu and Poku (2014), have studied the marketization of higher education in Africa particularly Ghana and found that marketing activities by institutions have significant influence on brand position and choice, which many public universities have not strategically used to their maximum advantage despite the advent of digital forms of communication such as social media platforms. In other words, marketing communication allows higher education institutions including public universities to reach success by strategically positioning their brands to attract students and other stakeholders. The objective of marketing communication in higher education is to support the recruitment of student, attract and retain world class academics, share research breakthrough and output, communicate the mission and values, facilitating stakeholder engagements, attracting investment, highlighting the impact of the university on society, and promoting their competitive status (Times Higher Education, 2023).

In this regard, the primary goal is to reach large audiences and promote their identities and influence their behaviours through information, persuasion and reminders to encourage patronage and brand loyalty (Dolphin, 2000). This is consistent with what Davies (2002) indicates that higher education institutions which craft persuasive branding messages and market them effectively position their brand identity and promises to audiences and stakeholders. In marketing higher education, institutions brand their uniqueness by defining the essence of what the universities are, what they stand for and what they want to be reputed for, which requires consistency and precision to commit and develop the brand (Boateng, 2015; Harsha & Shah, 2011). In their attempts to craft the brand identity of what higher education institutions seek to be known for and present their promises to target audiences, public universities use various communication strategies including social media to deploy user-generated content about their exceptional outputs and achievements of students, staff and other stakeholders to attract many people to their institution.

Branding Higher Education

The American Marketing Association describes a brand as a name, design, term, symbol, or feature that distinguishes the good or service of one seller or providers from another (AMA, 2009). This means that a brand distinguishes one item(s) or service(s) of a seller from another. Brodie, Glynn and Little (2006) conceptualize service brands in terms of making, enabling and keeping promises. As Boateng (2015) and De Chernatony (2006) concur, a brand does not only represent a name given to identify a product or service, but also gives personality and value. In higher education context, a brand denotes a psychological covenant between the brands and audience through which shared expectations are identified and addressed (Kapferer, 2004, 2005). This implies that a brand could be a perception which exists in the minds of audiences about institutions. The perceptions that stakeholders including future students and partners, among others hold about the reputation of university brands emanates from the impression created in their mindsets via communication about the institution and interactions with the university (Cole & Bruch, 2006; Times Higher Education, 2023). The role of branding has moved from just designating the ownership of services or products into a valuable source of information and tool which deliver promises to enhance relationships. This trend is significant with the emergence of digital technologies and social media platforms, which provide uncontrolled and unmediated platforms to showcase the brands and essence of institutions as distinct identities that differentiate and influence the decision making of stakeholder audiences (Boateng, 2015; Keller, 2008).

Identity is an important concept in branding that is applicable to every organization including public universities (Balmer & Greyser, 2006; Boateng, 2015). As Kapferer (2005) notes, the attention of branding literature has shifted to brand identity, which concentrates on the distinctiveness of a brand. While Aaker and Joachimsthaler (2000) refer to brand identity as the vision of how target audiences perceive about a brand, or what organizations, products and services want their brands to stand for; Keller (2008) noted that brand identity indicates the meaning of the brand as presented by an organization (Kapferer, 2008). The implication is that higher education institutions could decide on what and how they want to be known or perceived (Alsem & Kostelijik, 2008; Boateng, 2015). Service brands such as higher education institutions including public universities are particularly involved in corporate branding and identity. Corporate identity refers to what makes organizations unique and different that encompasses the communication, design, culture, behaviour, structure, industry identity and strategy of organizations (Boateng, 2015; De Chernatony & Cottam, 2008). This implies that corporate identity is concerned with understanding of the differentiating attributes or distinctive features of organizations, and how they are communicated to diverse stakeholder audiences. Several factors such as location, advertising, leadership and social responsibility programmes, among others contribute to creating, communicating and promoting corporate brand identity of organizations (Coleman, 2010), which could be undertaken through digital marketing.

Digital Marketing

Marketing higher education is an essential activity considering the intense local and international competition in the sector. One form of marketing that has become popular is digital marketing, which entails all marketing strategies that utilize the internet and technology to promote brands, products and services (Madhu & Verma, 2018). This form of marketing includes the use of email marketing, search engine optimization and advertising on different digital platforms including social media. An important advantage of digital marketing is that promotion through digital media promotes creativity and personalization, which enables organizations such as higher education institutions to respond and react to evolving trends and engage with target audiences and different stakeholders including students, future students and academics. The many digital marketing tools available could make it difficult for universities to choose the most relevant and effective strategies and approaches for their needs. Digital marketing communication strategy plays a key role in developing brand awareness of higher education institutions and promoting their university reputation (Times Higher Education, 2023). Given the interactive features and potentials of digital media, there have been concerns about the effectiveness of traditional marketing, which calls for further studies of the concept of digital marketing in the particular lens of social media. There have been attempts to redefine the concept of marketing in the context of digital and social media communication, which continues to change activities in practice (Gable et al., 2011). Patsiotis and Kapareliotis (2016) suggest that the concept of marketing must be broadened to consider the significance of technological developments and advancement in practice and theory. These assertions indicate the need to shift from the traditional to digital marketing and its implications on industries including higher education institutions such as public universities, which equip students and graduates with knowledge and skills to promote developments and innovations.

The concept of digital marketing and social media marketing may seem similar. However, the two concepts are not identical but rather seek to complement each other. It is important to strike a balance between the roles of each of the concepts to align them with organizational or institutional goals. Organizations could consider digital marketing and social media tactics as not only practical but also cost-effective forms of engagements with stakeholders; expand audience reach and promote brand loyalty beyond geographical boundaries (Clark et al., 2017; Nazeeer, 2017). For bigger organizations such as public universities, utilizing digital marketing and social media tactics is essential to reach their numerous stakeholder audiences globally (Time Higher Education, 2023). For public universities which focus on service as the primary form of exchange, interactivity, co-creation, social relationships and networking are relevant to their digital marketing activities. A major example of digital marketing is social media marketing, which presents several opportunities and challenges to organizations with regard to communication engagements and social relationships (Patsiotis & Kapareliotis, 2016). Following the bandwagon, higher education institutions in African are following the global trend of engagement beyond physical presence to adopt social media platforms to promote their brands. Digital engagements have become the practice due to the keen competition in the higher education sector, which requires innovative and result-oriented approaches to attract future students, academics and other stakeholders to patronize institutions. The need to attract diverse interest groups has raised concerns about how public universities could take advantage of social media to compete in the higher education industry. Universities could deploy various strategies social penetration, traffic analytics, social analytics, content analytics, pay-per-click and search engine optimization, among others, as well as adopt appropriate tools that can be used to assess their performance (Times Higher Education, 2023).

Social Media Marketing

Social media is a digital marketing strategy deployed by institutions as a response to the search for innovative and interactive ways of engaging with audiences and stakeholders. Social media platforms are internet-based applications that thrive on Web 2.0 which allow for the creation of user-generated contents (Kaplan & Haenlin, 2010, p. 61). Similarly, Carr and Hayes (2015) referred to social media as "internet-based, dis-entrained and persistent channels of mass personal communication facilitating perceptions of interactions among users, driving value primarily from user-generated content" (p. 8). Social media have unique features which include flexibility, convergence, participation, conversation, community and communality, openness, connectedness, immediacy or real-time feedback, performance, prominence and easy usability (Anena, 2014; Mayfield, 2008). Social media are electronic communication platforms which serve as websites for social networking and micro-blogging activities because of the opportunities they offer to users to establish communities online to connect, communicate, interact and exchange messages, ideas and contribute to content creation and participation (Fuchs & Trottier, 2015, p. 5). Drawing from the discussions, this study situates that social media marketing involves the specific use of social networking or micro-blogging platforms to promote and interact with brand users, audiences and other stakeholders.

Social media marketing entails the creation of profiles and posting brand messages, as well as engaging with followers via comments and direct responses or reactions on platforms such as Facebook, YouTube, TikTok, Instagram, Twitter and LinkedIn, among others. Social networking sites, especially Facebook are driving the craze of social media (Boyd & Ellison, 2007). In social media marketing, there is more emphasis on networking and interactivity to promote customer satisfaction through feedback. Institutions, particularly higher education institutions, can leverage their unique features and characteristics to reach stakeholder audiences with their brand messages to encourage patronage (Times Higher Education, 2023). Universities could post their programmes and other unique information about them for further details and enquiries on social networking platforms such as Facebook, or transform them into applications to promote their brands, achievements and global status by telling their narratives (Times Higher Education, 2023). Public universities could collaborate with other businesses for paid advertisements and blog posts, to promote their institutions. While some institutions promote their brands digitally by joining online communities, for example, on Facebook, Twitter and Instagram where they provide information about their brands to attract attention for consideration, others use their websites to drive traffic to showcase their content and information to persuade audiences to choose their brands (Times Higher Education, 2023). This study focuses on the use of Facebook as social media exemplar to explore how the University of Cape Coast markets and promotes its brand through advertising.

Facebook as Social Media Marketing Platform

The Facebook community was created by Mark Zuckerberg as a networking tool for students at Harvard University with the intention of providing online version of the publication of papers, pictures and information on freshmen in Harvard (Cassidy, 2006). The name was consequently changed from "thefacebook" to "Facebook" in 2005, which opened up the community to institutions and individuals outside the United States. Facebook provides interpersonal features which promote exchange of information via posts and responses or comments to messages, updating profiles, chatting and liking posts (Boateng, McCracken & Lubombo 2020; Kearney, 2013). Facebook promotes cognition, communication, networking and co-operation, involving communities and collaborative work, as well as sharing of user-generated and other contents. In the digital age, Facebook as an innovation cannot be relegated to the background due to its influence in shaping and forming opinions (Boateng, 2020). Facebook provides the platform for connecting with diverse brand stakeholders, where users turn to search, connect, comment, like and follow others. This is because Facebook offers an avenue for conversations, enabling individuals to share and obtain opinions and views about brands, organizations, products and services in real time. Facebook provides higher degrees of identity salience and prominence which means that as the online activities and engagements increase on the platform, individuals' behaviours are socially deregulated in diverse ways to provide a setting of face-to-face communication (Boateng, 2019; Halpern & Gibbs, 2013; Kearney, 2013). Facebook connects users with accessible profiles to promote friendship, active and sociable discussions, as compared to YouTube which provides users more anonymity (Halpern & Gibbs, 2013). This study used Facebook because the platform has huge global popularity with over 5.65 million users in Ghana than other social media like Twitter, YouTube, TikTok, LinkedIn and Instagram, which has an advertising reach of equivalent to 16.7% of the total population at the beginning of 2023 (Datareportal, 2023).

Presence of the University of Cape Coast on Facebook

As of 2023 the University of Cape Coast had over 78, 485 students, which runs various undergraduate and postgraduate study programmes (www.ucc.edu.gh/main/explore-ucc/summary-statistics). Given its growing brand image as one of the best universities in Africa to be ranked among the top 400 institutions by Times Higher Education global rankings, the University of Cape Coast has used various social media platforms including Facebook, Twitter, Flickr, Instagram, YouTube and LinkedIn, among others, to communicate its brand, advertise and attract audiences in digital marketing activities to globalize the university. As a digital marketing strategy, the University of Cape Coast attracts a significant portion of its social media and website traffic from its Facebook posts which enable the institution to reach and attract wider stakeholder audiences.

The University of Cape Coast is actively present on Facebook with regular posts to present its brand, many followers and visitors to its page. Since the creation of its Facebook account in December 2010, the University of Cape Coast has attracted over 93, 000 followers and 71, 200 likes onto its Facebook page. The University of Cape Coast uploads messages in different forms on Facebook designed to target different stakeholder audiences with diverse information on undergraduate and postgraduate student life, campus settings and virtual world, among others. The texts, videos, images and banners posted by the university on Facebook could influence audiences and followers to develop relationships with the institution. Given this, it is a relevant platform for studying digital marketing in higher education. Facebook advertisement is fundamental to marketing strategies with the capacity to reach billions of users; hence, it is a useful social networking site for examining digital marketing activities of the University of Cape Coast.

The University of Cape Coast uses Facebook to promote various posts. For example, on 23 May 2023, the University of Cape Coast posted that the school remained the number one higher education institution in West Africa and Ghana, which attracted over 1, 600 likes, 162 comments and 167 shares. The university made other posts to promote its programmes of study by encouraging audiences to take advantage of its competitive programmes for enrolment on 13 May 2023, which attracted over 555 likes, 79 comments and 54 shares. On the other hand, the University of Cape Coast use Facebook to engage with the public and stakeholders by inviting individuals and stakeholders including students, faculties and alumni to its programmes. This was evident in the post made by the university on 16 July 2023 announcing a special congregation for the award of degrees to distinguished personalities in Ghana, which attracted over 356 likes, 21 comments ad 12 shares. The recruitment of students also features in the Facebook marketing of the university brand, giving reminders of admission-in-progress and encouragement to audiences not to miss the golden opportunity of studying at the University of Cape Coast. This Facebook post regarding admissions made by the university on 26 August 2023 attracted over 256 likes, 27 comments and 15 shares. These posts (messages) on Facebook market and attract future students and stakeholder audiences to the university brand. Copy from sample Facebook posts made by UCC include the following:

1 *Post for Brand Promotion and Advertising*
UCC is still the No.1 University in Ghana and West Africa (Source: @UCC, 2023)
2 *Post for Programme Marketing*
Take advantage of these competitive programmes of the University of Cape Coast College of Distance Education. Apply Now!!! (Source: @UCC, 2023).
3 Post for Public and Stakeholder Engagement
UCC will confer honorary doctorate degrees on seven remarkable individuals for the substantial contributions to public life and the University in very different ways at a special congregation.
#UCC:#Universityof CompetitiveChoice (Source: @UCC, 2023).
4 *Post for Student Recruitment and Admission*
Admission in Progress
BSc. Sports and Exercise Science
Visit:
https://apply.ucc.edu.gh/ (Source: @UCC, 2023).

Theoretical Framework

Technology Acceptance Model

This chapter is underpinned by two theoretical frameworks. The Technology Acceptance Model (TAM) propounded by Davis (1989) theorizes how users come to accept and use particular technologies. The TAM provides understanding of the determinants of computer acceptance that is general and capable of explaining user behaviours across a broad range of end-user computing technology and user population, while at the same time being parsimonious and theoretically justified (Davis, 1989; Davis, Bagozzi & Warshaw, 1989). The key feature of the TAM is the perception of individuals, that is, potential users of the technology. The thrust of Technology Appropriation Model is that how users believe in the perceived usefulness and ease of use of technologies including the internet and social media could be used to explain why and how they accept these new innovations in communication (Dwivedi, Rana, Nripendra, Jeyaraj, Clement & Williams, 2019). Perceived usefulness refers to the degree to which an individual believes that the use of a particular technology would be beneficial (Davis, 1989; Wothington, Burke & Shiraz, 2020). When there is perceived usefulness of a technology, the intention to use increases (Burgess & Worthington, 2021). Perceived ease of use is the degree to which an individual believes that the use of technology will not be difficult or perhaps would be free from efforts (Burgess & Worthington, 2021; Davis, 1989; Davis, Bagozzi & Warshaw, 1989).

The TAM posits that the use of technology is determined by the intentions of an individual or organization to use the technology (Davis, 1989). This means that when the intention of an individual or organization to use a technology increases, they are more likely to use such technology. When an individual or organization's perception of ease of use of a particular technology increases, the intention to use such technology increases (Burgess & Worthington, 2021; Davis et al., 1989). The extent to which users of a particular technology believe that it is useful for their cause and the extent to which they feel they can use such technology influence their willingness to accept and use it (Inegbedion et al., 2021).

With the emergence of new technologies especially in communication and media, the TAM has been refined or in other words, modified to extend it in research to develop understanding of the intention of users of the internet and social media. For example, the TAM has been used to study other technologies beyond computers such as mobile phone applications (Min, So & Jeong, 2019), digital technologies (Scherer, Siddiq & Tondeur, 2019), e-learning platforms (Sukendro et al., 2020) and telemedicine services (Kamal, Shafiq & Kakria, 2020). TAM enabled this study to explain the reason and ease with which officials of the University of Cape Coast use social media as new forms of communication technology to promote their institution, programmes and activities in the marketing of its higher education brand. The model allowed the study to discuss the usefulness of social media marketing to the achievement of the marketing goals of the University of Cape Coast including the influence(s) of their adoption to Facebook in promoting its brand as a public university in the competitive environment from the perspectives of interviewees. The TAM is complemented by Kapferer's Brand Identity Prism.

Kapferer's Brand Identity Prism

The Brand Identity Prism was propounded by Kapferer (1986), who theorized brand identity in respect of six elements from a prism. Kapferer's Brand Identity Prism recognizes different parts of a brand's identity, which recommends a careful blend of six facets to contribute to the establishment and maintenance of strong brand identities (Kapferer, 1986, 2004, 2005). There are six important characteristics of a brand's identity that could interact as components of a whole in the form of a prism to tell a story. These six important features include physique, personality, culture, relationship, reflection and self-image. The physique entails the physical features of a brand, that is, everything that audiences could visually perceive about you (Haaften, 2009; Kapferer, 2004, 2005). The physique including logo, colour palette and location emphasizes the tangible visuals which make it much easier for audiences to grasp beyond the concept. The *personality* refers to the voice of the brand and face of the brand (Kapferer, 1986, 2004, 2005). The brand personality addresses what a brand says and how it says it, which is not limited to verbal communication (Kapferer, 2004, 2005). The *personality* referred to as the *human characteristics* of the brand portrays who the brand is in terms of a person, that is, what audiences would see, hear and discuss about the brand. *Culture* deals with the brand's story of origin, belief system and values that are ascribed to the brand and reasons for such ascriptions (Haaften, 2009; Kapferer, 2004).

Relationship involves the engagements between the brand and audiences, which goes beyond the functions of the brand to emotions attached to them (Kapferer, 2004, 2005). This relationship goes beyond monetary transaction, in particular terms of the brand maintaining a healthy relationship with diverse stakeholder audiences from the initial interaction to subsequent purchase or use of service (Kapferer, 1986, 2004). Social media could provide the platform for engagements to promote good relationship between a brand and target audiences. *Reflection* involves the source of identification, which envisages who the brand wants its stakeholder audiences to be or target audience the brand intends to reach (Haaften, 2009; Kapferer, 1986, 2004). *Self-image* involves how audiences visualize their ideal selves (Kapferer, 1986, 2004). Self-image provides inspiration for the brand and audiences, as users seek to view themselves in particular or ideal ways that the brand could help them to achieve. Kapferer's Brand Identity Prism allows this study to discuss the characteristics including the personality, culture, self-image, relationship, reflection and physique of the University of Cape Coast, as well as how social media platforms have contributed to marketing these features of the brand as a university of competitive choice. This article complements TAM with Kapferer's Brand Identity Prism to adequately understand and analyse how perceived usefulness and ease of use of Facebook could influence and enable the University of Cape Coast to digitally market its higher education brand identity.

Methodology

This study triangulates qualitative interviews with document analysis. Qualitative approaches involve studies that focus on the qualities of individuals, organizations and processes that are not examined in terms of numbers and quantity (Cresswell, 2013; Hastings, 2013). As this study sought to elicit the perspectives of how social media are used by the University of Cape Coast in promoting its brand in the competitive higher education environment to attract stakeholder audiences, the qualitative research approach is appropriate to engage respondents in natural settings to analyze the phenomenon in marketing the university. The study used a case study design, which refers to an intensive and systematic investigation of individuals, groups, organizations, communities, or any unit that a researcher examines for detailed data in relation to social variables (Heale, 2018). This article uses case study because it sought to gather detailed understanding of how social media have been accepted by the University of Cape Coast and how personnel responsible for marketing communication activities have responded in their widespread to promote its unique selling proposition and attract many stakeholder audiences to the institution. The study complements interviews with document analysis, which involves the evaluation of physical and electronic documents for interpretation and understanding of meanings based on information collected (Bowen, 2009). The study uses document analysis because it sought to examine and interpret data to elicit meaning, understand and gather empirical knowledge of social media marketing of public universities in Ghana (Corbin & Strauss, 2008). The use of document analysis enabled the study to compare, corroborate or disprove data gathered from interviews with respondents. The study focused on electronic documents to identify and extract useful information such as words, phrases and images as documents, and categories or patterns of data to address research questions. Such electronic documents could be social media posts, journals, blogs, email, flyers, posters and banners, among others. This article analyzed social media posts including texts, images flyers, posters, banners and other advertising documents on the Facebook page of the University of Cape Coast to allow the study to organize qualitative data into themes. The document analysis was conducted to compare, corroborate, or disprove data from interviews with respondents.

The population of the study includes public universities in Ghana. However, this study focused on the University of Cape Coast as the case of examination. The focus on the University of Cape Coast is because of its rapidly grown brand into the best university in Ghana and West Africa, as well as an African powerhouse university brand (www.timeshighereducation.com). Given such achievements, this study envisaged that the University of Cape Coast could provide an interesting case and experiences of officials regarding how social media marketing has contributed to the transformation of public universities in Ghana. This study did not seek to generalize but provide detailed insight into how social media marketing has influenced the brand of the University of Cape Coast. The study conducted qualitative interviews with six (6) respondents who are involved with social media marketing to explore how social media as new forms of communication technology have been accepted and used to market, promote and position the brand of the University of Cape Coast in the competitive global higher education environment. In gathering empirical evidence of the usage of social media marketing by the university, the study conducted document analysis of the Facebook page of the University of Cape Coast to corroborate or disprove the responses from interviewees. The study analysed fifty-five documents posted on the Facebook page of the University of Cape Coast to describe the nature of its social media advertising from March to May 2023, which is a period for matriculation, graduation and admission activities that could compel the university to market and advertise on the platform even if did not at other times.

Data were collected from document analysis and interviews with purposively sampled respondents, which were thematically analyzed. Purposive sampling refers to the deliberate selection of participants in a study due to the qualities they possess (Etikan, Musa & Alkassim, 2016). The study interviewed the six (6) respondents who were purposively selected for their knowledge and experiences in marketing communication and social media marketing activities at the University of Cape Coast to address the research objective and questions. Thematic analysis is a method for identifying, analyzing and reporting the patterns or themes in data (Braun & Clarke, 2006). Braun and Clarke (2006) outline a theme-development procedure in conducting thematic analysis, which includes six steps, such as becoming familiar with the dataset, generating codes, generating themes, reviewing themes, defining, and naming themes and locating examples. In line with Braun and Clarke's (2006) thematic analysis, the study read interview transcripts and screen shots of posts (documents) on Facebook page of the University of Cape Coast several times to immerse into the data and gather more insights to code for topics. These codes were sorted into higher level topics to cluster them into themes and sub-themes. The themes were reviewed and interrogated by revisiting the coded data which were also applied to content of documents. The names of themes were refined and issues discussed under them to address questions.

Findings and Discussion

This study sought to explore how public universities (University of Cape Coast) are using social media marketing to promote its higher education brand. Three major themes: usefulness of social media in marketing, social media marketing strategies, and nature of social media marketing documents recurred in the data collected and analyzed. The issues regarding acceptance and usage of social media in marketing the brand of the University of Cape Coast is discussed under these three major themes in the following sections.

Usefulness of Social Media in Marketing UCC Brand

The findings of the study show the acceptance and use of social media (Facebook) in marketing public universities (University of Cape Coast) influence the decisions of individuals to choose the institution as a brand of competitive choice. Officials of the University of Cape Coast responsible for marketing communication are aware of the impact of social media in marketing the institution to attract students, academics and other stakeholder audiences to their higher education brand. The usefulness of social media in marketing is recognized by the University of Cape Coast because these platforms help the institution to influence decisions and choices of future students, academics and other stakeholder audiences. These acknowledgements are consistent with the postulations of Anena (2014) and Mayfield (2008) that the capabilities and easy usability of social media are important features that drive their acceptance and intentions of users to appropriate them in communication and marketing activities. The acceptance of these platforms by the University of Cape Coast is evident in the regular use of social media (Facebook) in marketing and promoting its university brand, programmes, achievements and status, among others. This validates the recommendation by Times Higher Education (2023) that global powerhouse university brands need to take advantage of digital and social media platforms to reach many diverse stakeholder audiences and tell their stories, highlight their societal impact and promote their competitive status globally to solidify their brands as universities of competitive choice.

There is evidence of significant use of social media (Facebook) by the University of Cape Coast. This could be seen in the fifty-five posts made by the University of Cape Coast during the study period to market its brand on Facebook. In addition to the easy ability to use social media especially Facebook by the university, the respondents revealed that social media marketing reduces the cost of marketing the brand, programmes and achievements to the institution. The fact that social media platforms (Facebook) are found to be reducing the marketing cost to the university influence the decision of the University of Cape Coast to significantly utilize the platforms (Facebook) to market their institution's brand. For example, respondent 3 reported:

> Apart from the usefulness of social media, the cost effectiveness of these platforms in reaching out to global audiences makes it reasonable for us as one of the powerhouse universities in Africa to use them in marketing our brand. Social media have tremendously contributed to our marketing communication activities, that is why and how the University of Cape Coast is increasingly coming on top of higher education rankings as one of the best universities in Africa, West Africa and Ghana. These platforms are not too difficult to operate which makes the marketing of our brand easier because our personnel do not require so much skill to communicate using them.

The implication of social media significance to the higher education marketing activities of the University of Cape Coast lies in its perceived usefulness of the platforms to influence the brand choice of future students, academic and towards the university brand, as well as their simple operation and cost-effectiveness in marketing the brands and offerings of the institution. The thrust of the technology appropriation model is that how users believe in the perceived usefulness and ease of use of particular technologies including social media could influence why and how they accept to use these new innovations to communicate (Davis, 1989; Davis et al., 1989; Divivedi et al., 2017).

Social Media Marketing Strategies in Promoting UCC Brand

The University of Cape Coast deployed various social media strategies to market its brand and offerings. The university use Facebook, Twitter, TikTok, Flickr, Instagram, YouTube and LinkedIn, among others, which are used strategically to undertake the branding, marketing and promotion activities of the institution. The University of Cape Coast has very active social media presence on Facebook with over 93,000 followers as compared to other platforms, which rationalizes its usage as an exemplar in this study. Refer to Table 8.1 in the text.

The University of Cape Coast uses different strategies for different marketing activities depending on the goals, objectives and outcome the university seeks to achieve on specific social media platforms. In attesting to this, respondent 1 said:

> Strategically, we have various accounts on different social media and improve our profiles on these platforms frequently to promote the brand of the University of Cape Coast as the best in Ghana and West Africa, and the fourth best in Africa. As a reputable higher education institution, we cannot rely on only one social media because we need to explore and blend all the available platforms to maximize their use in marketing our university's brand. As part of our social marketing strategy, we have created profiles on Facebook, Twitter, Instagram, Twitter, LinkedIn, and YouTube, among others to reach and promote our brand to wider audiences as possible to attract them to have a stake in our rapidly growing university in Ghana.

This response indicates that public universities in Ghana and Africa are following the global trends in higher education marketing where global powerhouse university brands are making deliberate efforts to harness the potentials, usefulness and ease-of-use of new technologies especially social media and Facebook to position and enhance their reputation (Times Higher Education, 2023). Elaborating further on the strategies, respondent 5 narrated:

> We are particular about which strategies to use at any given time. For example, at the University of Cape Coast, we use Facebook to advertise our programmes, events, and achievements, as well as Instagram to create awareness of our university brand and others like LinkedIn to drive traffic to our university website as and when necessary. As a way of checking whether

Table 8.1 Social Media Platforms of the University of Cape Coast and their Followers

Social Media Platforms	*Number of Followers*
Facebook	93,000
LinkedIn	91,000
Twitter (X)	17,900
Instagram	8,691
YouTube	1,270
Flickr	7

> the social media marketing strategies we deploy are getting the results, we assess the click-through; track the number of story views and cost-per-click, among others to determine the success of communicating and promoting our brand. Basically, as we see more comments, likes, calls and shares of messages from the university advertised on our Facebook page, it signals that the brand is persuading audiences to recommend information from the institution to others.

These assertions validate the claim that universities use digital and social media and other digital platforms including websites to drive traffic to showcase their content and information to attract attention and persuade audiences to choose their higher education brands (Times Higher Education, 2023). In addition to the reports above, the study found that the University of Cape Coast uses media analytics that enable it to gather information about who and where its followers are located, and how they engage and interact with the university's brand on social media platforms. This helps the University of Cape Coast to identify what is working and what is not working in its social marketing activities. In this regard, respondents concurred that they compared their brand communication and promotion activities to other local and international institutions to determine any gaps in what the University of Cape Coast does or provides to address them. For example, respondents 2 and 4 noted:

> From time to time we conduct competitive analysis and social listening to identify what other competing universities in Ghana and beyond are doing on social media platforms especially what other institutions are marketing and sharing about their brands, programmes and achievements, as well as what audiences are saying about them.

The strategies deployed by the University of Cape Coast make it possible for the institution to showcase its unique brand identity to audiences. This situates social media as strategic platforms that public universities could resort to in creating user-generated content that depicts the various elements of their brand identity to attract their target audiences to patronize their brands.

Nature of Social Media Marketing Documents on Facebook

The University of Cape Coast makes daily posts in different document formats: videos, audios, pictures and texts that attract thousands of reactions, views, shares, likes and comments from audiences, which could be turned into conversations and relationships. This gives credence to the findings of Times Higher Education (2023) which suggest that reactions, shares, likes and comments features to documents posted by universities on social media indicate engagements of audiences with the content. This gives reason for the University of Cape Coast to accept and use social media to market its unique selling proposition to attract and convert many of its large followers, friends and other stakeholder audiences on social media to the brand of the institution.

However, the use of these platforms particularly Facebook for interactive engagements and conversations was not evident, making the platform to limit its usefulness of social media marketing of the brand of the University of Cape Coast on the platform to public information and advertisements. The University of Cape Coast disseminates advertisements on Facebook to reach global audiences using various documents (banners, images, texts, videos, audio and flash) to market and promote its brand. For example, the video document posted by the university in relation to its Special Congregation to award honorary doctorate degrees on TVUCC on Facebook on 29 July 2023 had over 810 views, 48 likes, two comments and six shares. The over 76 picture documents posted by the university on its Facebook platform on 23 August 2023 attracted over 203 likes, three comments and ten shares. This is inconsistent with the postulations of Kapferer (2004, 2005) that individuals and organizations need to explore opportunities to converse and build strong relationships by addressing the expectations of individuals and stakeholder audiences to earn brand loyalty (Kapferer, 2004, 2005). Copy from sample Facebook posts:

1 *Video Document*
   SPECIAL CONGREGATION FOR THE AWARD OF HONORARY DOCTORATE DEGREES (Source:@UCC, 2023)
2 *Picture Document Posted by UCC on 23 August 2023 (Source: @Facebook)*
   A selection of the best photos from some of the list of key events that transpired at the University of Cape Coast (UCC) during the Second Semester of the2022/23 Academic Year, which officially came to a close on Friday, 18 August, 2023 (Source: @UCC, 2023)

This gives credence to the recommendation to institutions that want to develop global powerhouse university brands to use social media platforms to share research breakthrough and output, highlight their societal impact and promote their competitive status to position their institutions in the competitive higher education sector attract stakeholder audiences (Times Higher Education, 2023).

The study found that the University of Cape Coast has linked its online television channel (TVUCC) to its Facebook page, which provides video and audio contents about the university including programmes and events of the institution to audiences on the platform (University of Cape Coast, 2016). This validates the findings that higher education institutions could link and transform their social media platforms into applications to promote the unique selling proposition and offerings of their brands (Times Higher Education, 2023). As part of promoting the brand, the University of Cape Coast markets the various features of its identity including its physique such as infrastructure on social media through online tour of its campus and facilities, as well as pictures and videos of other elements to stakeholder audiences across the world. This is consistent with the postulation by Kapferer (2004, 2005) and Boateng (2015) that organizations including higher education institutions have to search for innovative ways to market their personality, culture, physique, reflection, relationship and self-image to uniquely position them to attract audiences in competitive environments. The impact of social media particularly Facebook on the brand identity of the University of Cape Coast could not be ignored because these platforms have contributed to the marketing communication, advertising and popularity of the institution. In that regard, Facebook has enabled the University of Cape Coast to uniquely present and make itself more visible digitally to attract many people. Highlighting this significance, respondents 3 said:

> With the use of Facebook communication, the number of admission applications to the university increase every year because the transformation of our brand and achievements could be witnessed all over social media, and we are able to attract and respond quickly to inquiries and issues challenging audiences, which could have prevented potential stakeholder audiences from developing interest in the University of Cape Coast. Despite the relatively cheaper cost regarding the use of Facebook, its impact has been tremendous.

Facebook usage in marketing, the platform allows us to get to many people globally with posts about the university and its programmes, which could not have been possible without these digital forms of communication. These assertions re-emphasize the significance of the presence of the university on social media, especially how Facebook provides affordability in marketing and advertising to attract many stakeholder audiences to universities in real time on the internet as compared to traditional media.

African-Centric Trends

The mere posting of content does not maximize the usefulness of Facebook in social media marketing, which implies that the University of Cape Coast has to combine both promotional and informative messages (posts) to achieve desired results. Public universities in Ghana particularly the University of Cape Coast have not given critical attention to the use of Facebook to advance engagements, conversations and relations for feedback to secure brand loyalty. Beside the creation of awareness through advertising on Facebook, the university could promote engagements and interactions with friends, followers and audiences to secure their mutually beneficial relationships in the form of feedback. However, the failure of the university to respond to comments and inquiries on its Facebook page prevents them from taking maximum of the interactive features of the platform to advance relationship marketing. The improvement of use, engagements, interactions and generation of leads from Facebook marketing and advertising require strategic insights and professional experience in social media communication to position the University of Cape Coast in the competitive higher education industry. As the University of Cape Coast matures in its social media usage, it requires enlightened policies and investment to improve their functionality and develop multi-platform approaches to social media marketing in promoting the brand identities of public universities to attract stakeholder audiences. This includes the adoption of interactive applications by the university, for example, artificial intelligence into the university's social media communication especially Facebook to provide feedback and address marketing, information and interactive needs of stakeholder audiences. The uniqueness of Facebook advertising at the University of Cape Coast does not only lie in the acceptance of the platform to attract global audiences, but the institution's ability to cease opportunities it provides to engage with stakeholder audiences as leading university brands in the Global North do.

Study Limitations and Future Research

The views elicited in this study did not include questions that sought to gather detailed perspectives of respondents regarding university engagement levels and impressions on Facebook. Therefore, further studies could focus on questions to elicit responses from interviewees regarding their perspectives on how universities are engaging, interacting and impressing audiences on social media. This study focused on the digital (Facebook) marketing of the University of Cape Coast; hence it cannot generalize findings to other institutions, as respondents in private and other higher education institutions were excluded from this research. Further research can be conducted on other social media aside Facebook and to include other universities, as well as audience perspectives for generalization.

Bibliography

Aaker, D., A. & Joachimsthaler, E. (2000), *Brand Leadership*. New York: Free Press.

American Marketing Association (2009). *Definitions*. Retrieved on 23 September 2023 from http://www.marketingpower.com/_layouts/Dictionary.aspx?dLetter=B.

Ameyaw, S. (2021). The impact of social media use on the academic performance of students of private institutions in Ghana: The Valley view university perspective. *International Journal of Technology and Management Research* 6(2), 106–115.

Anena, H. (2014). *Social media and freedom of expression in Uganda: The case of Facebook*. Unpublished Dissertation, Makarere University: Kampala.

Bala, M. & Verma, D. (2018). A critical review of digital marketing. *International Journal of Management, IT and Engineering* 8(10), 321–339.

Balmer, J., M., T. & Greyser, S., A (2006). Corporate marketing: integrating corporate identity, corporate branding, corporate communications, corporate image and corporate reputation. *European Journal of Marketing 40*, 730–741.

Boateng, A. B. (2015). Branding public universities through advertising: A study of two public universities in Ghana, *Journal of Developing Country Studies* 5(21), 43–55.

Boateng, A. B. (2021). Twitter as political communication platform in election campaigns in Ghana. *International Journal of Communication and Media Studies 11*(2), 25–36.

Boateng, A., B., (2019). Facebook usage in political communication in Ghana. The case of two political parties. Unpublished doctoral thesis. University of Kwazulu-Natal, South Africa.

Boateng, A. B., McCracken, D. P., & Lubombo, M. (2020). Intra-party election campaigns in Ghana: An analysis of Facebook use. In M. Ndlela & W. Mano (Eds.), *Social media and electoral democracy in Africa* (Volume 1, pp. 215–232). Cham: Palgrave Macmillan.

Boateng. A., B. (2022). Social media usage and digital rights restrictions in the Republic of Chad. In F. A. Kperogi (Ed.), *Digital dissidence and social media censorship in Africa* (1st edition). London: Routledge.

Bowen, G. A. (2009). Document analysis as a qualitative research method. *Qualitative Research Journal 9*(2), 27–40.

Boyd, D. & Ellison, N., B. (2007), Social networking sites: Definition, history, and scholarship, *Journal of Computer-Mediated Communication 13*(1), 210–230.

Braun, V., & Clarke, V. (2006). Using thematic analysis in psychology. *Qualitative Research in Psychology 3*(2), 77–101.

Brodie, R., J., Glynn, M., S. & Little, V. (2006), The service brand and service-dominant logic: missing fundamental premise or the need for stronger theory? *Journal of Marketing Theory 6*(3), 363–379.

Burgess, L., G. & Worthington, A., K. (2021). *Technology acceptance model in persuasion theory in action: An open educational resource.* Retrieved on 10th February 2024 from https://ua.pressbooks.pub/persuasiontheoryinaction/chapter/technology-acceptance-model/.

Carr, C., T. & Hayes, R. (2015), Social media: Defining, developing and divining. *Atlantic Journal of Communication 23*(1), 46–65.

Clark, M., Fine, M., & Scheuer, C. (2017). Relationship quality in higher education marketing: the role of social media engagement. *Journal of marketing for Higher Education 27*(1), 40–58.

Cole, M., S. & Bruch, H. (2006). Organisational identity strength, identification, and commitment and their relationship to turnover intention: Does organisational hierarchy matter? *Journal of Organisational Behaviour 27*, 585–605.

Constantinides, E., & Stagno, M. (2012). Higher education marketing: A study on the impact of social media on study selection and university choice. *The International Journal of Technology and Education Marketing 2*(1), 41–58.

Corbin, J., & Strauss, A. (2008). *Basic qualitative research: Techniques and procedures for developing grounded theory* (3rd ed.). Thousand Oaks, CA: Sage.

Cresswell, J. W. (2013). *Qualitative inquiry and research design. Choosing among five approaches*. California: Sage.

Davies, S. (2002). *Marketing in higher education: Matching promises and reality to expectations. Responding to student expectation*s, OECD Report, 103–114.

Davis, F. D. (1989). Perceived usefulness, perceived ease of use, and user acceptance of information technology. *MIS Quarterly 13*(3), 319–340.

Davis, F. D., Bagozzi, R. P., & Warshaw, P. R. (1989). User acceptance of computer technology: A comparison of theoretical models. *Management Science 35*(8), 982–1003.

De Chernatony, L. (2006). *From brand vision to evaluation*, Oxford, Butterworth: Heinemann.

De Chernatony, L. & Cottam, S. (2008). Interactions between organisational cultures and corporate brands. *Journal of Product & Brand Management 17*, 13–24.

Degenhard, J. (2023). Facebook users in Ghana 2018–2027. Retrieved on 22 June 2023 from htpps://statistica.com/forecast/1136461/facebook-users-in-Ghana/.

Dolphin, R. R. (2000). Is corporate communications a strategic function? *Management Decision 38*(2), 99–106.

Donkor, E. S., & Kyei, K. A. (2020). Contribution to higher education in Ghana: Improving student enrolment through application of the 7ps of marketing. *The International Journal of Business Management 8*(9), 1–9.

Dwivedi, Y., K., Rana, N. Nripendra, P., Jeyaraj, A., Clement, M. & Williams, M., D. (2019). Re-examining the unified theory of acceptance and use of technology (UTAUT): Towards a revised theoretical model, *Information Systems Frontiers 21*(3), 719–734.

Etikan, I., Musa, S. A., & Alkassim, R. S. (2016). Comparison of convenience sampling and purposive sampling. *American Journal of theoretical and Applied Statistics 5*(1), 1–4.
Forrest-Lawrence, P. (2019). Case study research. In Pranee Liampultong (Ed.), *Handbook of research methods in health social sciences* (pp. 317–331). Singapore: Springer.
Fosu, F. F., & Poku, K. (2014). Exploring the factors that influence students' choice of higher education in Ghana. *European Journal of Business and Management 6*(28), 209–220
Gerring, J. (2006). *Case study research: Principles and practices*. New York: Cambridge University Press.
Gyasi, R. S., Owusu-Ampomah, Y., & Kusi, B. (2017). Brand communication of higher education institutions in Ghana: An overview. *British Journal of Interdisciplinary Research 8*(1), 339–351.
Haaften, R. V. (2009). Brand identity prism. Retrieved from http://www.vanhaaften.Nl/index.php?option=com_content&view=article&id=77&catid=48&Itemid=53&lang=en.15.07.2012].
Halpern, D. & Gibbs, J. (2013). Social media as a catalyst for online deliberation? Exploring the affordances of Facebook and YouTube for political expression. *Computers in Human Behaviour 29*(3), 1159–1168.
Harsha, P. P. & Shah, H. (2011). Creating brand value of higher education institution. *International Journal of Management and Tourism 19*(2), 152–158.
Hastings, J. (2013). *Qualitative data analysis from start to finish*. Los Angeles, CA: Sage.
Hemsley-Brown, J. & Goonawardana, S. (2007). Brand harmonisation in the international higher education market. *Journal of Business Research 60*, 942–948.
Hemsley-Brown, J., & Oplatka, I. (2006). Universities in a competitive global marketplace: A systematic review of the literature on higher education marketing. *International Journal of Public Sector Management 19*(4), 316–338.
Inegbedion, H. E., Inegbedion, E., Asaleye, A., Jasamu, F. & Obadiaru, E. (2021). Use of social media in the marketing of agricultural products and farmers' turnover in South-South Nigeria. *F1000 Research 9*(1220), 1–19.
Jothi, P., Neelamalar, S. & Prasad, R. S. (2011). Analysis of social networking sites: a study on effective communication strategy in developing brand communication. *Journal of Media and Communication Studies 3*(7), 234–242.
Kamal, S. A., Shafiq, M., & Kakria, P. (2020). Investigating acceptance of telemedicine services through an extended technology acceptance model (TAM). *Technology in Society 6*, 101212.
Kapferer, J. N. (2004). *The new strategic brand management: Creating and sustaining brand equity long term*. London: Kogan Page.
Kapferer, J. N. (2005). *The new strategic brand management*. London: Kogan Page.
Kapferer, J. N. (2008). *The new strategic brand management* (4th Edition). London: Kogan Page.
Kapferer, J. N. (1986). *Beyond positioning: Retailer's identity*. Esornar summer proceedings. Brussels. 4-6 june, 167–76.
Kearney, M. W. (2013), *Political discussion on Facebook: An analysis of interpersonal goals and disagreement*, Unpublished Master's Thesis, University of Kansas, Lawrence.
Keller, K. L. (2008). *Strategic brand management: Building, measuring and managing brand equity* (3rd Edition). Upper Saddle River, NJ: Pearson Prentice Hall.
Kolan, B. J., & Dzandza, P. E. (2018). *Effect of social media on the academic performance of students in Ghanaian universities: A case study of the University of Ghana, Legon*.

Legris, P., Ingham, J., & Collerette, P. (2003). Why do people use information technology? A critical review of the technology acceptance model. *Information and Management 40*(3), 191–204.

Manu, B. D., Ying, F., Oduro, D., & Boateng, S. A. (2021). Student engagement and social media in tertiary education: The perception and experience from the Ghanaian public university. *Social Sciences & Humanities Open 3*(1), 1–12.

Mayfield, A. (2008). *What is social media? An eBook from iCrossing*. Retrieved on 9 April 2018 from www.icrossing.co.uk/.../What_is_Social_Media_iCrossing_ebook.pdf.

Min, S., So, K. K. F., & Jeong, M. (2019). Consumer adoption of the Uber mobile application: Insights from diffusion of innovation theory and technology acceptance model. *Journal of Travel and Tourism Marketing 36*(7), 770–783.

Nazeeer, J. (2017). Impact of social media advertisements on university students. *Arts and Social Sciences Journal 8*(4), 1–6.

Patsiotis, A., G. & Kapareliotis, I. (2016). Digital marketing trends and the curriculum. *Journal of Management and Financial Sciences 9*(23), 11–21.

Sasu, D. D. (2022). Number of social media users in Ghana 2017–2022. Retrieved on 22 June 2023 from www.statistica.com/statistics/1171445/number-of-social-media-users-in-Ghana/.

Scherer, R., Siddiq, F., & Tondeur, J. (2019). The technology acceptance model (TAM): A meta-analytic structural equation modeling approach to explaining teacher's adoption of digital technology in education. *Computers & Education 128*, 13–35.

Sukendro, S., Habibi, A., Khaeruddin, K., Indrayana, B., Syahruddin, S., Makadada, F. A., & Hakim, H. (2020). Using an extended technology model to understand students' use of e'learning during Covid-19: Indonesian sport science education context. *Heliyon 6*(11), e05410.

Wong, B. (2023). Top social media statistics and trends of 2023. Retrieved on 20 June 2023 from https://www.forbes.com/advisor/business/social-media-statistics/.

Wothington, A. K., Burke, E. E., Shirazi, T. N., & Leahy, C. (2020).US women's perceptions and acceptance of new reproductive health technologies. *Women's Health Reports 1*(1), 402–412.

9 Africa Rising

Assessing How African Online Influencers Are Influencing Consumer Buying Decisions – A Study of the Nigerian Telecommunications Industry Using Lagos State as a Case Study

Adeola Kayode and Christiana Alex-Ojei

Introduction

Consumer buying decisions are the ultimate choice consumers make about whether to buy a product or service. This is not an instant process and involves several steps and factors which can influence whether consumers have a favourable perception or disposition to buy and use the product (Abdullahi et al., 2020; Chand, S., 2019; Qazzafi, 2019). One of the fastest-growing techniques deployed for the promotion of products and services is to leverage the popularity and credibility of online influencers in the marketing and promotion of products and services (Brown & Hayes, 2008; IntelligentHQ, n.d.). This technique, called Influencer Marketing, is a strategy used in promoting products and/or services by organizations by leveraging the popularity, credibility, and reach of online influencers – people who are perceived as credible within certain areas of human endeavour (Abdullahi et al., 2020; Geyser, 2023; Harris et al., 2020).

This commonly used technique in advertising helps businesses launch a new product, change perception, reinforce a behaviour, build social proof, reinforce the positioning of an existing product, or reach new audience segments (Gupta & Mahajan, 2019; Boone, Menon & Rogers, 2001; Geyser, 2023; Harris et al., 2020). While online influencers are classified based on the size of their following, this study focused on the macro, micro, and nano influencers – people who grew into popularity and influence using social and digital media (Geyser, 2023) (Table 9.1).

This study considers their effect on consumer buying decisions especially within the African continent.

Africa, the Rise of Digital Media and Online Influencers

Africa presents a unique understanding of the impact of mobile and digital technology on a continent's population and commerce. A continent with a very culturally diverse population of 1.5 billion, 52 countries, and 75 languages and tribes, the nuances regarding perception, usage, and behaviour vary slightly with every region and location (Ochab, 2018; Okafor, 2023). Accounting for about 18% of

DOI: 10.4324/9781032689654-9

Table 9.1 Different Levels of Influencers Based on Size of Followers. Influencer Marketing Hub

Type of Influencer	*Followers*
Mega-influencer	> 1 million
Macro-influencer	Between 100,000 & 1 million
Micro-influencer	Between 1,000 & 100,000
Nano-influencer	< 1000

the world's population, Africa is the world's youngest continent with about 70% of its population under the age of 30 (Habti, 2022; United Nations, n.d.). Mobile penetration is very extensive as 24 of its 52 countries have more than 75% mobile phone ownership with 11 of them over 90% – that is, almost everyone has a mobile phone (Edjo, 2023). Seventy percent of the world's $1 trillion mobile money transactions are happening on the continent, making it the most advanced Mobile Money continent in the world (Onyango, 2022). Africa's diversity, its young population, mobile penetration, growth of fintech, and mobile money industry make the understanding of online engagement on consumer behaviour unique and important. As access to the internet continues to grow (Feydeau et al., 2022; Njanja, 2022), potential customers have continued to shift their source of information from traditional media to the new and emerging digital and social media platform where online influencers are creating content (Abdullahi et al., 2020; Ezenwafor et al., 2021). Some of these online influencers, especially recognized by YouTube across Africa, include SisiYemmie, Agatha Nkirote, Banele Ndaba, Calen Orem, Carissa Magunde, Eniola Olanrewaju, Gina Ehikodi Ojo, Joanne Wanja, Juliet Kane, Kate Wanjiku, Kelechi Anyanwu, Latifat Omowunmi Kilanu, Louis Ihuefo, Maryam 'Taooma' Apaokagi-Greene, Debo 'Macaroni' Adedayo, Matlala Mokgehle, Muzikayifani Sambo, and Seithati Letsipa (Okosi, 2022).

Though internet penetration is growing rapidly (Feydeau et al., 2022; Njanja, 2022; Onyango, 2022), Africa's rich nexus of language, countries, interests, and cultures and the need to ensure effectiveness make identifying and working with online influencers are difficult to define and determine (Talkwalker, 2022). For instance, to deepen the relationship between the European Union and Africa, the commission launched an Africa-EU Campaign-themed 'We See Africa' project. In Nigeria, the EU Delegation collaborated with female music maestro, Teniola Akpata (Teni) and online influencer, Eniola Adeoluwa alongside nine other micro-influencers ('heroes') for the campaign in Nigeria while balancing regional and gender differences. To succeed in the execution, this campaign ran simultaneously in the same format using different influencers in Cameroon, Congo, Tanzania, and Zimbabwe regions of Africa (European Union, 2022; Olatunji & Onyenucheya, 2022). According to Njathi (2023), while it is generally agreed that these influencers create value for businesses, there is still a limited consensus on how compensation and commerce are organized and quantified, especially in Africa where the culture and transactions are differentiated. To ensure the effectiveness of any online influencer project, Zipporah and Mberia (2014) proposed that a careful assessment of the brand, each influencer, and the target audience is very important for success. To assess the effect of online influencers on consumers, this study considered the telecommunications industry in Nigeria where the use of influencers is common and frequently deployed.

Nigeria and Its Telecommunications Industry

Nigeria is a strategic template to understanding the African market. The country is Africa's most populous country and ranks sixth globally. One in every two West Africans, one out of every four Africans, and one out of every five persons of African origin is a Nigerian. It represents about 20% of the total population of sub-Saharan Africa, and it represents about 10% of the whole black population in the world (Ogunro, 2023; The Conversation, 2022). Before its telecommunication industry was deregulated in 2000, Nigeria had only about 400,000 phone lines (Ojobo, 2023; Okocha, 2023; Paul & Kolawole, 2021) but now boasts of over 226.8 million phone lines (NCC, 2023; Ojetunde, 2023). It is regarded as Africa's largest ICT market and accounts for 82% of the continent's telecommunications subscribers but only 29% of its internet usage. The rapid growth and evolution in the telecommunications industry have been a major driver of other critical sectors of the Nigerian economy in the last twenty years (USITA, 2023). This resulted in a rapid increase in the number of subscribers, mobile phone, and smartphone ownership, increase in the number of value-added services with extensions into other areas like data, mobile money, media, and mobile advertising which already raked in over N70billion in 2021 alone (Anyalewechi, 2021). The Sub-Saharan Africa region is affirmed to be the world's fastest-growing region with a compound annual growth rate (CAGR) of 4.6% and a projected additional subscriber base of over 167 million in the next five years. Nigeria is projected to account for over 55% of this growth (Guardian Newspapers, 2022; USITA, 2023).

With such a huge opportunity for growth and profit, the rivalry between the different telecommunication companies in the country will see them exploring new ways to compete for loyalty, subscription, and patronage. The existing players include MTN Nigeria, currently holding the largest market share with 39.66%, followed by Airtel Nigeria, Globacom, and 9mobile (NCC, 2023; USITA, 2023). The Nigerian Communications Commission's (NCC's) regulatory policy of Mobile Number Portability (MNP) also increased competition by giving subscribers the power to switch and change providers at will (Adepetun, 2022; Udo, 2013). This means a competitive industry like this will mean telecommunication companies will look to evolve new and innovative ways to keep customers loyal and engaged (Kotler & Keller, 2009). This is where the use of influencers as a marketing strategy comes in.

To gain competitive advantage, mobile telecommunications companies have been exploring collaboration with influencers, who are perceived to be more relatable, credible, believable, and knowledgeable and are seen as an effective additional opportunity to their products and services (Johansen & Guldvik, 2017). When Elon Musk launched his internet satellite company, Starlink, into the

Nigerian market, it relied on internet savvy and youthful technology influencers like Fisayo Fosudo, Oscar Frank, Izzi Boye, and a few others to review and introduce the product to the Nigerian market. In their own unique style of creative presentation, they created video content to introduce the product, demonstrate the use of its internet satellite stability and efficiency, compared its speed to other existing players in the market, and ultimately promote Starlink as the better and faster internet service provider to its Nigerian target audience (Adeduyite, 2023; Mohammed, 2023). Similarly, when mobile telecommunication giant, MTN, launched its 5G internet service into the Nigerian market, it leveraged several influencers in educating and demonstrating the use of the product (MTN Nigeria, 2022). Airtel worked with an internet-savvy final-year undergraduate student, Lade, to sing its widely received advert jingle 'Airtel 444' (Olowoyo, 2020). As the intensity of rivalry continues to grow, influencer marketing is one of the ways they look to gain competitive advantage.

Statement of the Problem

Though influencer marketing is a rapidly growing industry with a market size of approximately $11billion in 2021 and projected to reach $30 billion by 2030 (Guardian Nigeria, 2023), businesses using influencers for marketing need to ensure it is cost-efficient and effective. As businesses explore opportunities by leveraging these kinds of influencers to affirm some form of differentiation, distinction, and loyalty for their own products, there needs to be clear evidence on the business metrics that this is a valuable strategy that will improve business outcomes.

While there have been several studies globally (Brown & Hayes, 2018; Johansen I., & Guldvik C., 2017; Taylor, 2020) that have opened the debate on the impact of the influencer's personality and credibility on consumers' intention to purchase a product, this has not been comprehensively and exhaustively done with the African market in mind (Abdullahi et al., Dec 2020; Ezenwafor et al., 2021). Johansen and Guldvik (2017) concluded in their study that influencer marketing has no direct effect on consumers' purchase intention, and therefore not a more efficient marketing strategy than regular online advertisement. Taylor (2020) affirmed the popularity of influencer marketing among business professionals but opined that many factors continue to limit the conviction that it is effective. Abdullahi et al. (Dec 2020) concluded that there is significant positive effect of an influencer's credibility, attractiveness, and product-fit on impulse purchasing of MTN customers within the Lagos metropolis. However, in their own independent study, Ezenwafor et al. (2021) found that attractiveness, trustworthiness, and influencer and product match-up have significant predictive effects on purchase intention while expertise had no significant effect.

This study seeks to investigate the relationship between an influencer and consumer's buying decisions using the Nigerian telecommunication industry as a case study. As digital channels become more varied and segmented, there is a question of how much focus should businesses and budgets allocate to influencers as a fulcrum that drives their growth ambitions.

Objectives of the Study

The major objective of this study is to investigate the relationship between online influencers and consumer purchase decision with a focus on the telecommunications industry in Nigeria. Specific objectives include:

i To assess the relationship between online influencer marketing and African consumers' buying decisions using the Nigerian telecommunications industry as a case study
ii To assess the influence of online influencers on consumer buying decisions within the Nigerian telecommunications industry.

Research Questions

i What is the relationship between online influencers and consumers' buying decisions within the Nigerian Telecommunications industry?
ii What is the level of influence of online influencers on consumers' buying decisions within the Nigerian Telecommunications industry?

Research Hypotheses

The following research hypothesis were tested.

i There is no significant relationship between Influencers and consumers buying decisions in the Nigerian telecommunications industry.
ii Influencers have no significant influence on consumer buying decisions within the Nigerian telecommunications industry.

Significance of the Study

The focus of this study is to gain more understanding of the relationship between influencers and consumer buying decisions. This is important because doing business and succeeding in Africa requires more than a cursory perception and a cut-and-paste approach (Intradev, 2022; Ventureburn, 2021). Firstly, this study would serve as a guide to existing and emerging business professionals who are seeking to implement influencer marketing as a strategy in African Markets. Secondly, this study will show the importance and impact that influencers can have on consumers' buying decisions, especially within the African context. The outcome of this research will serve as a platform for other research in this area to explore the opportunities, effectiveness, and approach of using influencer marketing in growing their businesses in Africa.

Scope of the Study

While this research is focused on the relationship between online influencers and potential customers on the Africa continent, this study focused on mobile telecommunications subscribers within Lagos State Nigeria in 2022. The study was conducted in February 2022 and focused on examining the level of influence of online influencers on consumer choice decisions.

Literature Review

Endorsement as a Marketing Technique

Endorsement has continued to be a powerful marketing technique that businesses use to drive awareness, recruit new users, and change consumer perception and behaviour in a way that ensures profitability and business growth. Endorsements can be in different types, explicit – person endorses the product), implicit – person uses the product), imperative – person impels the product, or co-presentational – merely appearing with the product (Capanzana et al., 2006; Nam-Hyun Um, 2013). Endorsements are effective in a way that ensures celebrities give expert opinions, become a spokesperson, or demonstrate usage of the product (Lukas & Seno, 2007).

Celebrity Endorsement and the Rise of Online Influencers

Though businesses have always used celebrities to build trust, brand equity, loyalty, and patronage (Cheah, Ting, Cham, & Memon, 2019; Nwachukwu, 2019; Roll, 2018), the rise of social media, mobile, and digital technologies has given rise to online influencers as a new power block (Thurairatnam, 2021). Influencers are a new category of opinion shapers, 'microcelebrities' who leverage the power of the internet and the content they shape perception and behaviour (Evans et al., 2017). By concept and definition, celebrities and influencers are close but are not the same (Ekşioğlu, 2021). While celebrities are known for being popular outside the digital space, social media is integral to the popularity and reputation of influencers (Dhanesh & Duthler, 2019; Schouten et al., 2021; Tafesse & Wood, 2021). Online influencers are also perceived to be closer to the audience and hence perceived as more credible (Lou & Yuan, 2019; Sokolova & Kefi, 2019). They do these by driving engagement (Chmait et al., 2020, Hughes et al., 2019), making recommendations (Jiménez-Castillo & Sánchez-Fernández, 2019), and helping shape the awareness, perception, and attitude toward the brand (Abdullahi et al., 2020; Jin & Muqaddam, 2019; Lou & Yuan, 2019).

Consumer Decision Models

Armstrong., Kotler & Da Silva Buying Decision Model. (2006)

According to Armstrong et al (2006), the consumer buying decision process is a series of stages through which a consumer undergoes before finally making a purchase for the product they are interested in. This series of steps include Need Recognition, Information Search Alternatives Evaluation, Choice of Purchase, and Post Purchase Evaluation and Behaviour (Figure 9.1).

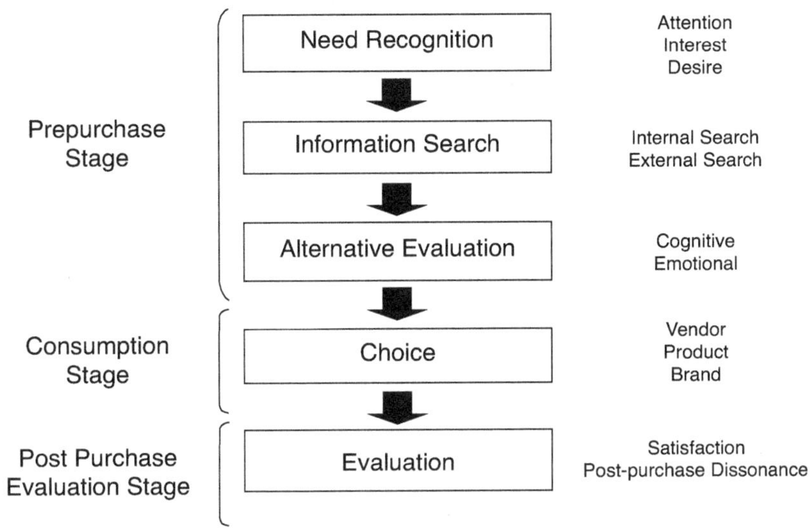

Figure 9.1 Armstrong et al's Buying Decision Model (2006)

Consider those businesses that use celebrities or influencers leverage the opportunity of giving the product or service visibility and to get the target audience to consider it by acting as a major 'billboard'. Source credibility is a phrase commonly used to explain that the credibility of the source or communicator will affect the way the audience receives the message being conveyed (Ohanian, 1990). This acceptance or rejection of the message depends on three factors of the online influencer – his degree of expertise, attractiveness, and trustworthiness (Hovland, Janis & Kelley, 1953; Hovland &Weiss, 1951; Ohanian, 1991).

Shimp's TEARS Model (2007)

The TEARS model refers to Trustworthiness, Expertise, Attractiveness, Respect, and Similarity as the key variable components of a Celebrity personality that help determine the effectiveness of a celebrity endorsement. This attribute affirms that consumers are more likely to respond positively if the celebrity endorser shares common features with them (Shimp, 2007).

In addition to the body of work, Apejoye (2013) researched on the influence of celebrity-endorsed advertisement on students' purchase intent. While it affirmed that celebrity-endorsed advert has a significant influence on students' purchase intention, it also proposed that celebrity-endorsed adverts need to be given adequate thought and preparation in a way that achieves the desired results. In research conducted by Ahmed, Ahuja, Paryani and Seedani (2015), it was shown that attributes exhibited by an online influencer and a positive relationship and perception of a celebrity have a significant influence on consumer choice decisions.

Conceptual Model

As shown in Figure 9.2, the conceptual framework derives its basis from the Celebrity Endorsement TEARS model, which is a framework that establishes the key independence variable of the celebrity as factors that affect consumer choice decision for products and brands within the telecommunications industry (Figure 9.3).

Methodology

Research Design

The examination of the relationship between online influencers and consumer buying decision took a descriptive approach which will further help to better understand and describe the relationship between two variables.

The design method deployed for this study is the survey design (Glasow, 2005; Groves et al., 2011). This allowed an effective way to explore and describe the profile and personality of online influencers in relation to consumer buying decisions of products and services within the telecommunication products in the industry. The research was also quantitative (Kleining & Witt, 2001) as it seeks to draw deductive conclusions based on analysis of the statistical data collated from the field.

Population of the Study

The population of study consists of all residents living and working in Lagos State, who are subscribed to a telecommunications network. While Nigeria represents

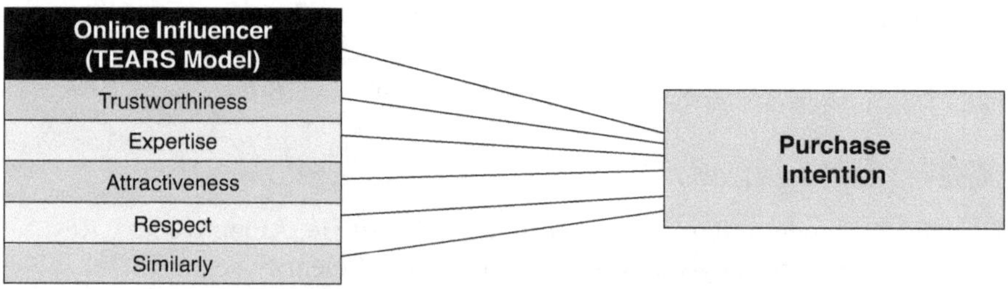

Figure 9.2 Shimp TEARS Model. Shimp, 1997

Figure 9.3 Conceptual model. (The researcher)

a balanced view of Africa in terms of population, diversity, and socioeconomic distribution, Lagos State is its commercial capital of Nigeria. Lagos State is a major economic distribution hub of the West African market and a fair representative balance in the age distribution, gender, tribe, mobile penetration rate, telecom subscriber distribution, and socioeconomic class (SEC). The total population of telecommunication subscribers in Lagos State as at this year (2022) is about 26,500,000 (Premium Times, 2023).

Sample Size

The sample size was determined using Taro Yamane's technique (Yamane, 1973). This technique is used to estimate the suitable sample size from a particular population using a given confidence level and tolerance margin for errors. It is determined using the formula below.

$$n = N \Big/ \left[1 + N(e)^2\right]$$

Where:

n = sample size required
N = total number of people in the population
e = margin of error

For the overall population of twenty-six million, five hundred thousand (26,500,000) telecommunication subscribers in Lagos and being desirous of a result with 95% confidence level and an error margin of 5%.

$$n = \frac{N}{\left[1 + N(e)^2\right]} = \frac{26,500,000}{1 + 26,500,000\left(0.05\right)^2} = \frac{26,500,000}{66,251} = 399.994$$

From the above calculation, n = 399.994 approximately 400 respondents.

Sampling Technique

The sampling was done through convenience sampling technique (Etikan et al., 2016; Obilor, 2023). The convenience of reaching and selecting respondents by chance, willingness to participate, and ensuring each member of the population has an equal chance of being included in the sample made this an efficient way to go.

Data Collection Method

Research instrument is the tool used to collect data from the respondents. Data was collected using a structured, closed-ended questionnaire (Stantcheva, 2023). The data was administered through closed-ended structured questionnaires which were created on Google Forms and administered through Computer-Assisted Personal Interviews, CAPI (Baker, 1992; Das & Emery, 2023). Respondents were also willing to participate in the field work resulting in a total number of 400 filled questionnaires being garnered, resulting in a 100% response rate.

Validity and Reliability of Instrument

The content and face validity were conducted and validated to ensure that the thinking is thorough and clearly highlights the variables and concept being measured (Asika, 2009). The reliability of the questionnaire was tested using a pilot questionnaire administration with 20 sample respondents. Data obtained from the pilot was tested to validate the consistency of the research instrument.

Data Analysis Method

The collated responses from the respondents were analysed using the standard statistical tool – Standard Package for Social Sciences (SPSS). The hypothesis was tested using Pearson correlation and regression analysis (Silverman et al., 2003). The resulting data was presented in the forms of tables and graphs in a way that highlights the frequency, mean, and standard deviation. The hypotheses and relationship between the variables were tested using correlation and regression analysis.

Data Analysis

Presentation and Analysis of Socio-Demographic Data

As shown in Table 9.2, the study revealed that a majority (49.6%) of the respondents are between the ages of 16 and 25 years old, with 57.0% of them being female. This showed that a larger percentage of the respondents were youthful and female. This implies the findings of this survey were taken from a largely youthful audience who are conversant with the telecommunication industry, have access to online influencers in a way that ensures they are more disposed to share their own experiences. Table 9.2 also showed that about half (49.5%) of the respondents earn below ₦50,000. About 107 respondents (26.9%) of the respondents earn between ₦50,000 and ₦100,000 every month. Only five (1.3%) of the respondents earn above ₦250,000 monthly. However, this implies the study focused on people with limited income and therefore the impact of online influencers on their buying behaviour was tested. Table 9.2 also revealed that over half of the respondents (50.6%) considered secondary education as their highest qualification. About 84 respondents (21.1%) had OND/NCE. Forty-six of the respondents (11.5%) had a BSc/Higher National Diploma while about 67 (16.8%) of the respondents have a master's degree.

Table 9.2 Socio–Demographic Characteristics of Respondents

Variable	*Frequency (N=400)*	*Percentage (%)*
Age (in years)		
<16	9	2.3
16–25	198	49.6
26–35	114	28.6
36–45	49	12.3
46+	29	7.3
Gender		
Male	172	43.0
Female	228	57.0
Income		
Below ₦50,000	197	49.5
₦50,001– ₦100,000	107	26.9
₦100,001– ₦150,000	74	18.6
₦150,001– ₦250,000	15	3.8
Above ₦250,000	5	1.3
Education		
*SSCE	202	50.6
**OND/ ***NCE	84	21.1
****BSc/*****HND	46	11.5
Master's Degree & above	67	16.8

Key: *SSCE – Senior Secondary Certificate Examination, **OND – Ordinary National Diploma, ***NCE – National Certificate in Education, ****BSc – Bachelor of Science, *****HND – Higher National Diploma

Presentation and Analysis of Screening Questions and Responses

As shown in Table 9.3, it revealed that most of the respondents (45.8%) use only one mobile network provider, while about 37.8% use two mobile networks. 65 respondents representing about 16.3% say they use three mobile networks while only one of the respondents use four mobile networks.

Table 9.3 also revealed that 81.3% of the respondents will prefer marketing communication messages that are endorsed by an online influencer, while 18.7% said they will prefer them without celebrities. 65.4% of them say they often see a product endorsed by an influencer while 34.3% said they often buy these products. 24.7% say they occasionally see products endorsed by an online influencer while 39.8% of them say they occasionally buy products endorsed by an online influencer. However, only 3.8% of the target audience say they have never seen a product endorsed by an online influencer. Table 9.3 also revealed 73.6% of the respondents affirmed that online influencer helps them remember a brand to buy though 4.8% of the respondents say an online influencer has never helped them remember a brand they intend to buy.

Table 9.4 revealed that the majority of the respondents (53% & 49.5%) agreed that MTN uses online influencers the most and has been the most successful at using it.

Table 9.3 Respondent's Disposition to Advertisements and Online Influencers

Variable	*Frequency (N=400)*	*Percentage (%)*
Number of mobile networks used		
1	183	45.8
2	151	37.8
3	65	16.3
4	1	0.3
Types of marketing communication preferred		
Influencer endorsed	321	81.3
Not-influencer endorsed	74	18.7
Ever bought a product endorsed by an influencer?		
Yes	326	83.8
No	63	16.2
How often do you see a product endorsed by an influencer?		
Often	256	65.4
Occasionally	*98*	*24.7*
Rarely	28	7.1
Never	15	3.8
How often do you buy a product endorsed by an influencer?		
Often	136	34.3
Occasionally	158	39.8
Rarely	77	19.4
Never	26	6.5
Does an influencer help you remember a brand to buy?		
Yes	293	73.6
No	38	9.5
Sometimes	48	12.1
Never	19	4.8

Table 9.4 Online Influencers and Consumer Buying Intent in the Telecommunications Industry

Variable	*Frequency (N=400)*	*Percentage (%)*
Which Network uses Online Influencers most?		
MTN	212	53.0
Glo	93	23.3
Airtel	80	19.2
9 Mobile	14	3.5
Which of the mobile networks do you think has been the most successful in positioning their brand with Online Influencers		
MTN	198	49.5
Glo	96	24.0
Airtel	93	23.3
9 Mobile	13	3.2
How likely are you to switch telecommunication provider because of an influencer?		
Very likely	*143*	*36.1*
Likely	25	6.3
Not sure	19	4.8
Very unlikely	73	18.4
Not likely	136	34.3

Presentation and Analysis of the Respondents' Responses to Online Influencer Attributes

Table 9.4 revealed that 56.3% of the respondent strongly agreed that it is important for the online influencer to be trustworthy, believable, and dependable, 48% agreed that it is important for the online influencer to be an expert in an area relating to the product, 43% also agreed that the physical attractiveness of an influencer is an important factor when buying a product, about 45% of the respondents also strongly agreed that it is important for them to respect and admire the online influencer for them to buy and use the product, and 40% strongly agreed that it is important for the online influencer to match and represent someone like them in age, gender, and race, while only about 5% disagreed that it is important for the online influencer to be relevant with the products that they endorse (Table 9.5).

Presentation and Analysis of the Respondents on Consumer Buying Decision

As shown in Table 9.6, the study revealed that about 48% of the respondents strongly agreed and an additional 34.4% agreed that an online influencer is important for them to notice or be aware of a product. Only 3.1% of the respondents strongly disagreed with this. About 43% agreed and an additional 38.1% strongly agreed that an online influencer is important for them to seek more information about a product or service. Only 3.6% of the respondents strongly disagree with this.

Table 9.6 also shows that about 41% strongly agreed and an additional 38.3% agreed that online influencers are important for them to consider buying a product. However, only 4.3% strongly disagreed with this. 41% agreed and an additional 38.8% strongly agreed that the kind of online influencer is ultimately the most important factor in helping them decide whether to buy a product. Only about 4.8% disagreed with that.

About 40% of the respondents agreed, and an additional 36.4% strongly agreed that negative news or publicity around an online influencer will affect whether they should buy a product. Only about 6% of the respondents disagreed with this.

Table 9.5 Online Influencer Attribute Scale

CPA Tool	*Min*	*Max*	*Mean*	*Std. D*
It is important for the online influencer to be trustworthy, believable, and dependable.	1	5	4.35	.979
It is important for the online influencer to be an expert in an area relating to the product.	1	5	4.14	.995
The physical attractiveness of an online influencer is an important factor when buying a product.	1	5	4.12	1.070
It is important for me to respect and admire the online influencer for me to buy and use the product.	1	5	4.12	1.104
It is important for the online influencer to match and represent someone like me in age, gender, and race.	1	5	4.11	1.095
It is important for the online influencer to be relevant with the products that they endorse.	1	5	4.21	1.022

Table 9.6 Consumer Buying Decision Attribute Scale

Descriptive Statistics				
Consumer Choice Decision	*Min*	*Max*	*Mean*	*Std. D*
An online influencer is important for me to notice or be aware of a product.	1	5	4.12	1.111
An online influencer is important for me to seek for more information about a product or service.	1	5	4.02	1.092
An online influencer is important for me to be consider buying a product.	1	5	4.01	1.143
The kind of online influencer is ultimately the most important factor in helping me decide whether to buy a product.	1	5	3.99	1.131
Negative news or publicity around an online influencer will affect whether I should buy a product.	1	5	3.90	1.185
My dislike for an online influencer will affect whether I buy a product.	1	5	3.94	1.210

41% of the respondents strongly agreed, and an additional 35.1% agreed that their dislike for an online influencer will affect whether they buy a product. Only about 6.5% disagreed with this.

Hypotheses Testing

Hypothesis 1

There is no significant relationship between online influencer and consumer buying intent in the Nigerian telecommunications industry.

Table 9.7 reveals the relationship between online influencer attributes and consumer choices of products within the telecommunications industry. With a correlation coefficient of.872, it was revealed that the personality attributes of an online Influencer influences consumer choices on products in the communication industry.

Hypothesis 2

Online influencers have no significant influence on consumer buying decision within the Nigerian telecommunications industry.

To assess the influence of online influencers on consumer buying decision, a regression analysis was conducted (Table 9.8).

The correlation coefficient for online influencer attributes and customer buying decision. Online influencer is 0.923, with an R-squared of 0.852 and Standard error estimate of 2.17437. Making the relationship between these 2 variables a positively strong relationship (Table 9.9 and 9.10).

Table 9.7 Correlation Matrix of online Influencer and Consumer Buying Decision

Variables	*Online Influencer*	*Consumer Buying Decision*
Online Influencer	-	.872
Consumer Buying Decision	.872	-

Table 9.8 Model Summary

Model	*R*	*R Square*	*Adjusted R Square*	*Std. Error of the Estimate*
1	.923[a]	.852	.852	2.17437

[a] Predictors: (Constant), CBDecisionOnline
[b] Dependent Variable: OI Atttributes

Table 9.9 ANOVA[a]

Model		*Sum of Squares*	*df*	*Mean Square*	*F*	*Sig.*
1	Regression	10368.741	1	10368.741	2193.112	.000b
	Residual	1796.589	380	4.728		
	Total	12165.330	381			

[a] Dependent Variable: OI Atttributes
[b] Predictors: (Constant), CB Decision Online

Table 9.10 Coefficients[a]

		Unstandardized Coefficients		*Standardized Coefficients*		
Model		*B*	*Std. Error*	*Beta*	*t*	*Sig.*
1	(Constant)	3.093	.480		6.443	.000
	CBDecisionOnline	.449	.010	.923	46.831	.000

[a] Dependent Variable: OIAtttributes

The regression analysis above revealed the relationship between online influencers and consumer buying decision in within the telecommunications industry. With a beta coefficient of 0.449, it was revealed that the endorsement of a product by online influencers influences consumer buying decisions in the communication industry, this relationship is highly statistically significant with p-values <0.001.

Table 9.11 revealed the residual statistics for the variables. The mean predicted value is 8.4823, and the Standard residual is −2.907. The standard predicted value has an overall average of -3.158, making the model fit a good one (Figure 9.4).

The correlation coefficient for the relationship between online influencer and consumer buying decision in the telecommunications industry is 0.923. This means

Table 9.11 Residual Statistics[a]

	Minimum	*Maximum*	*Mean*	*Std. Deviation*	*N*
Predicted value	8.4823	30.0409	24.9581	5.21676	382
Residual	–6.32110	14.82286	.00000	2.17151	382
Std. Predicted value	–3.158	.974	.000	1.000	382
Std. Residual	–2.907	6.817	.000	.999	382

[a] Dependent Variable: OIAtttributes

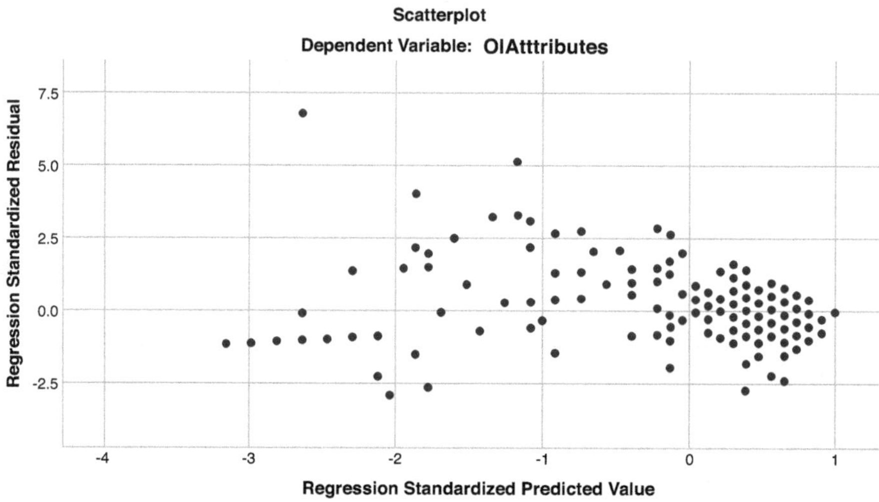

Figure 9.4 The relationship between online influencers and consumer buying decision in the telecommunications industry. (The researcher)

that the association between online influencers and consumers choice is highly correlated. If the online influencer's behaviour is good, consumers will like/buy the product.

Findings, Implications, and Imperatives for Brands in Africa

The study affirmed the positive effect of influencer marketing on consumer buying intent. This finding, however, contradicts an earlier report by Johansen and Guldvik (2017) who concluded that influencer marketing is not a more efficient strategy than regular online advertisement. This has, however, been contradicted by Ezenwafor et al. (2021) who affirmed the outcome of this research by confirming that attractiveness, trustworthiness, and influencer and product match-up have a significant predictive effect on purchase intention but concluded that expertise has no significant effect on purchase intention. Abdullahi et al. (2020) in a similar study in the telecommunications space also affirmed that social influencers credibility has a significant effect on the impulse buying behaviour of MTN subscribers in

Lagos. It also affirmed that perception of credibility can affect consumers' beliefs, opinions, attitudes, and behaviours with capacity to be more persuasive and capable of driving consumer purchase intention and loyalty.

While these studies affirm the significant effect of online influencers, it also establishes the need for proper evaluation in the selection of an online influencer if it is going to be effective.

Trends Shaping Influencer Marketing in Africa

In context, there are, however, trends that make online influencer marketing a bit nuanced from implementing elsewhere.

- i Adapting for culture, region, and interests: Identifying and working with online influencers for Africa is not usually a one-size-fits-all approach. Selection and implementation usually lead to having more than one to cater for the diversity of religions, languages, locations, and interests.
- ii The rise of more influencer marketing and e-commerce platforms: As online influencer grows in usage and popularity, it means more and more influencer marketing and ecommerce startups like Selar, Peppa, Vzy, VendorStack, Flutterwave Store, Twvia, Aifluence will continue to be launched. These kinds of apps help bring effectiveness and efficiency in the selection, management, and collaboration with influencers.
- iii More jobs for the young continent: In the last three years, Microsoft, Meta, and Google have made significant investments into internet access for Africans (Clark, 2022), which is one of the most important aspects of growing strong and impactful online influencers.

Summary of Findings, Conclusion, and Recommendations

Summary of Findings

- i This means that the association between online influencers and consumers' buying decisions is highly correlated ($r = 0.876, p < 0.05$). If the online influencer's behaviour is good, consumers will like/buy the product. Therefore, it is affirmed that online influencer endorsement is significantly related to consumers' buying decisions among telecommunication subscribers.
- ii Online influencers significantly predicted consumers' buying decision ($r = 0.760$, $p < 0.005$)

Conclusion

This study investigated the link between online influencer endorsement and consumer buying decision with subscribers within the Nigerian Telecommunications business. After extensive fieldwork and the subsequent analysis of the data obtained, the study affirmed the significant influence of online influencers on consumer buying decisions. It also remains a faster way to connect with consumers and to leverage an influencer's credibility, reach, and familiarity to increase consumer adoption of products and services.

In conclusion, this study affirms that using an online influencer to endorse a product can have a significant impact on influencing consumer choice decision on which network to subscribe to depending on how they perceive the online influencers that endorse them. A company using highly rated online influencer is more likely to influence a consumer choice decision than the one that does not use any. With this technique been used across several industries across industries in the country, business managers and marketing professional will continue to see this as a worthy investment to reach their desired target groups in a meaningful way.

Recommendations

Based on the findings and conclusion of this study, the following recommendations need to be considered to help the Nigerian telecommunication industry as well as the management of the network providers in reducing ineffective and inefficient results gotten from the use of influencer marketing as a strategy.

- i In as much influencer marketing has an impact on customer buying decision, it cannot make up for a poor product. Businesses need to deliver on consumer expectation and product promise for any marketing effort to be long-lasting and effective.
- ii Quality and relevance of the online influencer to the product category and industry needs to be examined as well. This will help the effectiveness and strength of impact of the influencer.
- iii Influencer marketing needs to be in alignment with the overall business strategy and brand positioning and other marketing elements.

Limitation of the Study and Suggestion for Further Research

The study focused on only telecommunication subscribers in Lagos State as a microcosm of Africa. While Lagos represents a proportionate and diverse population of Africans, it is possible that the response will be different in other states and countries in Africa. The study was also limited to online influencers and brands within the telecommunications industry in Nigeria, meaning responses may differ based on the industry. The study of the impact of online influencers is not exhaustive one. Further studies can go into assessing the strength of each influencer in relation to specific regions, industries, and from one influencer to another.

Bibliography

Abdullahi, H., Adedeji, I., & Otori, Y. A. (2020). Social media influencer and customer impulse buying behavior: A study of MTN Nigeria. *Lapai International Journal of Administration (LIJAD)*, December 2020.

Adeduyite, Okiki. (2023). *Elon Musk's Starlink Partners Jumia to Expand Services in Africa*. https://punchng.com/elon-musks-starlink-partners-jumia-to-expand-services-in-africa/
Adepetun, A. (2022). Nigerians shun number porting, activate new SIMs. *The Guardian*. https://guardian.ng/technology/nigerians-shun-number-porting-activate-new-sims/
Ahmed, R., Seedani, S., Ahuja, M., & Paryani, S. (2015). Impact of celebrity endorsement on consumer buying behavior. Available at SSRN 2666148.
Alvarez-Monzoncillo, J. M. (2023). *The Dynamics of Influencer Marketing: A Multidisciplinary Approach* (p. 220). Taylor & Francis.
Apejoye, A. (2013). Influence of celebrity endorsement of advertisement on students' purchase intention. *Journal of Mass Communication & Journalism*, 3(03), 2–7.
Armstrong, G., Kotler, P., & Da Silva, G. (2006). *Marketing: An Introduction: An Asian Perspective*. Pearson/Prentice Hall.
Asika, L. K. (2009). *Essentials of Research Methodology*. Spring Publishers.
Baker, R. P. (1992). New technology in survey research: Computer-assisted personal interviewing (CAPI). *Social Science Computer Review*, 10(2), 145–157.
Boone, L. E., Menon, K., & Rogers, H. P. (2001). Celebrity Advertising: An assessment of its relative effectiveness. In *Proceedings of the Society for Marketing Advances Conference*, New Orleans, Louisiana. Retrieved from http://citeseerx. ist. psu. edu/viewdoc/download.
Brown, D., & Hayes, N. (2008). *Influencer Marketing: Who Really Influences Your Customers?* Elsevier Publishing.
Capanzana, D. T., De Guzman, M. P., & Mendis, K. C. (2006). *Sleeper Effect: Modes of Endorsement and Sources of Message as Determinants of Purchase Intent*. Retrieved from https://animorepository.dlsu.edu.ph/etd_bachelors/7267
Chand, S. (2019). *Consumer Behavior: Meaning/Definition and Nature of Consumer Behavior*. http://www.yourarticlelibrary.com/marketing/market-segmentation/consumerbehaviour-meaningdefinition-and-nature-of-consumer-behaviour/32301
Cheah, J. H., Ting, H., Cham, T. H., & Memon, M. A. (2019). The effect of selfie promotion and celebrity endorsed advertisement on decision-making processes: A model comparison. *Internet Research*, 29(3), 552–577.
Chidinma Anyalewechi. (2021). MTN mobile lending, VAS rakes in N70 billion in 2021. *Nairametrics*. https://nairametrics.com/2022/01/31/mtn-mobile-lending-vas-rakes-in-n70-billion-in-2021/
Chinedu Okafor. (2023). *Top 10 African Countries with the Largest Population Mid-Way into 2023*. https://africa.businessinsider.com/local/lifestyle/top-10-african-countries-with-the-largest-population-mid-way-into-2023/pzy8td5
Chmait, N., Westerbeek, H., Eime, R., Robertson, S., Sellitto, C., & Reid, M. (2020). Tennis influencers: The player effect on social media engagement and demand for tournament attendance. *Telematics and Informatics*, 50, 101381.
Clark, R. (2022). *Google, Meta Cables Will Be 'Game-Changers' for Africa*. https://www.lightreading.com/cable-technology/google-meta-cables-will-be-game-changers-for-africa
Das, M., & Emery, T. (2023). Digital technologies and the future of social surveys. *Research Handbook for Digital Sociology*. Edgar Publishing, Vol 1. P. 87–100.
De Feydeau, A., Menski, M., & Perry, S. (2022). *Africa's Digital Infrastructure Transformation: Affordable, Universal Digital Access Is Key to Africa's Growth and Development*. https://www.whitecase.com/insight-our-thinking/africas-digital-infrastructure-transformation
Dhanesh, G. S., & Duthler, G. (2019). Relationship management through social media influencers: Effects of followers' awareness of paid endorsement. *Public Relations Review*, 45(3), 101765.

Edjo, Muriel. (2023). Africa: Five countries have near 100% mobile phone ownership (survey). *ITC & Telecom News*. https://www.ecofinagency.com/telecom/1601-44176-africa-five-countries-have-near-100-mobile-phone-ownership-survey

Emmanuel Paul, E., & Kolawole, O. (2021). Inside 2 decades of mobile telecommunications in Nigeria. *Techpoint Africa*. https://techpoint.africa/2021/04/27/20-years-mobile-telecommunications-nigeria/

Etikan, I., Musa, S. A., & Alkassim, R. S. (2016). Comparison of convenience sampling and purposive sampling. *American Journal of Theoretical and Applied Statistics*, 5(1), 1–4.

Evans, N. J., Phua, J., Lim, J., & Jun, H. (2017). Disclosing Instagram influencer advertising: The effects of disclosure language on advertising recognition, attitudes, and behavioral intent. *Journal of Interactive Advertising*, 17(2), 138–149.

Eyo, Ekeno, Soyemi, Khadeejat, & Uzo, Uchenna. (2022). Doing influencer marketing right in Africa. *The Afritail Blog*. https://afritail.com/doing-influencer-marketing-right-in-africa/

Ezenwafor, E. C., Olise, C. M., & Ebizie, P. I. (2021). Social Media Influencers and Purchase Intention amongst Social Media Users in developing African economy. *Quest Journal of Management and Social Sciences*, 3(2), 217–228.

Glasow, P. A. (2005). *Fundamentals of Survey Research Methodology*. Retrieved January, 18, 2013.

Groves, R. M., Fowler Jr, F. J., Couper, M. P., Lepkowski, J. M., Singer, E., & Tourangeau, R. (2011). *Survey Methodology*. John Wiley & Sons.

Gupta, S., & Mahajan, R. (2019). Role of micro-influencers in affecting behavioural intentions. *International Journal of Recent Technology and Engineering*, 8(45), 189–192.

Harris, A., Karamustafic, S., Palladina, S., Perloff, R., & Stockmaster, T. (2020). Social media influencers: Who they are and how they influence. *Student Scholarship*. https://engagedscholarship.csuohio.edu/stu_pub/1

Hicham El Habti. (2022). *Why Africa's Youth Hold the Key to its Development Potential*.https://www.weforum.org/agenda/2022/09/why-africa-youth-key-development-potential/

Hovland, C. I., Janis, I. L., & Kelley, H. H. (1953). Communication and persuasion. Yale University Press.

Hovland, C. I., & Weiss, W. (1951). The influence of source credibility on communication effectiveness. *Public Opinion Quarterly*, 15(4), 635–650.

Hughes, C., Swaminathan, V., & Brooks, G. (2019). Driving brand engagement through online social influencers: An empirical investigation of sponsored blogging campaigns. *Journal of Marketing*, 83(5), 78–96.

Iheanyi Nwachukwu. (2021). *Lagos Tops Nigeria's Investment Destination with $8.304bn Capital Inflow*. https://businessday.ng/exclusives/article/lagos-tops-nigerias-investment-destination-with-8-304bn-capital-inflow/

Intradevadmin. (2022). *Want to Expand Your Business in Africa? Toss the Cut-and-Paste Strategy*. https://intradevafrica.com/want-to-expand-your-business-in-africa-toss-the-cut-and-paste-strategy/

Jiménez-Castillo, D., & Sánchez-Fernández, R. (2019). The role of digital influencers in brand recommendation: Examining their impact on engagement, expected value and purchase intention. *International Journal of Information Management*, 49, 366–376.

Jin, S. V., & Muqaddam, A. (2019). Product placement 2.0: "Do brands need influencers, or do influencers need brands?" *Journal of Brand Management*, 26, 522–537.

Johansen, I., & Guldvik, C. (2017). Influencer marketing and purchase intentions: How does influencer marketing affect purchase intentions? *Norwegian School of Economics*. https://openaccess.nhh.no/nhh-xmlui/bitstream/handle/11250/2453218/masterthesis.PDF?sequence=1

Kleining, G., & Witt, H. (2001, February). Discovery as basic methodology of qualitative and quantitative research. Qualitative and Quantitative Research: Conjunctions and Divergences (Vol. 2, No. 1). *Forum Qualitative Social Forum.* https://www.qualitative-research.net/index.php/fqs/article/view/977

Kotler, P., Keller, K. L., Ang, S. H., Tan, C. T., & Leong, S. M. (2018). *Marketing Management: An Asian Perspective*. London: Pearson.

Lou, C., & Yuan, S. (2019). Influencer marketing: How message value and credibility affect consumer trust of branded content on social media. *Journal of Interactive Advertising*, 19(1), 58–73.

Marketing, R. (2019). *Influencer Marketing Global Survey Consumers*. Rakuten Marketing, San Mateo.

Mohammed, A. (2023). Tech influencers review Starlink capacity, price in Nigeria. *Marketing Edge*. https://marketingedge.com.ng/tech-influencers-review-starlink-capacity-price-in-nigeria/

MTN Nigeria. (2022). The wonder of 5G is coming! Ready to experience lightning-fast internet? *Facebook*. https://www.facebook.com/watch/?v=1043929892977968

Nam-Hyun Um. (2013). The Role of Culture in Creative Execution in Celebrity Endorsement: The Cross-Cultural Study. *Journal of Global Marketing*, 26(3), 155–172. https://doi.org/10.1080/08911762.2013.804613

NCC (n.d.). Indusry Statistics. Nigerian Communications Commission website. https://ncc.gov.ng/statistics-reports/industry-overview

Nicosia, F. M. (1966). *Consumer Decision Processes; Marketing and Advertising Implications*. Prentice Hall.

Njanja, A. (2022). *As Africa's Digital Economy Grows, Expensive Internet Hinders Investor Activity in Some Countries*. https://techcrunch.com/2022/07/27/as-africas-digital-economy-grows-expensive-internet-hinders-investor-activity-in-some-countries/

Nwachukwu, I. (2019). *What Do Recent Celebrity Endorsements in Nigeria Mean?* http://www.financialnigeria.com/what-recent-celebrity-endorsements-in-nigeria-mean-blog-474.html

Nwagwu, I., & Oni, T. (2015). Lagos and Its potentials for economic growth. *Heinrich-Böll-Stiftung Report*. https://ng.boell.org/en/2015/07/02/lagos-and-its-potentials-economic-growth

Obilor, E. I. (2023). Convenience and purposive sampling techniques: Are they the same. *International Journal of Innovative Social & Science Education Research*, 11(1), 1–7.

Ochab, R. (2018). *How Many Languages Are There in Africa*? https://www.cetra.com/blog/many-african-languages/

Ogunro, J. (2023). Nigeria's population time bomb. *The Cable Newspaper*. https://www.thecable.ng/nigerias-population-time-bomb

Ohanian, R. (1990). Construction and validation of a scale to measure celebrity endorsers' perceived expertise, trustworthiness, and attractiveness. *Journal of Advertising*, 19(3), 39–52.

Ohanian, R. (1991). The impact of celebrity spokespersons' perceived image on consumers' intention to purchase. Journal of advertising Research, 31(1), 46–54.

Ohetunde, O. (2023). Nigeria's mobile subscribers hit 226.8m, grow 15% in one year. *Dataphyte*. https://www.dataphyte.com/latest-reports/telecoms/nigerias-mobile-subscribers-hit-226-8m-grow-15-in-one-year/

Okocha, S. (2023). *Giants Strides in Nigeria's Technology Industry and Building on Successes Recorded*. https://von.gov.ng/giants-strides-in-nigerias-technology-industry-and-building-on-successes-recorded/

Okosi, Alex. (2022). Meet the YouTube Black voices creator, artist, singer and songwriter class of 2023. *Google Africa Blog*. https://blog.google/intl/en-africa/company-news/technology/meet-the-youtube-black-voices-creator-artist-singer-and-songwriter-class-of-2023/

Ojetunde, O. (2023). Nigeria's mobile subscribers hit 226.8m, grow 15% in one year. *Dataphyte*. https://www.dataphyte.com/latest-reports/telecoms/nigerias-mobile-subscribers-hit-226-8m-grow-15-in-one-year/

Ojobo. (2023). Sustaining the revolution in Nigeria's communications sector. *The Cable Newspaper*. https://www.thecable.ng/sustaining-revolution-nigeria-communications-sector

Ojo, B. (2013). 15 things Nigerians need to know about how mobile number portability works. *Premium Times*. https://www.premiumtimesng.com/business/131102-15-things-nigerians-need-to-know-about-how-mobile-number-portability-works.html?tztc=1

Olatunji, K., & Onyenucheya, A. (2022). Nigeria, four others to deepen EU's partnership with Africa. *The Guardian Newspapers*. https://guardian.ng/business-services/nigeria-four-others-to-deepen-eus-partnership-with-africa/

Olowoyo, G. (2020). Interview: How Airtel 444 advert threw me into limelight – Singer, Lade. *Premium Times Newspaper*. https://www.premiumtimesng.com/entertainment/416990-interview-how-airtel-444-advert-threw-me-into-limelight-singer-lade.html?tztc=1

Onyango, S. (2022). *Africa Accounts for 70% of the World's $1 Trillion Mobile Money Market*. https://qz.com/africa/2161960/gsma-70-percent-of-the-worlds-1-trillion-mobile-money-market-is-in-africa

Qazzafi, S. (2019). Consumer buying decision process toward products. *International Journal of Scientific Research and Engineering Development*, *2*(5), 130–134.

Seno, D., & Lukas, B. A. (2007). The equity effect of product endorsement by celebrities: A conceptual framework from a co-branding perspective. *European Journal of Marketing*, 41(1/2), 121–134.

Schouten, A. P., Janssen, L., & Verspaget, M. (2021). Celebrity vs. Influencer endorsements in advertising: The role of identification, credibility, and product-endorser fit. In *Leveraged Marketing Communications* (pp. 208–231). Edited by Alexander P. Schouten, Loes Janssen, Maegan Verspaget: Routledge.

Shimp, T. E. (1997). *Advertising, Promotion and Supplemental Aspects of Integrated Marketing Communication* (4th ed.). Fort Worth: The Dryden Press.

Sıla Ekşioğlu. (2021). *Celebrities vs. Influencers: What Sets Them Apart*. https://inflownetwork.com/celebrities-vs-influencers-what-sets-them-apart/

Silverman, S. G., Zou, K. H., & Tuncali, K. (2003). Correlation and simple linear regression. *Radiology*, 227(3), 617–628.

Social Sprout. (2023). *What Is Influencer Marketing: How to Develop Your Strategy*. https://sproutsocial.com/insights/influencer-marketing/

Sokolova, K., & Kefi, H. (2020). Instagram and YouTube bloggers promote it, why should I buy? How credibility and parasocial interaction influence purchase intentions. *Journal of Retailing and Consumer Services*, 53, 101742.

Stantcheva, S. (2023). How to run surveys: A guide to creating your own identifying variation and revealing the invisible. *Annual Review of Economics*, 15, 205–234.

Stefan Thurairatnam. (2021). How Technology Influences social media. *Entrepreneur Magazine*. https://www.entrepreneur.com/en-in/social-media/how-technology-influences-social-media/378476

Tafesse, W., & Wood, B. P. (2021). Followers' engagement with Instagram influencers: The role of influencers' content and engagement strategy. *Journal of Retailing and Consumer Services*, 58, 102303.

Talkwaker (2022). *Africa's top marketing influencers. Talkwalker Blog*. Retrieved from https://www.talkwalker.com/blog/africa-marketing-influencers-twitter

Taylor, C. R. (2020). The urgent need for more research on influencer marketing. International Journal of Advertising, 39(7), 889-891.

The Conversation. (2022). Nigeria's large, youthful population could be an asset or a burden. *The Conversation Blog*. https://theconversation.com/nigerias-large-youthful-population-could-be-an-asset-or-a-burden-186574

Toni O. (2021). 7 most popular African music genres. *The African Exponent*. https://www.africanexponent.com/post/7769-7-most-popular-african-music-genres

United Nations. (n.d). *Young People's Potential, the Key to Africa's Sustainable Development*. https://www.un.org/ohrlls/news/young-people%E2%80%99s-potential-key-africa%E2%80%99s-sustainable-development

US International Trade Administration [USITA]. (2023). *Nigeria - Country Commercial Guide*. https://www.trade.gov/country-commercial-guides/nigeria-information-and-communications-technology

Ventureburn. (2021). *New Report Calls for Changes to VC Strategy in Africa*. https://ventureburn.com/2021/01/new-report-calls-for-changes-to-vc-strategy-in-africa/

Werner Geyser. (2023). *What Is An Influencer? – Social Media Influencers Defined*. https://influencermarketinghub.com/what-is-an-influencer/

Yamane, T. (1973). *Statistics: An Introductory Analysis* (3rd ed.). Harper and Row.

Zipporah, M. M., & Mberia, H. K. (2014). The effects of celebrity endorsement in advertisements. *International Journal of Academic Research in Economics and Management Sciences*, 3(5), 178–188.

10 Digital Ecosystem in Africa

Unfolding Regulatory Practices, Gaps, and Trends

Anne W. Njathi, Grace Mutung'u and Yinka Ajibola

Introduction

An exponential uptake of digital platforms in African countries has led to policy and regulatory challenges related to digital platform access, acceptance, adoption, and usage. Such challenges include criminalizing content, internet shutdowns, and taxation that stifle the full embrace of the digital economy. The proliferation of digital platforms and platform governance in African countries is currently at a crossroads. Although a few regulations do exist, in some cases they are less explicit when considering striking a balance between regulating and significantly increasing digital platforms' uptake while promoting human rights and protecting consumers (Freedom House, n.d.-a). In most African countries, digital platforms have become marketplaces, spaces for knowledge production, and workplaces for individuals and companies seeking to leverage internet affordances. For example, Kenya and Nigeria are among the pillars of innovation and high-tech entrepreneurship which make up Africa's most thriving economies. These economies, known as KINGS—Kenya, Ivory Coast, Nigeria, Ghana, and South Africa—are named such due to strong economic growth, entrepreneurial ecosystems, vibrant telecoms, tech infrastructure, and supportive policies (Osiakwan, 2017).

Due to increased digital connectivity, there is an increased uptake of digital platforms leading to massive online socioeconomic interactions. While Nigeria has 122.5 million internet users, with 31.60 million active social media users, Kenya is rising, with 17.86 million internet users, with 10.55 million active social media users (Kemp, 2023). However, both countries are caught up in nonexistent, insufficient, or weak judicial institutions that execute digital regulations and policies. If anything, both countries are faced with the contradictory efforts of their governments to increase internet access. For instance, the Kenyan government has heavily invested in internet connectivity initiatives that include five undersea fiber optic cables, [1] Universal Access,[2] and Digital Economy Blueprint, and in Nigeria's case widening internet access (Adepetun, 2022) while paying less attention to controlling and regulating the ferocious usage of the internet, which is broadening and complicating the regulatory framework by the day.

This chapter examines the digital platforms' regulatory gaps, challenges, and trends in African countries, specifically Kenya and Nigeria, and how these

DOI: 10.4324/9781032689654-10

regulatory trends affect the uptake, usage, and adoption of digital platforms among actors that include the government, users, brands, and civil society organizations (CSOs). The chapter analyzes platform regulatory and legal frameworks from Kenya and Nigeria using case studies on content moderation, taxation, internet shutdowns, and political interference. Our approach gleans into select secondary sources, such as existing tech regulatory laws and policies, published reports, popular case studies, popular press articles, and publications of digital platforms policy issues from the past three years. The aim is to demonstrate the prevalence of the emerging regulatory gaps in line with the research questions and to help inform debates over increased digital connectivity and content moderation, internet shutdowns, and taxation. Although many other eras are worthy of reflection, this chapter focuses on the post-pandemic era where digital regulatory gaps became more prominent as the digital platforms' uptake heightened. Incidents of digital regulatory gaps included the Twitter (X) shutdown in Nigeria (Amnesty International, n.d.; Anyim, 2021; Princewill & Busari, 2021; The Punch, 2021). This chapter is structured into three parts: case studies and examples specifically from Kenya and Nigeria, emerging gaps and implications, and recommendations.

Emerging Regulatory Trends in African Markets

The lack of scholarly inquiry on emerging regulatory trends and gaps in Africa, and to what extent these factors influence the uptake, usage, and adoption of digital platforms, tends to heighten the implications for improved digital platform operations. These implications for digital regulatory gaps remain largely understudied. Although popular press articles highlight the regulatory trends and gaps in Africa, they are mostly anecdotal without substantial evidence, failing to capture the entire scope of policy formation gaps, actors, and processes in Africa related to platform governance. A substantial body of literature on platform governance (de Kloet et al., 2019; Gillespie, 2018; Gorwa, 2019; Helberger et al., 2018; Poell et al., 2019; Popiel, 2021; Van Dijck, 2020, 2021) is Western-centric. Considerably less is known about platform governance from an African context. A few scholars (see Arewa, 2021; Kwet, 2019; Njathi, 2023; Tamale, 2020) have focused on Africa and shown the implications of the regulatory gaps that include digital colonialism borne from the oligopolistic mode of the GAFAM operations; overexploitation of users, including digital workers; undercutting; and digital pay gaps among other digital harms.

In addition, there is scant discourse about nonmarket issues, such as content moderation and digital taxes. For instance, the new Africa Continental Free Trade Agreement (ACFTA; African Union, 2018) leverages digital technologies to achieve free movement of people and e-commerce. Negotiations for a digital trade and e-commerce protocol began after the agreement came into force. Key issues featured in protocol negotiations include data governance, data flows, payment systems, taxation, liberalization of digital trade, and consumer protection (Hagos, 2022, Lemma et al., 2022). Issues of content policy are not featured, suggesting that content policy is not prioritized in trade discussions. However, content production, moderation, and consumption are regulated in terms of information and from the perspectives of labor, tax, and employment.

The objective of this study is to interrogate, analyze, and understand how regulation and policy will shape the unfolding of digital platforms for Africa, with a specific focus on professions like advertising, public relations, and marketing that rely on digital platforms for business activities in the digital economy. The study sits at the broader intersection of platform governance and regulation, digital economy, law, globalization of technology, and the country's development priorities to explicate the complex regulatory and governance challenges facing Africa's fast technological uptake.

Examples of Emerging Digital Economies in Africa: Nigeria & Kenya

Nigeria

Nigeria's rise as a digital economy can be attributed to its large population and strong economy. With over 200 million inhabitants, Nigeria is the continent's most populated country. It is also Africa's largest economy, valued at over $477 billion USD in 2022 (The World Bank, 2023). The country has an internet penetration rate of 55.4% and an estimated 31.6 million social media consumers (DataReportal, 2023). The Nigeria Communications Commission gauged the contribution of the telecommunication sector to be 12.61% the gross domestic product (GDP) in 2021. Over the past two decades, Nigeria has incubated successful start-ups in financial technology, entertainment, e-commerce, and services (Bayen, 2018; Olurounbi, 2021; Oluwole, 2022).

Although Nigeria comprises 36 independent states and the Federal Capital Territory, policies for the digital sector are mainly developed by the federal government. In 2023, Nigeria enacted the Data Protection Act, and other legislation that would reshape the legal landscape for internet content in Nigeria remains under consideration including a bill to regulate online content hosts and a bill that would expand criminal penalties for online speech (Freedom House, n.d.-a). In 2022, the National Information Technology Development Agency (NITDA), whose task is to implement information technology (IT) policy and oversee IT development in Nigeria, rolled out a draft regulation for online platforms. The regulation titled, "Code of Practice," is a measure to realign the connection between online platforms and Nigerians to maximize advantages shared by both parties and to advance a long-term digital economy. This regulation is specifically directed at interactive computer service platforms/internet intermediaries, such as Meta platforms, Twitter (X), and TikTok, providing conditions for operating in Nigeria (NITDA, 2022).

Kenya

Kenya's digital economy is shaped by both government and private sector investment and is governed by policies that support mobile telephony, a precursor to the digital economy. The country has a population of about 50 million, the majority of whom are under the age of 30 years (Kenya National Bureau of Standards [KNBS], n.d.). Over the last two decades, the mobile phone boom has reached a penetration of 114.2%. While *Digital 2022: Kenya* (Kemp, 2022) indicates that internet and social media use lag, with 42% and 23% respectively, the country also has many phone-based applications that serve even non-smartphone users. The most well-known application is Mpesa, a mobile money platform. Besides financial technology, Kenya also has notable start-ups in information services and logistics all situated in Nairobi. Nairobi, the capital city of Kenya, is known as the innovation hub of East Africa (van der Meer, 2018), as a strong entrepreneurial hub with a strong technological service. Nairobi is referred to as the Silicon Savannah (Akamanzi et al., 2016; Donner & Locke, 2019; Friederici et al., 2017).

Kenya has large e-government services and has won the prestigious United Nations Public Service Award (UNFPA) award for public service delivery (Nation Correspondent, 2015). Recent digital economy laws include the Data Protection Act of 2019; the Computer Misuse and Cybercrimes Act of 2018; and the digital service tax (DST) that falls under the 2021 Finance Act. The traditional Communications Authority and Competition Authority oversee and regulate licensed players. Other regulators such as the Central Bank of Kenya (CBK, 2022), is regulating the emerging digital aspects of their subject matter, such as their own digital lending apps.

Case Studies: Nigeria and Kenya

Through convenience sampling, we explore and interrogate eight content moderation, taxation, internet shutdown, and political interference cases using published reports, case studies, popular press articles, and publications of digital platforms' policy issues from the past five years (2018–2023) to analyze platform regulatory and legal frameworks from Kenya and Nigeria. The selected cases involve varying degrees of complexity in content moderation, platform content access, content regulation, user protection and privacy rights, actors' responsibility from mundane to cutting-edge technology, and everyday lived experiences of individuals and organizations in the digital realm. In addition, we provide a comparative overview of Nigerian- and Kenyan-specific cases (see Table 10.1). We submit our criticism of policy violations from the intermittent patterns, frequency, and severity of isolated incidents. Our analysis is quite timely and relevant given the plethora of content creation on digital platforms in Africa, which are particularly curated by African youth who spend 80% of their time online (Kemp, 2023), and by organizations seeking to leverage platforms for their goods and services. The next sections present the case studies on these two countries that are understood as leading and thriving economies in Africa (Osiakwan, 2017). The case studies addressed include EndSars and Twitter (X) shutdown from Nigeria and content moderation laws such CMCA, DST, Facebook Worker's Legal Battle from Kenya. In both countries, we shine a light on the role and actions of bodies such as NITDA and SERAP, which are intricately tied to this discourse.

Table 10.1 Case Studies Explored

Case Study	*Nigeria*	*Kenya*
1	EndSars	CMCA***
2	Twitter (X) Shutdown	DST****
3	NITDA*	Facebook worker's legal battle
4	SERAP**	Data breaches

* National Information Technology Development Agency (NITDA)
** Socio-Economic Rights and Accountability Project (SERAP)
*** Computer Misuse and Cybercrimes Act (CMCA)
**** Digital Service Tax (DST)

Case Study 1: Nigeria

Content Moderation Cases

The most recent national instance of conflict over internet content moderation can be traced to 2017, when 21 pro-Biafra websites were arbitrarily blocked by the Nigerian Communications Commission (Freedom House, n.d.-b; Nigerian Communications Commission, 2021). Biafra was a separatist state (1967–1970) that declared independence from Nigeria (Diamond, 2007). Using Biafra as precedence, in fiscal year 2020–2021, the NCC imposed a ban in accordance with Section 146 of the 2003 Nigeria Communications Act, highlighting national security matters and mandating internet service providers (ISPs) to work with the NCC to protect national security and deter crime in the country (Freedom House, n.d.-a). Some of the websites were eventually restored, raising uncertainty about the blockade's rationale as a nationwide ban related to national security. The Nigerian government's inconsistent action signaled a lack of internet content transparency.

#EndSars Protest

The most notable discourse around content moderation within the past three years is associated with the #EndSars protest in Nigeria (Adepetun, 2020). In October 2020, Nigerian youth and activists called for the dissolution of the Special Anti-Robbery Squad (SARS), a division of the Nigerian Police Force (Ajisafe et al., 2021).

The world watched as the #EndSARS movement took social media by storm. The youth of the country utilized platforms such as Twitter (X) and Facebook to discuss the protests and violence they were experiencing on the ground. The Nigerian government's response to the protests was contradictory to the messages being conveyed online; the government deemed information disseminated by citizens as *fake news*. The #EndSARs movement was one of many emanating from developing countries since social media platforms became mainstream. Meta, Facebook's parent organization, claimed that automated technologies blocked posts using the #EndSARS hashtag to draw attention to police assaults on demonstrators, indicating its failure to take local context into consideration. Meta alleged its automated systems mistakenly identified COVID-19 as fake information when they misinterpreted the hashtag *activism against police brutality* (Ilori, 2020). The ramifications of these actions by Meta AI technologies are varied, showing that social media platforms can serve as a transformative tool (Ajisafe et al., 2021), but underlying issues remain regarding how Meta administers their content moderation policies.

Twitter (X) Shutdown

On June 5, 2021, Nigerian President Buhari tweeted out a promise to deal with anyone instigating disturbance in the country using "the language they understand," referring to the 1967–1970 civil war, which killed millions of Nigerians (Amnesty International, n.d.; see Figure 10.1).

The post sparked significant worry around the world and resulted in millions of comments that were heavily criticized and condemned. Eventually, those concerns led to the suspension of the President's Twitter (X) account (Anyim, 2021). In response, the Nigerian government placed a ban on Twitter (X) from operating domestically for 222 days, only allowing Twitter (X) to operate again after it consented to closer government collaboration (The Punch, 2021). Over 39 million Twitter (X) users in Nigeria were affected by the ban, while other users resorted to circumventing the ban by using a virtual private network (VPN) under a viral hashtag, #ThankGodforVPN (Princewill & Busari, 2021). The Nigerian Bar Association vowed to sue the federal government if the ban was not reversed. Similarly, the Socio-Economic Rights and Accountability Project (SERAP), a Lagos-based civil society group, also took steps to sue the Nigerian government (Ejekwonyilo, 2021; Global Freedom of Expression, n.d.). In a significant ruling, the Economic Community of West African States (ECOWAS) ordered the federal government to make sure the illegal suspension does not happen again (Kelley, 2022). Twitter (X) conceded to several of the Nigerian government's demands in exchange for renewed access within the nation (Maclean, 2022).

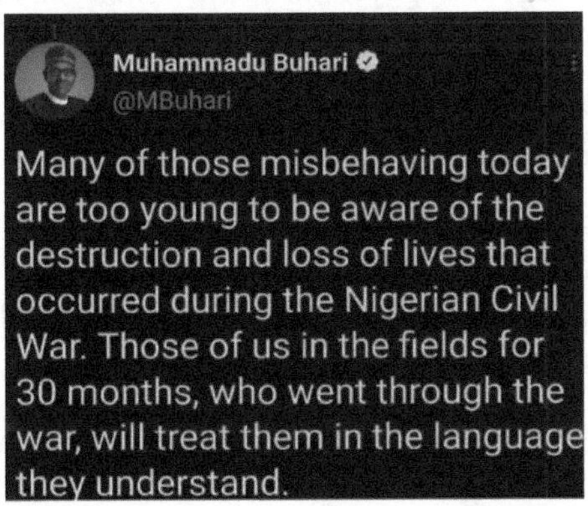

Figure 10.1 Lai Mohammed reacts to Twitter (X) deleting Buhari's "civil war" tweet

Source: The Punch, 2021

Case Study 2: Kenya

Content Moderation Laws

Content regulation in Kenya is greatly influenced by moments. The late 1990s market liberalization only focused on broadcast content, while more recent laws were enacted after elections. The Computer Misuse and Cybercrimes Act (CMCA, 2018) is the latest legislation to attempt consolidation of content regulation through criminalization of content, such as fake news (CMCA, 2018, secs. 22 and 23). These offenses, while intended to clean the information environment, effectively reintroduced information offenses from previous eras. For example, the provision also includes criminal defamation. Notably, criminal defamation had been nullified by the High Court of Kenya in 2017 in Jacqueline Okuta & another v Attorney General & two others [2017] eKLR (Kenya Law, 2016).

CMCA co-opts private companies, such as internet service providers (ISPs) into cybercrime investigations, including content moderation. ISPs are required to keep records and preserve data under investigation, collect real-time traffic data, and intercept content (Walubengo & Mutemi, 2018). While cooperation between state investigation agents and ISPs is supervised by the judiciary, there are no provisions for investigatory agencies to give annual reports on procedures taken under the CMCA. The lack of a reporting mechanism under the CMCA removes the public from participating.

Content Moderation Cases

As policymakers and regulators struggle to make appropriate regulations for the online space, citizens are turning to the judiciary to protection. Petitioners raise concerns about the economy of content moderation by social media, namely marketing through dominant languages, market entry into regions with less dominant languages, and liability for offline harm arising from online content. Even as platforms increasingly engage with governments (i.e., Meta announced it would assist the Kenyan government in gathering data on online tax defaulters), legal cases are filed about inadequate regulatory practices (Mwenda, 2022). In three recently filed cases, digital workers and victims of harmful content raised concerns on labor and health rights.

Meta Worker's Rights

In the yet-to-be decided case of Abraham Meareg, Fisseha Tekle, and Katiba Institute v. Meta, Petitioner 1: Abraham seeks accountability from Facebook for failing to take down posts calling for his father's murder, despite repeated reports to the platform. Petitioner 3: Katiba Institute, a civil society organization, is aggrieved by Facebook's inaction regarding content shared on its platform in Kenya and Ethiopia (Perrigo, 2021). In another undecided case, Kiana Monique and James Agada Mark and 182 others vs Meta Platforms, Inc., Meta Platforms Ireland, Ltd., and nine others, the petitioners, who were employed by Samasource as content moderators, are seeking compensation for being declared redundant and are claiming a lack of adequate psychosocial support leading to employee mental health damage (Perrigo, 2021, 2022). In an earlier suit involving a former Samasource employee, Daniel Motaung argued he was wrongfully terminated while trying to unionize and address Samasource's working environment. Motaung claimed he suffered damage to his mental health because of content moderation work but lacked adequate psychosocial support to address his needs (Perrigo, 2021, 2022).

Digital Service Taxes

As issues of content moderation are debated, the Kenyan government is attempting to secure a share of revenue derived from digital marketplaces through taxation. In 2021, the Kenyan government introduced the digital services tax (DST) for resident and nonresident persons who transact over digital marketplaces in Kenya (KPMG, 2021; Mwangi, 2021; Nyawira, 2021). The DST is aimed at collecting Sh13.9 billion ($114 million USD) from the digital marketplace over the next three years (Mwenda, 2022). Global policy-making bodies and technology companies oppose the tax and argued for the uniform Organization of Economic Co-operation and Development (OECD)-led global digital tax initiative (Ngugi, 2023). However, Kenya remained steady in its resolve that taxes should be charged in Kenya where the digital marketplaces occur (Kenya Revenue Authority, 2021). Similarly, in early 2022, the federal government of Nigeria implemented a 6% tax on turnover on overseas enterprises that offer digital services to domestic customers in Nigeria (Arise News, 2022; Reuters, 2022). The tax is applicable to apps, high-frequency trading, electronic data storage, and online advertising (Oriola, 2022). In the case of taxing creatives in Nigeria, there is an imminent plan to tax content creators (Oparada, 2022)

The 2023 Kenyan national budget not only retains the DST, which is computed at 1.5% of the transaction amount, but also introduces new taxes to capture digital content creators and users (The Finance Bill, 2023). The bill includes a 3% tax on income derived from trade in digital assets, such as cryptocurrencies, and a 15% withholding tax on income derived from digital content creation. In addition, taxes on mobile money transactions are increased from 12% to 15% (The Finance Bill, 2023). Digital taxes demonstrate both the Kenyan and Nigerian governments' view of the digital platform space as a new economic frontier that can also raise government revenue. However, there are questions on how the tax trickles down from the platform owner to the user, corporate brands, and the government, and to whose benefit it works (Njathi, 2023).

Analysis + Discussion: Emerging Regulatory Gaps & Trends

The above case studies from Kenya and Nigeria raise concerns, ambiguities, and complexities that thwart regulation of legal and policy-related platforms when it comes to content moderation, taxation, internet shutdowns, and political interference. Altogether, they present a conundrum of threats and challenges to provide a legal and social framework by which the principles and standards of the digital economy could abide. These cases underscore Helberger et al.'s (2018) question of who is responsible for platform governance and to whose agenda platform governance is serving and why. Our analysis draws attention to four key overlapping findings, which evolve in juxtaposition with the need for sustainable policy strategies: (a) reactionary ad hoc policy strategies in response to regulatory crises; (b) main actors' privileges; (c) competition to regulate among actors; and cumulatively, (d) the enormous power that platforms hold, presenting tensions and potential harms to the platform economy. Each finding represents a challenge tied to the state of platform governance, including safety and security, privacy of user rights, freedom of expression, and more. A brief overview of each finding follows.

Reactionary Ad Hoc Policy Strategies

A first observation when studying content moderation on platforms in Kenya and Nigeria is an overarching pattern of the rationality by which most recent content moderation policy interventions continue to proliferate, and are intrinsically reactionary, often existing only temporarily. Recent policy interventions were put in place following trigger moments and incidents like #endSars, the Twitter (X) shutdown in Nigeria, Kenya's general elections in 2017, or violations of data privacy, such as the Kenya Revenue Authority cases of mining Kenyans' data online to combat tax and financial fraud (Ngila, 2022). Take for instance, NITDA's (2022) draft, "Code of Practice" for the regulation of online platforms, which is a response to the 2021 Twitter (X) shutdown in Nigeria. Some of the provisions include regulatory compliance, platform guidelines, and take-down actions. The NITDA provision is a starting point for conversation around content moderation in Nigeria. Although it is key, users and human rights must be placed as a priority in all discussions. However, a critique of the provision highlights the vagueness of some of the provisions. For instance, the code stipulates that data from these platforms, even information that has been removed or marked as restricted by the government shall be retained. However, the amount of time that such data can be stored is not mentioned. Indefinite access to user data that the user no longer has access to violates both their right to privacy and their Nigeria Data Protection Regulation (NDPR) right to be forgotten (Communications, 2022).

Such policy interventions are formulated as urgent remedies to radically navigate and respond to severe cases of ongoing content moderation violations. These kinds of reactive policy interventions reveal not only how tech policies are an afterthought in African countries but also how the governments fail to forerun the unpredictability of fast-evolving technology, nor significantly anticipate, drive, validate, and proactively uphold public interest with the uptake of digital technologies. Importantly, the reactive approach leads to a lack of comprehensive policy response to policy problems that undermine key public values, such as violation of data rights and privacy, information access, and freedom of expression. Such mindsets are unprepared to embrace the shared responsibility that comes with regulating content on digital platforms' uptake, usage, and adoption. While there are some pre-existing ad hoc regulatory frameworks, such as CMCA, the majority fail to recognize the dynamic nature of the digital platforms that are constantly undergoing reconfiguration of existing business models due to datafication and platformization (Cohen, 2019; Srnicek, 2018; Zuboff, 2019). Inevitably, this restructuring poses a major challenge to advancing policy goals and values that foster public interests. Even more, none of the ongoing cases of content moderation violations have won legal battles due to a lack of firmly grounded regulatory frameworks for recourse with digital technologies. For example, the Meta legal battle with the Kenyan government turned into a political contestation (Wangari, 2023) over whether Meta could be locally sued for a toxic work environment in Nairobi (Perrigo, 2021, 2022). Ultimately, the concern disputed the role of Kenya's jurisdiction to hold Meta accountable.

Actors' Privilege

The question of who can "set the legal boundaries of what can be exchanged on platforms and who can determine how content can be created, distributed, marketed, and monetized online" (Poell et al., 2022, p. 81) remains largely unanswered. Unlike platforms, which own infrastructure and are some of the wealthiest companies across the globe (Kwet, 2019), local governments such as Kenya and Nigeria may not have the financial power to push their agendas to the interests of their own people. The platform's commercial interests interfere with the welfare of its users and public institutions as well as its regulatory actors (Helberger et al., 2018). At the same time, platform governance is not simply the responsibility of each individual nation, Nyabola et al. (2022) argued. Some policies are best implemented and upheld by national governments, including policies related to speech. Other policies, such as who has the right to accumulate data, and transparency in the advertisement, require a global response. Helberger et al. (2018) argued that there is a need to understand who bears the responsibility to hold platforms "accountable, legally and morally, for what is 'shared' through them" (p. 2).

Subsequently, less powerful actors, such as users who are increasingly "platform-dependent" (Poell et al., 2022, p. 197), are at the mercy of the government, platforms, and corporations who set the digital economy agenda, replicating existing power structures. At a macro level, when Twitter (X) was shut down in Nigeria, those actors with financial means turned to virtual private networks (VPN), isolating those without the knowledge or finances to turn to VPN. Similarly, the CMCA in Kenya caters to the needs of those in power, such as politicians. According to Madung (2022), people have economic interests, such as political influencers who are seeking to make livelihoods on platforms by pushing for political agendas that work in their favor. Recent political moments in Kenya demonstrate how platforms grow and tell the government how the platforms will help the country's political, national security, and control interests. In return, the government is willing to collaborate with and listen to the platforms' requests, leaving the people's interests unchampioned. For example, in 2017, Meta offered financial incentives to combat fake news ahead of the Kenyan general elections (Miriri,

2020), but this attempt to regulate misinformation demonstrated a contradiction. The effort to curb misinformation seems to protect the powerful, including the political elite (Mutahi & Kimari, 2017). There is an economy around misinformation, where social media users are hired to spread and amplify messages and, as a consequence, distort the information environment (Madung, 2022).

The unraveling content moderation debate polarizes the use of digital platforms along the lines of power and privilege while obscuring accountability and transparency in platform governance. Such oppressive structures tend to favor the haves more than the have-nots. The Kenyan and Nigerian governments are trying to play catch up with premature policies, which continually harm vulnerable actors, such as everyday internet users, and impede Africa from competing with the global digital economy. A closer look at our analysis reveals that the government's content creation policy intervention and efforts are limited related to the content moderation practices of global social media companies by the obfuscated business models and the size of operation and resources required. Within the same lens, organizations such as UNESCO (2023) have designed Guidelines for Regulating Digital Platforms that are serving as proxy policies for African nations. Such efforts are designed to cultivate safe, healthy online interactions and support freedom of expression, ensuring the availability of accurate and reliable information in the public sphere on platforms.

While assessing UNESCO's guidelines on the human content moderation we recognized these provisions can be reinforced by providing a minimum threshold to which digital platforms should adhere. Such efforts delineate colonial undertones with the need to save Africa, because Africa cannot save herself. Researchers (e.g., Arun, 2021; Díaz & Hecht-Felella, 2021) showed that some platforms use human rights lingo to conceal and camouflage their content moderation policies. As part of ongoing ICT innovations, social media is an important tool in building and connecting the global world. Despite the fact that social media corporations position their content moderation rules in terms of human rights, their activities are primarily motivated by financial imperatives, the prospect of government regulation, and external pressure from the general public and mainstream media (Díaz & Hecht-Felella, 2021, p. 3).

In addition, Global Network Initiative (n.d.)[3] criticized the scope of UNESCO's (2023) guidelines as "extremely ambitious" and one that requires "engaging in robust, thematic consultations with experts in each of the specific fields that remain within scope" (p. 1). We argue that social media companies have the autonomy to decide how to administer content moderation, but these efforts are marred by incompetency and a lack of accountability, amongst other factors. Is it time to push for an industry standard pertaining to content moderation? If companies are held to a particular standard, an industry standard on content moderation could be a starting point for accountability. This reiterates our position that a fundamental paradigm shift is required to localize content moderation policy interventions and transfer the authority and resources to the national and municipal levels.

Worryingly, our analysis, viewed from the various actors and their points of interest, shows that the interests held by businesses, platforms, and government are likely to coalesce. There is a possibility of platforms promising to help governments pursue their interests as long as platforms are given *soft* treatment. In this regard, people are sometimes caught between the government and the platforms' interests, leading to digital harms, such as data breaches. The over-privileging of the elites and platforms, whilst further entrenching the agendas of both the platforms and the government, is explicitly at the expense of social media users. Inevitably, the platforms set the conditions of the rules of profit-making because governments face the "threat of losing investments in their countries" (Fuchs, 2014, p. 104); as a result, government entities must implement company-friendly policy measures that favor tax incomes, employment, and publicly funded internet infrastructure expansion projects.

Competition to Regulate

The attempt to regulate online content when there is no law in place or when there is loosely bound regulation is fundamentally contested rather than embraced. Because of the heterogeneous, amorphous, and ubiquitous nature of online content that cuts across industries and businesses, there are multiple actors moderating content from competing positions. For example, in Kenya, the Kenya Film Classification Board (KFCB, 2023) has popularly offered alternative explanations for censoring online content by defining what digital content is morally upright on platforms (see Figure 10.2). In several instances, KFCB has called out companies, bloggers, and content creators for sharing offensive, potentially harmful content to national security threats or minors (KFCB, 2023), bringing to question whose role it is to regulate online content in Kenya. Oftentimes, KFCB contradicts the assigned government agency, Communications Authority, whose legal mandate is ICT policy and regulation in Kenya. For instance, in a Netflix content regulation ongoing debate, Barnes (2016) argues,

> There has been uncertainty about how to regulate Netflix as it makes in-roads into the African market. The KFCB was contradicted by the Communications Authority, who ruled that the streaming service does not require a broadcasting license, as it is an internet TV network, not a traditional broadcaster.
> (para. 6)

Notwithstanding the competing needs among policy actors, many actors nonetheless contribute to the agenda setting of content moderation trending topics and themes. These topics are not just popular conversation starters since they do receive an overwhelming amount of attention, especially by Kenyans on Twitter (X) (KOT). The topics and themes present a need to understand what constitutes online content and the actor responsible for regulation. However, such a position is difficult to sustain. Despite the shared interest by the competing actors, content moderation not only leads to conflict but also duplication of roles, which is expensive to maintain for already resource-strained countries like Kenya and Nigeria. More importantly, between these competing actors, there is constant conflict about which

Figure 10.2 Criticism of content creators' use of social media
Source: KFCB, 2023

policies are (il)legitimate, which makes content moderation a far more complex phenomenon. More often, as the complication reigns, users are caught up in discussions that discredit, prioritize, or deprioritize the perceived radical and eccentric policies. The existence of multiple regulators may call for coregulation (Helberger et al., 2018) as more domains of content that were previously regulated separately become platformized. As seen from Kenya's example of guidelines jointly developed between the Communications Regulator and the National Cohesion and Integration Commission, coregulation also requires public input and views from communities of users (Wamathai, 2017). In addition, the ongoing litigation in Kenya may therefore be an important moment for the localization of content moderation policies and procedures. Such debates imply that there is no single source of truth, as a clear gap exists in content moderation and regulation.

The Power That Digital Platforms Hold

The final observation from this study considers more broadly how platforms hold the power to facilitate or constrain different forms of community building among various actors. The global domination of online platforms by U.S.-based corporations known as the GAFAM, which includes Google, Apple, Facebook, Amazon, and Microsoft (Helberger et al., 2018; Kwet, 2019), obscures the nature of platform governance and agendas that local governments, such as Kenya and Nigeria can push. GAFAM exerts considerable power over African countries, advancing beliefs that they can dictate platform policy—paving the way to a system of capitalist exploitation and digital colonialism (Kwet, 2019). This form of exploitation is regarded as the "new scramble" for Africa (Obadare, 2023, para. 3), or the competition between superpowers China and the United States for Africa's alliance (Hussein, 2022; Obadare, 2023). The expansion of superpowers is shaped over time by a continuum of connected and contextually determined interests, including economic, political, and ideological paradigms (Paterson & Nothias, 2016). These interests are typically portrayed as a vision of progress from the economically privileged to the economically disadvantaged and are geared toward various development initiatives launched by or carried out in Global South countries. For instance, China and the United States, among other actors who take various approaches in their engagement with Africa, are perpetuating an ongoing rush for an artificial intelligence economy (Mutung'u, 2023).

The power inequality that exists within platforms, referred to as "notoriously difficult" (Helberger et al., 2018, p. 2), obfuscates the question of who is primarily responsible for the governance of platforms, especially in countries like Kenya and Nigeria where there is a scarcity of resources, capacity, and skills to govern. In addition, funding concerns and the reality of the two parallel policy interventions—local governments and platforms—further complicate the notion of platform governance. As suggested by Njathi (2023), platform capitalism (Srnicek, 2018) erodes the idea of platform governance, which happens to be intricately embellished by platform power. This is because platforms generally police content and monitor user behavior for economic purposes (Gillespie, 2018). Popiel (2021) argues that "datafication, platformization, and platform power exceed national jurisdictions, challenging existing policy paradigms and traditional legal frameworks" (p. 32). Based on the most recent research (Boateng et al., 2017; Kwet, 2019), the GAFAM is heavily investing in African countries. While Boateng et al. (2017) argue that such actions are part of GAFAM's relentless search for profit, the question emerges of whether African countries are ready to deal with datafication amidst unregulated content moderation practices.

Acknowledging the powers that platforms hold calls for greater transparency and involvement of people/democratic institutions in the regulation of platforms, particularly where various actors collaborate with governments. Even in instances where it appears like governments are trying to assert themselves, as in the case of digital taxation, it is important to acknowledge the complexities of platform power and ensure that public interest is protected. Platform governance regulation should therefore attempt to rebalance power through creating local mechanisms for grievance redress, and local judicial oversight, as opposed to copy and pasting existing policies like in the case of the GDPR as (Díaz & Hecht-Felella, 2021) has shown in their study.

African Centric Trends on Platform Regulatory and Legal Frameworks from Kenya and Nigeria

The study of Kenya and Nigeria has provided important insights on how large platforms are localized in terms of use and regulation. Cases from these two countries also provide interesting precedents that are likely to influence other countries in Africa to adopt similar platform regulatory policies and frameworks. Platforms, such as GAFAM, argue that they do not get significant revenue from Africa; hence, they offer a lower investment of content moderation, among other features, to protect African consumers. Approaches like digital taxation appear to test the validity of such claims by pushing for a share of the scant revenue generated by platforms. Digital taxation in tech-active countries such as Kenya and Nigeria is a trend to watch. If the numbers show significant revenue, more countries are likely to adopt similar regimes.

The value of large markets, such as Nigeria, on localization is made apparent by Nigeria's Twitter (X) ban. While the ban demonstrated government overreach, it also showed there is value in vibrant online discourses beyond the revenue derived from direct sales, such as advertisements on a platform. Another example of this value is Kenya's display of influencer networks' organization and the ways in which the networks capitalize on moments, such as elections. As more African countries advance their internet penetration, variants of such models may also be adopted for marketing, influencing, and political campaigning. Without engaging the real sources of power—platforms and marketers who supply business to networks of influencers—content moderation regulation is likely to focus on the wrong target. Consequently, the importance of localization of digital policies and governance to best serve the dynamics of emerging economies such as Africa is underscored.

Localization of Policies

We advocate for the localization of effective content moderation policies to support the optimal participation of African countries in the digital revolution, particularly in the context of emerging economies, and call for practical solutions to unlock and bridge the gaps in digital transformation. As we pushback, we agree with Nyabola et al.'s (2022) view that there are some policies that require a global response. At the same time, localization of platform governance is a capital and capacity intensive venture with geo-political dynamics that might obstruct the process. In addition, drawing inspiration from other digital legislative policies could prove helpful. Using an African-centric perspective, Africa should evaluate already established policies, learn from them, and localize them as needed. For instance, the European Union (EU) policy assessment found that too much regulation can stifle technological innovation (Ndemo, 2023). In addition, the EU's Digital Markets Act (DMA), which governs the digital conglomerates that dominate the digital economy, is a more pertinent issue relevant to the African setting (Ndemo, 2023).

Two lessons can be learned and adopted within the African context. First, excessive regulation can hinder technological innovation (Ndemo, 2023. It is crucial that policies are targeted and not redundant. Second, there is a need for a comprehensive policy that addresses the dynamics of the African digital market. It is critical for African countries to learn from the experiences of other countries, but it is even more crucial to adopt laws in a way that makes sense for each individual nation. Although having an African policy can be a unifying initiative, we believe that each nation should also concentrate on its local policies. However, policy localization can be a daunting task given the dynamics of regulating digital platforms that transcend geographic borders (Popiel, 2021). Like other international policy-making processes, initiatives on technology policy are linked to market forces (Hurel & Lobato, 2018). Nevertheless, global powers have not concurred on the emerging issues brought about by digital platforms. In the meantime, regions such as the European Union have developed laws to regulate competition and protect consumers in their markets. This means that platform governance initiatives, such as UNESCO's (2023) *Guidelines for Regulating Digital Platforms* may only be taken up in regions such as Africa. Initiatives such as the UNESCO platform guidelines policy play into the new ways of governing the internet leading to geo-political tensions.

Limitations & Future Research

This chapter focused on two countries with similar legal structures and fast-growing markets and innovation. It would be important to compare emerging trends in other parts of Africa and more regulated markets. Future researchers could conduct a comparative study of other parts of Africa. Another limitation to this study is the assumption that the market dynamics will hold and that democratic spaces shall remain relatively open. The trends may be different with market disruption or more closure of civic space. Future studies could be conducted to examine countries with other conditions.

Notes

1 Kenya has five undersea fiber optic cables: SEACOMS, EASSy, TEAMS, KDN reliance, and FLAG Falcon. The Kenyan government owns SEACOM, with various multinational companies in partnership with local companies owning the rest.
2 To complement private sector initiatives toward meeting universal access objectives to the grassroots level (Communications Authority of Kenya, n.d.). Republic of Kenya (2019). Digital Economy Blueprint: Powering Kenya's transformation. Ministry of ICT.
3 Global Network Initiative Submission: UNESCO Guidelines for regulating digital platforms Draft 2.0.

Bibliography

Adepetun, A. (2020, October 25). *Social media and carnage that trailed #EndSARS protest.* The Guardian. https://guardian.ng/features/social-media-and-carnage-that-trailed-endsars-protest/

Adepetun, A. (2022, June 10). *Nigeria to benefit as governments, firms pledge $18.5b to widen Internet access.* The Guardian. https://guardian.ng/business-services/nigeria-to-benefit-as-governments-firms-pledge-18-5b-to-widen-internet-access/

African Union. (2018, March 21). *Agreement establishing the African continental free trade area.* https://au-afcfta.org/wp-content/uploads/2022/06/AfCFTA-Agreement-Legally-scrubbed-signed-16-May-2018.pdf

Ajisafe, D., Ojo, T. A., & Monyani, M. (2021, July 20). The impacts of social media on the #EndSARs# youth protests in Nigeria. *Proceedings of the ICTeSSH 2021 Conference.* https://doi.org/10.21428/7a45813f.638ef816

Akamanzi, C., Deutscher, P., Guerich, B., Lobelle, A., & Ooko-Ombaka, A. (2016, Spring). *Silicon Savannah: the Kenya ICT services cluster.* Microeconomics of Competitiveness. https://www.isc.hbs.edu/Documents/resources/courses/moc-course-atharvard/pdf/student-projects/Kenya%20ITC%20Services%202016.pdf

Amnesty International. (n.d.). *End Twitter suspension in Nigeria.* https://www.amnesty.org/en/petition/end-twitter-suspension-in-nigeria/

Anyim, W. O. (2021, August). Twitter ban in Nigeria: Implications on economy, freedom of speech and information sharing. *Library Philosophy and Practice (e-journal),* Article 5975. https://digitalcommons.unl.edu/libphilprac/5975

Arewa, O. B. (2021). *Disrupting Africa: Technology, law, and development* (1st ed.). Cambridge University Press.

Arise News. (2022, January 6). *Nigeria introduces 6% tax on digital services, non-resident companies.* https://www.arise.tv/nigeria-introduces-6-tax-on-digital-services-non-resident-companies/

Arun, C. (2021, March 15). Facebook's faces. *Harvard Law Review Forum, 35.* Advance online publication. https://doi.org/10.2139/ssrn.3805210

Barnes, H. (2016, January 21). *Kenya's film censor: Netflix a threat to 'moral values and national security.'* The Guardian. https://www.theguardian.com/film/2016/jan/21/netflix-threat-kenya-film-classification-board-censor-moral-values-terrorism

Bayen, M. (2018, March 22). *Africa: A look at the 442 active tech hubs of the continent.* GSMA. https://www.gsma.com/mobilefordevelopment/blog-2/africa-a-look-at-the-442-active-tech-hubs-of-the-continent/

Boateng, R., Budu, J., Mbrokoh, A. S., Ansong, E., Boateng, S. L., & Anderson, A. B. (2017). *Digital enterprises in Africa: A synthesis of current evidence* (Paper No. 2). Economic & Social Research Council. https://diodeweb.files.wordpress.com/2017/04/diode-paper-2-digital-enterprises-in-africa.pdf

Central Bank of Kenya (Digital Credit Providers) Regulations 2022, Pub. L. No. Legal Notice No. 46 (2022). https://www.centralbank.go.ke/2022/03/21/central-bank-of-kenya-digital-credit-providers-regulations-2022/

Cohen, J. E. (2019). *Between truth and power: The legal constructions of informational capitalism.* Oxford University Press.

Communications. (2022, October 21). *An open call to NITDA to review the updated code of practice.* Paradigm Initiative. https://paradigmhq.org/an-open-call-to-nitda-to-review-the-updated-code-of-practice/

Computer Misuse and Cybercrimes Act, Act No. 5 of 2018 (2018). http://kenyalaw.org:8181/exist/kenyalex/actview.xql?actid=No.%205%20of%202018

DataReportal. (2023). *Digital 2023: Kenya.* https://datareportal.com/reports/digital-2023-kenya

De Kloet, J., Poell, T., Guohua, Z., & Fai, C. Y. (2019). The platformization of Chinese society: Infrastructure, governance, and practice. *Chinese Journal of Communication, 12*(3), 249–256. https://doi.org/10.1080/17544750.2019.1644008

Diamond, S. (2007). Who killed Biafra? *Dialectical Anthropology, 31*(1), 339–362. https://doi.org/10.1007/s10624-007-9014-9

Díaz, Á., & Hecht-Felella, L. (2021). *Double standards in social media content moderation.* Brennan Center for Justice. https://www.brennancenter.org/our-work/research-reports/double-standards-social-media-content-moderation

Donner, J., & Locke, C. (2019). Platforms at the margins. In Mark Graham (Ed.), *Digital economies at Global margins* (pp. 39–42). MIT Press.

Ejekwonyilo, A. (2021). *Reverse Twitter suspension or face legal action, NBA threatens Nigerian govt.* https://www.premiumtimesng.com/news/headlines/465697-reverse-twitter-suspension-or-face-legal-action-nba-threatens-nigerian-govt.html?tztc=1Freedom House. (n.d.-a). *Freedom on the Net 2021: Nigeria.* https://freedomhouse.org/country/nigeria/freedom-net/2021

Freedom House. (n.d.-b). *Nigeria: Freedom on the Net 2022 Country Report.* https://freedomhouse.org/country/nigeria/freedom-net/2022

Friederici, N., Ojanperä, S., & Graham, M. (2017). The impact of connectivity in Africa: Grand visions and the mirage of inclusive digital development. Electronic *Journal of Information Systems in Developing Countries*, *79*(1), 1–20. https://doi.org/10.1002/j.1681-4835.2017.tb00578.x

Friederici, N. (2019). Innovation hubs in Africa: What do they really do for digital entrepreneurs? *Digital entrepreneurship in Sub-Saharan Africa* (pp. 9–28). Cambridge: The MIT Press. [Pdf] Retrieved from the Library of Congress, https://www.loc.gov/item/2020719940/.

Fuchs, C. (2014). Digital prosumption labor on social media in the context of the capitalist regime of time. *Time & Society, 23*(1), 97–123. https://doi.org/10.1177/0961463X13502117

Gillespie, T. (2018). *Custodians of the internet.* Yale University Press.

Global Freedom of Expression. (n.d.). *Twitter Ban Amicus Brief, EWCS/CCJ/APP/23/21.* Columbia University. https://globalfreedomofexpression.columbia.edu/wp-content/uploads/2022/08/ECOWAS-Nigeria-Twitter-Ban-Amicus-Brief-AN_EFF_ONA.docx.pdf

Global Network Initiative. (n.d.). *Global Network Initiative submission: UNESCO guidelines for regulating digital platforms draft 2.0.* https://globalnetworkinitiative.org/wp-content/uploads/2023/03/GNI-Comments-on-UNESCO-Guidelines-2.0-All-comments-final.docx.pdf

Gorwa, R. (2019). What is platform governance? *Information, Communication & Society, 22*(6), 854–871. https://doi.org/10.1080/1369118X.2019.1573914

Hagos, B. A. (2022, December 7). *Digital trade in the African continental free trade agreement: Exploring its promises and challenges.* AfronomicsLaw. https://www.afronomicslaw.org/category/analysis/digital-trade-african-continental-free-trade-agreement-exploring-its-promises-and

Helberger, N., Pierson, J., & Poell, T. (2018). Governing online platforms: From contested to cooperative responsibility. *The Information Society, 34*(1), 1–14. https://doi.org/10.1080/01972243.2017.1391913

Hurel, L. M., & Lobato, L. C. (2018). Unpacking cyber norms: Private companies as norm entrepreneurs. *Journal of Cyber Policy, 3*(1), 61–76. https://doi.org/10.1080/23738871.2018.1467942

Hussein, S. N. (2022). Win or lose: An examination of China's supply of mass surveillance technologies in exchange for African's facial IDs. *University of Pretoria Journal, 16*, 73–89. https://doi.org/10.29053/pslr.v16i1.4506

Ilori, T. (2020, October 27). *Facebook's content moderation errors are costing Africa too much.* Slate. https://slate.com/technology/2020/10/facebook-instagram-endsars-protests-nigeria.html

Kelley, J. (2022, July 20). *Nigerian Twitter ban declared unlawful by court.* Electronic Frontier Foundation. https://www.eff.org/deeplinks/2022/07/nigerian-twitter-ban-declared-unlawful-court-victory-eff-and-partners

Kemp, S. (2022, February 15). *Digital 2022: Nigeria.* DataReportal. https://datareportal.com/reports/digital-2022-nigeria

Kemp, S. (2023, February 23). *Digital 2023: Nigeria.* DataReportal. https://datareportal.com/reports/digital-2023-nigeria

Kenya Law. (2016). *Petition 397 of 2016.* http://kenyalaw.org/caselaw/cases/view/130781/

Kenya National Bureau of Statistics. (n.d.). *Home.* https://www.knbs.or.ke/

Kenya Revenue Authority (KRA). (2021). *Digital service tax.* https://kra.go.ke/images/publications/Brochure-Digital-Service-Tax-Website.pdf

KFCB. (2023, April 26). *KFCB concerned over rampant sharing of inappropriate audio-visual content.* https://kfcb.go.ke/kfcb-concerned-over-rampant-sharing-inappropriate-audio-visual-content

KPMG. (2021, July). *Finance Act 2021: KPMG Analysis of the Finance Act, 2021.* https://assets.kpmg.com/content/dam/kpmg/ke/pdf/tax/2021/KPMG%20Analysis%20of%20the%20Finance%20Act%202021%20-%20Final.pdf

Kwet, M. (2019). Digital colonialism: U.S. empire and the new imperialism in the Global South. *Race & Class, 60*(4), 3–26. https://doi.org/10.1177/0306396818823172

Lemma, A., Mendez-Parra, M., & Naliaka, L. (2022, July 13). *The AfCFTA: Unlocking the potential of the digital economy in Africa.* Overseas Development Institute. https://odi.org/en/publications/afcfta-unlocking-the-potential-of-the-digital-economy-in-africa/

Maclean, R. (2022, January 13). *Nigeria lifts 7-month ban on Twitter.* The New York Times. https://www.nytimes.com/2022/01/13/world/africa/nigeria-lifts-twitter-ban.html

Madung, O. (2022). *From dance app to political mercenary: How disinformation on TikTok gaslights political tensions in Kenya* [NGO Research]. Mozilla. https://foundation.mozilla.org/en/campaigns/kenya-tiktok/

Miriri, D. (2020, June 15). *Credit from Safaricom's farming app sows seeds of change in Kenya.* Reuters. https://www.reuters.com/article/kenya-safaricom-agriculture-idUSL8N2DH3EW

Mutahi, P., & Kimari, B. (2017). *The impact of social media and digital technology on electoral violence in Kenya* [Working Paper]. https://www.chrips.or.ke/wp-content/uploads/2017/08/The-impact-of-social-media-and-digital-technology-on-electoral-violence-in-kenya.pdf

Mutung'u, G. (2023, February). Kenya: A selectively thriving digital economy. In A. Pannier (Ed.), *The technology policies of digital middle powers.* The French Institute of International Relations (Ifri), pp. 35–41. https://www.ifri.org/sites/default/files/atoms/files/etude_pannier_techpolicies_2023.pdf

Mwangi, D. (2021, November 8). *KRA gets gadgets to monitor Kenyans on social media and on the road.* Pulse Live. https://www.pulselive.co.ke/news/kra-gets-gadgets-to-monitor-kenyans-on-social-media-and-on-the-road/05ffcwh

Mwenda, E. (2022, October 27). *Facebook to share trade data with KRA, police.* Nation: Kenya edition. https://nation.africa/kenya/business/facebook-to-share-traders-statistics-with-kra- police-3999174

National Information Technology Development Agency (NITDA). (2022, September 26). *Code of practice for interactive computer service platforms/internet intermediaries.* https://nitda.gov.ng/wp-content/uploads/2022/10/APPROVED-NITDA-CODE-OF-PRACTIVE-FOR-INTERACTIVE-COMPUTER-SERVICE-PLATFORMS-INTERNET-INTERMEDIARIES-2022-002.pdf

Nation Correspondent. (2015, May 11). *Huduma Centre wins top UN award for improving service delivery.* Nation. https://nation.africa/kenya/news/huduma-centre-wins-top-un-award-for-improving-service-delivery-1092760

Ndemo, N. (2023, June 28). *Lessons from the EU's digital agenda.* Business Daily. https://www.businessdailyafrica.com/bd/opinion-analysis/columnists/lessons-from-eu-s-digital-agenda--4286732

Ngila, F. (2022, May 12). *Kenyans are protesting plans by tax authority to snoop on their online chats.* Quartz. https://qz.com/africa/2164861/kenyas-tax-authority-to-snoop-on-online-chats-to-combat-fraud

Ngugi, B. (2023, February 8). *Kenya's digital services tax on tech giants must go, IMF says.* The Standard. https://www.standardmedia.co.ke/

Nigerian Communications Commission (NCC). (2021, February 22). *Press statement: Telecoms sector, others take Nigeria out of recession as sector boosts GDP by 12.45%.* https://ncc.gov.ng/media-centre/news-headlines/960-press-statement-telecoms-sector-others-take-nigeria-out-of-recession-as-sector-boosts-gdp-by-12-45

Njathi, A. W. (2023). *The glitz and glamour platform economy: Issues for Instagram monetization for influencers in Nairobi, Kenya* [Doctoral dissertation, North Carolina State University]. NC State University Libraries. https://repository.lib.ncsu.edu/handle/1840.20/40891

Nyabola, N., Owen, T., & Tworek, H. (2022, June 13). *Platform governance needs a global response.* Centre for International Governance Innovation. https://www.cigionline.org/articles/platform-governance-needs-a-global-response/

Nyawira, S. (2021, June 16). *Treasury expands taxation net for digital incomes.* The Star. https://www.the-star.co.ke/business/kenya/2021-06-16-treasury-expands-taxation-net-for- digital-incomes/

Obadare, E. (2023, May 2). *A "new scramble for Africa"?* Council on Foreign Relations. https://www.cfr.org/blog/new-scramble-africa

Olurounbi, R. (2021, March 17). *Paystack, Interswitch, Flutterwave ... Nigeria's fintech revolution.* Arbiterz. https://arbiterz.com/paystack-interswitch-flutterwave-nigerias-fintech-revolution/

Oluwole, V. (2022, February 23). *Egypt, Nigeria, Kenya have the most advanced ecosystem for tech developers in Africa, according to Google.* Business Insider Africa. https://africa.businessinsider.com/local/markets/egypt-nigeria-kenya-have-the-most-advanced-ecosystem-for-tech-developers-in-africa/sb5ry4f

Oparada, P. (2022, October 6). *Nigerian government sues Facebook, Instagram, WhatsApp over adverts, demands N30 billion.* Legit. https://www.legit.ng/business-economy/technology/1495989-nigerian-government-sues-facebook-instagram-whatsapp-adverts-demands-n30-billion/

Oriola, M. (2022, April 23). *Digital taxation, an infant in Nigeria, a giant abroad.* Business Day. https://businessday.ng/bd-weekender/article/digital-taxation-an-infant-in-nigeria-a-giant-abroad-mobolaji-oriola/

Osiakwan, E. M. (2017). The KINGS of Africa's digital economy. In B. Ndemo & T. Weiss (Eds.), *Digital Kenya* (pp. 55–92). Palgrave Macmillan.

Paterson, C., & Nothias, T. (2016). Representation of China and the United States in Africa in online global news. *Communication, Culture & Critique*, *9*(1), 107–125. https://doi.org/10.1111/cccr.12133

Perrigo, B. (2021, September 23). *'I sold my soul.' WhatsApp content moderators review the worst material on the internet. Now they're alleging pay discrimination.* Time. https://time.com/6080450/facebook-whatsapp-content-moderators/

Perrigo, B. (2022, February 14). *Inside Facebook's African sweatshop*. Time. https://time.com/6147458/facebook-africa-content-moderation-employee-treatment/

Poell, T., Nieborg, D., & van Dijck, J. (2019). Platformization. *Internet Policy Review, 8*(4), 1–13. https://doi.org/10. 14763/2019.4.1425

Poell, T., Nieborg, D. B., & Duffy, B. E. (2022). Spaces of negotiation: Analyzing power in the news industry. *Digital Journalism*. Advance online publication. https://doi.org/10.1080/21670811.2022.2103011

Popiel, P. (2021). Regulating datafication and platformization: Policy silos and tradeoffs in international platform inquiries. *Policy & Internet, 14*(1), 28–46. https://doi.org/10.1002/poi3.283

Princewill, N., & Busari, S. (2021, June 4). *Nigeria bans Twitter after company deletes President Buhari's tweet*. CNN. https://www.cnn.com/2021/06/04/africa/nigeria-suspends-twitter-operations-intl/index.htmlReuters. (2022, January 21). *Nigeria to prioritize taxes from digital non-resident firms in 2022. Reuters*. https://www.reuters.com/world/africa/nigeria-prioritise-taxes-digital-non-resident-firms-2022-2022-01-20/

Srnicek, N. (2018). *Platform capitalism*. Polity.

Tamale, S. (2020). *Decolonization and Afro feminism*. Daraja Press.

The Finance Bill, 14 of 2023, National Assembly of Republic of Kenya (2023). http://www.parliament.go.ke/sites/default/files/2023-05/THE%20FINANCE%20BILL%20%2C%20 2023_compressed.pdf

The Punch. (2021, June 2). *Lai Mohammed reacts to Twitter deleting Buhari's "civil war" tweet*. Punch Newspapers. https://punchng.com/video-lai-mohammed-reacts-to-twitter-deleting-buharis-civil-war-tweet/

The World Bank. (2023, March 31). *The World Bank in Nigeria*. https://www.worldbank.org/en/country/nigeria/overview

UNESCO. (2023). *Safeguarding freedom of expression and access to information: Guidelines for a multistakeholder approach in the context of regulating digital platforms* [Conference program].

Van der Meer, B. J. (2018). The internet antenna of Silicon Savannah: How startups perceive the impact of internet services on the Nairobi business environment and enterprise development challenges [Master's thesis, Utrecht University]. Utrecht University Repository. https://dspace.library.uu.nl/handle/1874/368435

Van Dijck, J. (2020). Governing digital societies: Private platforms, public values. *Computer Law & Security Review, 36*, Article 105377. https://doi.org/10.1016/j.clsr.2019.105377

Van Dijck, J. (2021). Seeing the forest for the trees: Visualizing platformization and its governance. *New Media & Society, 23*(9), 2801–2819. https://doi.org/10.1177/1461444820940293

Walubengo, J., & Mutemi, M. (2018). Treatment of Kenya's internet intermediaries under the Computer Misuse and Cybercrimes Act, 2018. *The African Journal of Information and Communication, 21*, 1–19. https://doi.org/10.23962/10539/26114

Wamathai, J. (2017, July 5). Statement by BAKE on CA's 'guidelines for prevention of dissemination of undesirable political messages'. *IFreedoms Kenya*. https://ifree.co.ke/2017/07/statement-by-bake-on-cas-guidelines-for-prevention-of-dissemination-of-undesirable-bulk-political-sms-and-social-media-content-via-electronic-communications-networks/

Wangari, N. (2023, February 15). *Lawsuit against Meta in Kenya paves the way for African countries to sue tech companies*. GlobalVoices. https://globalvoices.org/2023/02/15/lawsuit-against-meta-in-kenya-paves-the-way-for-african-countries-to-sue-tech-companies/Zuboff, S. (2019). *The age of surveillance capitalism: The fight for a human future at the new frontier of power*. Public Affairs.

11 Trends in Public Relations and Marketing Research in Africa

Brandi Watkins and Anne W. Njathi

Introduction

The increasing attention from multinational corporations seeking to expand into the up-and-coming African market casts a spotlight onto the various communication management practices that are unique to the culture of Africa. However, in many ways, the practice of public relations and marketing in Africa is still evolving. As Watkins notes in Chapter 2, the practice of modern public relations, in particular, has been in existence for about 50 years on the African continent. Contrast this with the practice of public relations in the West, which dates to the late 1800s and early 1900s. Despite the relative newness of the practice, many of the leading international public relations agencies expanded their offices to Africa (Kiambi & Nadler, 2012). As Kiambi and Nadler (2012) suggested more than a decade ago,

> Western nations should pay closer attention to the ongoing development of public relations in less developed countries in this era of globalization. Particularly, practitioners and scholars need to recognize the unique role that culture plays in the practice of public relations.
>
> (p. 506)

Publication of African-based public relations and marketing research in Western academic journals and books is one method of highlighting the significant contributions that Africa can make to the discipline. In her review of African-based public relations research, Watkins (Chapter 2) identified 40 published articles from six public relations journals published between 1986 and 2023. And while Watkins noted a slight increase in the number of articles published in the 2010–2023 range, more effort is needed to incorporate African practice and culture into the globalization of public relations and marketing.

The purpose of this book was to compile a collection of research reflecting the state of public relations, marketing, and communication research in Africa with an emphasis on the emerging role of digital technology. The research presented in the chapters of this book answered a call for scholarship that addressed the complexities of the practice of communication management on a continent that was once deemed "The Dark Continent." Contributing scholars and practitioners, many of whom

DOI: 10.4324/9781032689654-11

have direct ties to Africa, highlight the ways that African countries are overcoming obstacles of the past to join the global digital revolution of the 21st century. Africa itself provides a compelling backdrop for such research as it is a "continent where pre-modern, modern, and post-modern characteristics are all present" (Rensburg, 2007, p. 38), and what makes Africa compelling also makes it a challenge for researchers and practitioners alike. Africa has more countries than any other continent, which creates an interesting mosaic of economic, political, and social factors (Kiambi et al., 2023). Oksiutycz and Enombo (2011) note that the complexity of these factors can have an influence on how stakeholders perceive public relations work as well as the ways in which public relations is practiced and practitioners are trained. In reflecting on the contributions of work presented in these chapters, three key trends related to communication management in Africa emerged: (1) digital communication is a global phenomenon, (2) the practice of public relations and marketing in Africa is still evolving, and (3) Africa-centric research trends. This chapter discusses those trends and provides recommendations for future research.

Digital Communication Is a Global Phenomenon

This book has elaborately demonstrated the uniquely yet contrasted digital environments of African countries when compared to the Westernized Eurocentric everyday digital cultures and realities. Although these realities and cultures have been assumed to be distinctively different from Western countries (Arora, 2019; Srinivasan, 2019), due to an entrenched digital divide (Bukht & Heeks, 2017; Graham, 2019; Graham et al., 2017; Heeks, 2022), the digital behaviors, practices, and perceptions discussed in this book show that consumption and participation are not different from other parts of the world. Contrary to expectations, Africans are participating in the digital economy just like their counterparts in Western countries. They are using the internet and digital technologies for economic purposes that include utilitarian reasons such as healthcare, education, or employment (Arora, 2019). Arora (2019) argues, "Although this is a readily accepted fact of contemporary digital life in the West, many still cling to the belief that the global poor are inherently different from typical users" (p. 2). Conflicting with the long-standing notions of global digital inequality around the global growth of digital connectivity, this book shows that Africans are participating in the digital economy just like their counterparts in Western countries. To Arora's (2019) point, Africans, living in major cities in Africa, use digital technology like anyone else in the world despite the digital divide and socio-economic, political, and cultural dynamics.

The chapters collected for this book embody the diversity of public relations and marketing practice in Africa. For example, in Chapter 9, Kayode and Alex-Ojei discussed the rising use of online influencers and content creators by the telecommunications industry such as MTN and Airtel in Lagos, Nigeria. Similarly, Moyo et al. (Chapter 4) delved into the use of social media in Zimbabwe's telecommunications industry while analyzing the impact on corporate reputation management. Chari (Chapter 3) presents opportunities and challenges of using social media by examining the experiences of public relations practitioners in Zimbabwe. In addition, how public relations, marketing, and communications professionals use social media platforms to market themselves in Egypt and Ghana are explored in Chapters 7 and 8 by Bassyouny and Boateng, respectively. Njathi and Wamanji (Chapter 5) explicated a surge in the use of social media platforms such as Twitter by Kenyans in holding brands, individuals, and governments responsible. Digital activism happenings propelled by KOT include #BoycottKFC, #SomeoneTellCNN, #SomeoneTell TDJakes, #SwitchOffKPLC, #kenyans4kenyans have amassed global popularity, gaining attention from international media, and sometimes warranted responses. Nzau and Capizzo (Chapter 6) analyzed the Twitter crisis management of General Muhoozi on Uganda-Kenya Relations.

Altogether, these chapters highlight the presence and growing use of digital platforms and technologies, the development potential of Africa's digital economy, and how the African youth population bulge, the rise of internet penetration, and data panoply are shaping the way marketing, public relations, and communication are becoming increasingly digital through consumption, adoption, and trends. In addition, these trends underscore how Africans are overcoming digital inequalities (Srinivasan, 2019), using similar digital strategies and cultures, not that different from the West to maximize opportunities in the digital world, presented by the exponential internet penetration in the continent. However, in a separate chapter, Njathi et al. (Chapter 3) looked at the limited yet complex technology policies, laws, and regulations impeding the full embrace of digital technology, such as the indefinite suspension of Twitter in Nigeria, digital service tax (DST) in Kenya, and Facebook Worker's Legal Battle in Kenya. They argue that African governments (Kenya and Nigeria) are playing catch-up with the fast-evolving technology, widening the existing regulatory gaps. Findings from the chapter not only show how the adoption of digital technologies may be a double-edged sword that presents opportunities discussed in the majority of the chapters but also accentuate regulatory risks associated with the globalization of technologies.

The Role of Digital in Marketing and Public Relations Is Evolving

Although the wave of digital disruption is taking over the African market, just like other parts of the world, the use of digital technologies and tools in public relations and marketing is relatively low. Inasmuch as Chapters 3, 4, 5, 6, 7, and 8 discussed the use of social media in managing public relations, marketing, and communications campaigns, none mentioned the use of Artificial Intelligence (AI), data and analytics, marketing automation, user experience (UX), and design as well as content management or other forms of emerging digital marketing tools. This is not surprising, according to Tirziu (2018), only a handful of African countries, Kenya, Nigeria, South Africa, Ghana, and Ethiopia are undertaking AI initiatives, but at a significantly small scale, pilot and ad hoc, mostly targeting financial services, agriculture, and healthcare with AI solutions. Partially, the lack of use of emerging technologies in public relations, marketing, and communications in Africa can be attributed to resource constraints and a lack of accessibility to modern technological solutions that require high financial and human capital investment, as elucidated by various chapters in the book. Tirziu (2018) argues that "many African countries remain incapable of requisite reforms in the areas of data collection and data privacy, infrastructure, education and governance" (p. 1). Despite practitioners being cognizant of the potential of new technologies and tools to accelerate the growth and productivity of companies, lagging internet infrastructure (Heeks, 2022; Graham et al., 2017) and the lack of suitable and affordable digital solutions force businesses to resign to basic use of social media. However, as Watkins (Chapter 2) and Njathi et al. (Chapter 3) argue, global digital solutions and tools may not necessarily work in local African markets. Thus, even with emerging technologies, local and regional adaptation is strongly recommended to cater to the complex African socio-economic, political, and cultural dynamics.

As discussed by Njathi et al. (Chapter 3), Africa's slow response to emerging technological and regulatory gaps might prevent the continent from evolving in the fast-changing digital era. As policymakers and regulators struggle to make appropriate regulations for the online digital marketplace and workplace, business transactions and consumer participation might not be fully realized. As Njathi et al. substantiate in Chapter 3, digital policies and regulatory challenges such as taxation, internet shutdowns, and criminalizing content stifle the full embrace of the digital economy for most African countries. This is because fast-emerging regulatory issues of platform governance, including safety and security, privacy of user rights, and freedom of expression, are largely unaddressed. In other words, professions in communication management fields like public relations and marketing that rely on digital platforms for business activities in the digital economy may experience slow adoption in the African continent especially in comparison to countries in the global North. In addition, when strategic communication professionals are faced with digital harms, dangers, and other unethical issues presented by digital opportunities, they may go unregulated as seen with examples like the Facebook worker rights and digital service tax mentioned in Chapter 3 and the lack of proper recourse for the Twitter crisis mentioned in Chapters 6 (General Muhoozi on Uganda-Kenya Relations) and 5 (#BoycottKFC).

In sum, in Africa, there's a huge untapped audience, with potential markets waiting to be exploded and revolutionized—particularly in the KINGS countries (Kenya, Ivory Coast, Nigeria, Ghana, South Africa), with a critical mass of youthful people, strong economic growth, entrepreneurial ecosystems, vibrant telecoms, tech infrastructure, and supportive policies (Osiakwan, 2017). Unless African governments build an inclusive digital economy by removing barriers such as access, the high cost of the internet, and improving digital skills, the continent will remain a nice-to-have in delivering audiences but not in meaningful participation in the digital economy.

Africa-Centric Research Trends

Rensburg (2007) proclaimed that there is an urgent need to establish communication management in Africa. In regard to the evolving nature of public relations and marketing practices in Africa, Mersham et al. (2011) note:

> The emerging generation of African practitioners will carry a huge responsibility to act as change agents and boundary spanners in the economic, political, and social spheres. They will act as brokers and counsellors to managements and governments to ensure that corporate responsibility becomes generic to Africa businesses and government programs in pursuit of mutuality of interest and concerns.
>
> (p. 205)

Practice and scholarship should work together to create a cohesive body of knowledge on the practices of communication management that are unique to the African context to meet the requirements outlined by Mersham et al. (2011). Further, to Rensburg's (2007) point, effective communication management, including public relations and marketing communication, benefits from an in-depth understanding of the practice through the lens of academic scholarship. While efforts are being made to contextualize African public relations and marketing research, more research is needed.

The chapters presented in this book contribute to the growing body of research on public relations and marketing with an emphasis on social media. As such, this research represents a step forward in establishing a research tradition on the use of digital technology on the African continent. To that end, collectively, these chapters highlight three trends where strategic communication practice is evolving: (1) corporate reputation management, (2) integration of social media as a communication tool, (3) employing one-way communication on social media, and (4) opportunities and challenges for the use of social media in public relations and marketing.

Corporate Reputation Management

Two chapters explicitly looked at the impact of social media on corporate reputation management (Chapters 3 and 4). In Chapter 3, Chari wrestled with the double-edged sword of using social media as a tool for corporate reputation management. Chari's research points to a number of opportunities for using social media in corporate reputation management that are oftentimes offset by challenges concluding that "the deployment of social media in corporate reputation management in Africa might be another case of 'change without change'." Whereas in Chapter 4, Moyo et al. presented a theory-based conceptual model and found empirical support for the use of social media, and Twitter (X) specifically, for reputation management. Their research emphasized how the integration of social media into reputation management represents a transition from more traditional approaches to corporate reputation management. They go on to recommend practitioners focus on the use of Twitter (X), Facebook, and YouTube for reputation management.

Other chapters also noted the relationship between social media and reputation management. Both chapters on crisis management (Chapters 5 and 6) noted the impact that social media crises can have on reputation management. For example, Njathi and Wamanji (Chapter 5) noted that social media, and Twitter (X) in particular, presents a special set of opportunities and challenges for reputation management. Nzau and Capizzo (Chapter 6) suggested that even humorous attacks on political figures could result in reputational damage. Both Bassyouny (Chapter 7) and Boateng (Chapter 8) concluded that social media provides public relations and marketing professionals with an outlet for defending a company's reputation.

Chari (Chapter 5) noted the dearth of research on corporate reputation in the global South and Africa, in particular. Reputation management is an important topic for African public relations and marketing scholarship as evidenced by the number of chapters that reference reputation management. The research presented in this book contributes to a growing body of literature examining the impact of social media and digital technologies on communication management practices in Africa. Additional research is needed, particularly in how to overcome some of the challenges discussed within the chapters in this book.

Social Media Integration

As Watkins notes in Chapter 2, much of the current research on Africans in Western journals is centered on the practice of public relations. Additionally, in Chapter 3, Njathi et al. note that digital platforms have become marketplaces in and of themselves. The research presented in the chapters contribute to the body of knowledge on the ways in which social media is integrated into public relations and marketing practice. For example, in Chapter 4, Moyo et al. looked at how social media has been integrated into corporate reputation management. They surveyed communication professionals working in Zimbabwe's telecommunications sector and found that they used Twitter (X) more as a conversational tool. In Chapter 7, Bassyouny noted that Egyptian communication professionals viewed social media as a way around the nation's complex traditional media system. In their view, social media was a useful channel for distributing messages to publics. Boateng (Chapter 8) examined how the University of Cape Coast in Ghana integrated Facebook into its efforts to market the university and attract potential students. In this case, the university was using Facebook to disseminate advertising messages but was not taking full advantage of the interactive features to engage and build relationships with potential stakeholders. Finally, Kayode and Alex-Ojei (Chapter 9) looked at how social media influencers can be leveraged as a marketing strategy.

There are important limitations to the use of social media that also warrant consideration. Notably, there is the issue of the digital divide and a lack of access to the internet, which is impacted by political, economic, and infrastructure factors. Bassyouny notes in Chapter 7 that Egypt has faced significant limitations to the adoption of technology and challenges of working with a population with lower media literacy rates. Publics not educated on how to use the internet are often more susceptible to disinformation and misinformation, which impacts the ability of public relations and marketing professionals to communicate effectively with these audiences.

When considering the integration of social media into public relations and marketing practice, it is also prudent to consider the role of regulations on social media platforms, which has been neglected in research on Africa. Njathi et al. (Chapter 3) addressed this gap in the literature by analyzing regulatory and legal frameworks in Kenya and Nigeria that impact the usage of social media. Their analysis revealed four key findings: "(a) reactionary ad hoc policy strategies in response to regulatory crises; (b) main actors' privileges; (c) competition to regulate among actors; and cumulatively, (d) the enormous power that platforms hold, presenting tensions and potential harms to the platform economy." In response, they recommend localizing content moderation and policy that reflects the complexity of African countries. As has been noted many times within this volume, countries in Africa represent a panoply of distinct cultures, economies, and access to technology. Future research on regulatory and legal frameworks on a country-specific basis is needed to further scholarship on the impact of political action in the adoption of new technologies. Such research can have a ripple effect to the global practice of public relations and marketing.

One-Way Communication Trends

Watkins noted in Chapter 2 that there was a dearth of research on social media and digital technology in the African context. And while this book, as a whole, is an attempt to fill that gap in the research, findings from several of the chapters point to an interesting trend in African-based social media research that warrants further investigation. Chapters 3, 4, 5, 6, 7, and 8 all noted that African communication professionals tended to use social media in a manner consistent with one-way or asymmetrical communication. For example, Chari noted in Chapter 3 that "the use of social media is not informed by a symmetrical two-way communication aimed at understanding the behaviors and attitudes of the audience to influence message strategy and creation for the ultimate benefit of the organization." Chari identified this use of social media as more instrumental for corporate reputation management that reflects the two-way asymmetrical model used with traditional media. Boateng (Chapter 8) echoed this sentiment in findings related to how the University of Cape Coast used Facebook in its digital marketing strategy. Boateng wrote, "the university could promote engagements and interactions with friends, followers, and audiences to secure their mutually beneficial relationships" and "the failure of the university to respond to comments and inquiries on its Facebook page prevents them from taking maximum of the interactive features to advance relationship marketing."

In their individual chapters on online crisis communication, both Njathi and Wamanji (Chapter 5) and Nzau and Capizzo (Chapter 6) found that neither the organization nor the public official embroiled in the crisis responded to pressure from Kenyans on Twitter (KOT). In regard to KFC's handling of the crisis, Njathi and Wamanji report the organization only tweeted once informing audiences about the potato shortage but never responded directly to the KOT, instead opting to send messaging through traditional media sources. In these cases, a lack of response from the organization and political figure indicated one-way communication on their part and consequently allowed the KOT to set the online narrative about the situation.

Bassyouny's (Chapter 7) interviews with Egyptian marketing and public relations professionals found that most of the professionals viewed social media as a tool to engage and interact with audiences, but in practice government institutions used social media platforms for disseminating one-way messages like press releases rather than engage with the dialogic features of the platforms. This is similar to Chari's (Chapter 3) suggestion that feedback or engagement from the public through social media is not necessarily part of organizational strategic communication plans. Thus, these findings of over-reliance on one-way communication and a lack of engagement on the organization's part reflect similar findings from Western-based studies. What is interesting about this finding is that previously scholars have noted that Africa's mostly collectivist culture lends itself to a more relationship-based practice of public relations. For example, researchers have noted that African public relations practitioners tend to employ the cultural interpreter and personal influence models of public relations (Kiambi & Nadler, 2012; Wu & Baah-Boakye, 2009), which emphasizes relationship building in public relations practice. These models better reflect the collectivist, interpersonally driven African culture (Anani-Bossman, 2021; Wu & Baah-Boakye, 2009). Moyo et al. (Chapter 4) reinforced the importance of relationships between organizations and publics in recommending that social media and social capital form the basis of contemporary African corporate reputation management.

Collectively, these findings continue the earlier work of scholars on the practice of public relations in Africa, specifically looking at what models of communication inform the practice (see Holtzhausen et al., 2003; Kiambi & Nadler, 2012; Tindall & Holtzhausen, 2012; Wu & Baah-Boakye, 2009). However, an important distinction must be made—the chapters in this book focused on social media specifically, whereas existing research primarily looked at the practice of public relations in general. The dichotomy between the existing practice-based research and the social media-based research presented in this book represents an interesting direction for future research that can have far-reaching implications on the development of African-based public relations and marketing theory and model development.

Opportunities and Challenges

Many of the opportunities for the use of social media as a reputation management tool reflect findings from more Western contexts. Benefits identified in the chapters in this book include immediate, interactive communication with feedback capabilities; cost-effectiveness; the ability to reach wide and diverse audiences; direct control of messaging; networking; opportunities for collaboration with stakeholders; a method to assess public opinion; reputation management; communicate corporate social responsibility; expedited method for communicating with stakeholders; and provide clients with measurable key performance indicators (see Chapters 3, 7, and 9). In Chapter 4, Moyo et al.'s research revealed that different social media platforms can support different components of corporate reputation management. While Boateng (Chapter 8) highlighted the use of social media marketing in persuading students to attend university in

Ghana. Kayode and Alex-Ojei (Chapter 9) found influencer marketing to have a positive effect on consumer purchase decisions.

A particular challenge to the practice of public relations and marketing noted within several chapters is the diverse range of audiences and publics whose perceptions of and interactions with an organization can impact reputation management. Several chapters in this book mention the precarious nature of reputation management, given that social media enables the publics to easily mobilize against an organization. This is particularly relevant in Chapters 5 and 6, which both look at the Kenyans on Twitter (KOT) phenomenon and how their online activity created a paracrisis situation. Bassyouny (Chapter 7) made an interesting point about how the socio-economic status of many Egyptians directly impacts the efforts of public relations and marketing professionals. In Egypt, there is a wide gap between "the few rich and many poor" and oftentimes social media users will attack businesses and organizations online and mock marketing campaigns as an act of frustration and noted this as a major challenge for communication management in Egypt.

Establishing the challenges and opportunities of using social media for public relations and marketing provides a template for future research. Scholarship should engage in quantitative and qualitative analyses to determine how organizations can maximize the benefits and opportunities of social media and mitigate some of the drawbacks. A significant area of research for public relations and marketing in general is analytics and measurement of social media effectiveness. Bassyouny's chapter (Chapter 7) reported that Egyptian practitioners noted the ability of social media to provide measurable key performance indicators, thus emphasizing the importance of continued research on this topic. Moreover, research on effective social media measurement would have benefits for public relations and marketing scholarship and practice on a global level.

Concluding Thoughts

The research presented in this book contributes to the growing interest in scholarship focused on public relations and marketing communication practices in African countries. More specifically, researchers focused on the influence of digital technology and social media and discussed the theoretical and practical implications for the ever-evolving practice of strategic communication management. As has been mentioned in several chapters, many African countries represent an up-and-coming market with a youthful population eager to embrace technology and modernity of the Western world. However, it is prudent to not forget that while some African countries have embraced technology and globalization, other countries on the continent face a myriad of challenges that prohibit them from taking part in the digital economy. Limitations such as access to the internet, affordability, and media/digital literacy must be considered when engaging in scholarship on African public relations and marketing practices.

African countries provide a compelling backdrop for the development of digital communication management. For instance, some have noted that in South Africa, scholars have a unique opportunity to study the development of professional communication in the context of a country that has weathered drastic political change in transitioning from apartheid to democracy (Holtzhausen, 2005). Other countries, like the KINGS countries (Kenya, Ivory Coast, Nigeria, Ghana, and South Africa; Osiakwan, 2017) provide insights into the ways African countries have embraced technology and opened their economies to multinational corporations. Many of the studies in this volume include interviews with working communication professionals and in-depth analysis of the artifacts of strategic communication on social media, thus answering a call from Anani-Bossman (2021) for research based on the practices of local professionals in Africa. African countries represented in the research in this book include the Sub-Saharan countries Ghana, Kenya, Nigeria, Zimbabwe, and Uganda. Further, Chapter 7 focuses on Egypt, which is a Northern African country. African countries and their people are not monoliths but rather distinct cultures and economies that must be considered in continuing African-based research on public relations and marketing communication.

This book is a first step in unpacking the influence of digital technology on the practice of public relations and marketing communication in Africa. Throughout the chapters in the book and existing research on public relations and marketing in Africa, there is a call for more research. As editors of this book, we echo this call for continued research that will allow for African-specific theory and models to contribute to our global understanding of public relations and marketing practice—a discipline that, to date, has been dominated by Western practice and ideology. Modern public relations practice and scholarship emphasize the development of mutually beneficial organization-public relationships. Perhaps that same ethos should be applied to the study of communication management through public relations and marketing in the African context where each party learns from the other: Western theory and practice can inform the developing scholarship and practice on the African continent, and likewise, the unique characteristics of African countries and their approach to public relations and marketing communication could breathe new life into Western ideology and practice.

Bibliography

Anani-Bossman, A. A. (2021). An exploration of strategic public relations management in Ghana. *Public Relations Inquiry, 10*(1), 73–96. https://doi.org/10.1177/2046147X20979292

Arora, P. (2019). *The next billion users: Digital life beyond the West.* Cambridge, MA: Harvard University Press.

Bukht, R., & Heeks, R. (2017). *Defining, conceptualizing and measuring the digital economy* (Development Informatics Working Paper No. 68). SSRN. https://doi.org/10.2139/ssrn.3431732

Graham, M. (2019). Changing connectivity and digital economies at global margins. In M. Graham (Ed.), *Digital economies at global margins* (pp. 1–19). MIT Press.

Graham, M., Ojanperä, S., Anwar, M. A., & Friederici, N. (2017). Digital connectivity and African knowledge economies. *Questions de Communication*, *32*, 345–360. https://doi.org/10.4000/questiondecommunication.11579Heeks, R. (2022). Digital inequality beyond the digital divide: Conceptualizing adverse digital incorporation in the Global

South. *Information Technology for Development, 28*(4), 688– 704. https://doi.org/10.1080/02681102.2022.2068492

Holtzhausen, D. R. (2005). Public relations practice and political change in South Africa. *Public Relations Review, 31*, 407–416. https://doi.org/10.1016/j.pubrev/2005.05.011

Holtzhausen, D. R., Petersen, B. K., & Tindall, N. T. J. (2003). Exploding the myth of the symmetrical/asymmetrical dichotomy: Public relations models in the new South Africa. *Journal of Public Relations Research, 15*(4), 305–341. https://doi.org/10.1207/S153275XJPRR1504_02

Kiambi, D., Arceneaux, P., & Golan, G. (2023). Organization-government relationships in sub-Saharan Africa: The emerging public affairs industry in Kenya. *Journal of Communication Management, 27*(4), 433–450. https://doi.org/10.1108/JCOM-07–2022–0093

Kiambi, D., & Nadler, M. K. (2012). Public relations in Kenya: An exploration of models and cultural influences. *Public Relations Review, 38*, 505–507. https://doi.org/10.1016/j.pubrev/2012.01.007

Mersham, G., Skinner, C., & Rensburg, R. (2011). Approaches to African communication management and public relations: A case for theory-building on the continent. *Journal of Public Affairs, 11*(4), 195–207. https://doi.org/10.1001/pa.413

Oksiutycz, A., & Enombo, M. P. (2011). Public relations in private sector companies in Gabon. *Public Relations Review, 37*, 274–280. https://doi.org/10.1016/j.pubrev.2011.03.011

Osiakwan, E. M. (2017). The KINGS of Africa's digital economy. In B. Ndemo & T. Weiss (Eds.), *Digital Kenya* (pp. 55–92). Palgrave Macmillan.

Rensburg, R. (2007). Communications management in the Africa context: Implications for theory, research, and practice. *International Journal of Strategic Communication, 1*(1), 37–51. https://doi.org/10.1080/15531180701285269

Srinivasan, R. (2019). *Beyond the Valley. How innovators around the world are overcoming inequality and creating the technologies of tomorrow*. Cambridge, MA: The MIT Press.

Tindall, N. T. J., & Holtzhausen, D. R. (2012). Toward an integrated model of communication: The case of South Africa. *Journal of Communication Management, 16*(4), 371–387. https://doi.org/10.1108/13632541211279003

Tirziu, A. G. (2018, November 14). *Coming to life: Artificial intelligence in Africa*. Atlantic Council. https://www.atlanticcouncil.org/in-depth-research-reports/issue-brief/coming-to-life-artificial-intelligence-in-africa/

Wu, M.-Y., & Baah-Boakye, K. (2009). Public relations in Ghana: Work-related cultural values and public relations models. *Public Relations Review, 35*, 83–85. https://doi.org/10.1016/j.pubrev.2008.09.015

Index

Note: **Bold** page numbers refer to tables; *italic* page numbers refer to figures and page numbers followed by "n" denote endnotes.

FSC
www.fsc.org
MIX
Papier | Fördert
gute Waldnutzung
FSC® C083411

Kolibri 360 GmbH
Ferdinand-Jühlke-Straße 7
99095 Erfurt, Deutschland
produktsicherheit@kolibri360.de